OPERATING BAIL

FIONA PATERSON
CLAIRE WHITTAKER

THE SCOTTISH OFFICE
CENTRAL RESEARCH UNIT

First published 1994

ISBN 0 11 495173 X

FOREWORD

At a time when there is widespread anxiety about the use and abuse of bail the results of this research study present an account of the operation of bail in three court areas which leads the researchers to question some of the assumptions which are often made about the significance of recorded bail abuse.

While those alleged to offend between charge and court appearance are undoubtedly a concern to those involved in the criminal justice system, the report clearly indicates that the level of bail abuse, as presently recorded, is in part a reflection of the way in which the system is monitoring the behaviour of those accused of crime. This has significant implications for the way in which those charged with bail abuse are subsequently treated.

It is hoped that the findings of this research will stimulate both a reconsideration of commonly held beliefs about bail and its abuse and a wider appreciation of the implications of different policies which can be adopted in responding to current concerns.

I am sure that the report will be of interest to all those who work within, and who are concerned about, the criminal justice system.

Dr C P A Levein

Chief Research Officer

CONTENTS

ACKNOWLEDGEMENTS

This research was commissioned by the Scottish Office Home and Health Department. The study would not have been possible without the co-operation of sheriff court staff, police, procurator fiscal staff, defence agents, crown counsel, members of the judiciary in the study areas and in the high court who helped us by participating in the research. We are grateful to all who gave of their time to speak to us about their work. Others have also been generous in assisting the research. In particular, Scottish Criminal Records Office helped us in collecting information about new alleged charges for people in the study sample. Bill Gilchrist of Crown Office has helped us to avoid legal inaccuracies and ambiguities in the report. Andrew Piggott of Central Research Unit undertook the collection of police statistical data and provided administrative support throughout the project. We are especially indebted to those professional colleagues who have supported this research from its infancy as a small pilot research project in 1988 - in particular to Jackie Tombs and Ann Millar of Central Research Unit. Any defects remain, of course, solely our own responsibility. Finally we would like to acknowledge the forbearance of our families who tolerated our long absences on fieldwork.

Fiona Paterson

Claire Whittaker

PART I

OVERVIEW

SUMMARY

The purpose of this research was to describe how bail decisions are made in Scotland. Only the courts have the authority to grant or refuse bail in Scotland. Nevertheless, decisions under the Bail etc. (Scotland) Act 1980 are also taken daily by police and prosecutors[1] (see figure 1.1). While the purpose was simple, the research needed to be designed to enable an examination to be made of the complexity of socio-legal relations between police, prosecutors and courts which produce bail decisions. Although the making of bail decisions is commonplace for criminal justice practitioners, there is little information about those decisions and their significance, as none of the institutions within the criminal justice system collects routine data about their bail decisions.[2] Practitioners may be clear about their individual decisions and aspects of their local experience but how these relate more generally to the way in which bail is being operated in Scotland remains opaque. This restricts the possibility of understanding the operation of bail and of assessing its effectiveness.

Yet, or perhaps because of this, over recent years there has been a great deal of concern about bail. During the 1980's a Scottish Office study of the use of custodial remand found that Scotland held proportionately more people on remand than almost any other country in Europe.[3] More recently, the press has run stories about so-called 'bail bandits' who, it is often claimed, are responsible for a high proportion of crime. Indeed, the level of offending while on bail which has been recorded by the police has risen from just under 3,000 offences in 1983 to nearly 20,000 in 1991. This dramatic increase is in part explained by the fact that police have been working to improve their recording of bail statistics during this period. Nevertheless, the study has been undertaken at a time of increasing anxiety about bail and it is against this background that the findings need to be understood.

The present research assessed the effectiveness of the operation of the Bail etc. (Scotland) Act 1980 by looking at police, prosecution and sheriff court decision making in three areas of Scotland (Doon, Tweed and Braid[4]). The areas were chosen because access could be agreed for the research with all criminal justice agencies in the locality. The areas are therefore illustrative of working practices for different types of locality but were not chosen because they were known to represent different patterns of use of bail. Findings illustrate the implications of pursuing particular policies in relation to bail. The study was undertaken during 1991 and 1992. A census of bail decisions was conducted in the study courts and a detailed examination was made of a sample from all arrests where police made a decision to detain people in custody or release them on an undertaking to appear in the sheriff court. (Figures A, B and C at the end of this summary show the criminal justice process and outcome for sample

---

1 Public prosecutors are known as procurators fiscal. Strictly, procurators fiscal are senior prosecutors usually responsible for a number of prosecutors, known as procurator fiscal deputes, working in a locality. The prosecutors who participated directly in this research were usually (though not always) procurator fiscal deputes. In this report the terms 'fiscal', 'depute' , 'procurator fiscal' are used to refer to prosecutors and do not imply the seniority of the particular prosecutor who is being referred to.

2 This issue has been under examination since April 1992 by the Scottish Office Working Group on Offending While on Bail. The group has representatives from all institutions in the criminal justice system.

3 .E Wozniak, P.Scrimgeour & L.Nicholson; Custodial Remand in Scotland; 1988; Central Research Unit.

4 To anonymise the study areas names of Scottish rivers have been used. The locations of the rivers chosen do not reflect the locations of the areas studied.

accused.) The variations in practice were not accounted for by differences in the seriousness of cases. Doon police had a high use of custody and the court had a high use of bail. Tweed police had a lower use of custody and the court had a higher use of unconditional release. In contrast, police at Braid had a low use of custody and the court had a high use of remand. The report argues that different patterns of use of bail and remand can be explained by variations in local criminal justice culture and that, by assessing the implications of the cultures identified, it is possible to assess the broader implications of fostering those cultures more widely, or of inhibiting them.

Release on bail is release by the court on trust that the bailee will appear at court on the appointed date, will not interfere with witnesses or otherwise obstruct the course of justice, will not commit offences while on bail and will conform to any other (special) conditions of release stipulated by the court. Most people in all areas were not alleged to have breached the court's trust by failing to appear, committing offences while on bail or by breaching any special conditions attached to their bail order. Doon, the area with the high use of bail, had the highest proportion of accused who were not ultimately convicted. Of those who were ultimately not convicted, a higher proportion of people at Braid, the area with a high use of remand, had spent time in prison while their case was being processed than was the case in Doon and Tweed.

Bail abuse is a generic term for breach of any condition of a bail order. In Scotland breaches of bail conditions can involve failing to appear at court or breach of any other bail condition by committing an offence while on bail, interfering with witnesses or evidence, or failing to adhere to a special condition imposed by the court. Prosecutors and courts regard any offence under the Bail Act as a breach of the court's trust. The most commonly recorded breach is that of committing an offence while on bail.

The problem of a high level of recorded offending while on bail, which is sometimes taken to be an indication of the court's failure to remand those who are involved in serious repeat offending, has been found in this study to be a consequence of the way in which bail is used in a locality. Police use of custody or undertaking brings accused to the attention of prosecutors and the court more quickly (within one day for custodies and between one and two days for undertakings) than if they had been simply reported to the prosecutor for summons to the court (this can take several weeks). Police detention in custody or release on undertaking is therefore interpreted by some prosecutors and courts as a signal that if an accused is to be released, they should not be ordained (that is, released unconditionally) but should have bail conditions set. These accused would not necessarily have otherwise been candidates for remand, but would have simply been ordained for a subsequent court appearance.

A high use of police custody can therefore promote a high use of bail by the court and allows these accused, because they are on bail, to be identified statistically as having had recent contact with the criminal justice system. If they commit offences during their release they will be identified as having breached the court's trust and therefore as having abused bail. A low use of police custody means that cases take longer to come to the attention of the prosecutor and the court. For this reason those who are committing further offences within a short time of their release by police will not have breached the trust of the court since they would not be on bail. Their offending would not therefore be identified statistically as bail abuse. Many of those who were found to have committed offences while on bail were not involved in committing serious offences for which a custodial sentence was a likely outcome. Areas with a culture of bail can be expected to have higher recorded levels of bail abuse since, by making greater use of bail, they enable those with recent criminal justice contact to be more easily identified. Whether this use of bail implies either more difficulties with the administration of justice or a greater danger to the public is considered in the report.

Chapter 1 BAIL IN SCOTLAND describes concerns about bail and looks at previous research on bail and risk. The study and its aims are described, and a framework for understanding bail decision making is presented. The chapter concludes with a description of the structure of bail decision making.

Police, prosecutors and courts all regularly make decisions under the Bail Act. When someone is arrested and charged with having committed a crime or an offence, police have the options of releasing them and reporting them to the prosecutor for possible summons to court; releasing them on a signed undertaking that they will appear at court on a specified date (which will be within one week); or detaining them in custody until the prosecutor decides whether they should appear in court, which will be on the next lawful day. The prosecutor, if they decide to proceed with a case in court can, if the accused person pleads not guilty in court, oppose that person's release prior to trial; ask for any release to be subject to the conditions of a bail order; or agree that the person should be released unconditionally (known as ordained) prior to trial.

Once a case comes to court the sheriff must consider, if the plea is one of not guilty, whether that person should be detained in custody (known as remanded) until trial, released on bail conditions or ordained. If the plea is guilty and the sheriff decides to defer sentence then the same custody release decisions must be made by the court.

Once guilt has been established an offender becomes the court's prisoner and the fiscal no longer has the authority to agree or oppose bail. (see Figures 1.1 and 1.2 in this Chapter).

Chapter 2 CRIMINAL JUSTICE DECISIONS IN DOON, TWEED AND BRAID describes the three study areas of Doon, Tweed and Braid. Information about custody/release decisions was extracted from police detention records and it was found that Doon police had a high use of custody and release on undertaking, Tweed police had a lower use of these and that Braid, which had the lowest use of custody, rarely used undertakings but instead released most people for summons. A census of sheriff court bail decisions was conducted in the study areas and outcomes of cases were checked for all accused recorded in the first twelve weeks of the census. Doon sheriff court was more likely to release accused on bail and less likely to either ordain or remand them; Tweed and Braid sheriff courts used bail for a similar percentage of accused, however Tweed ordained more accused and remanded people much less frequently than Braid. Accompanying the high level of remand at Braid there was a lower proportion of applications for bail and here there was a greater likelihood of prosecution opposition to bail. When cases were followed through to final disposal it was found that in Doon which had the highest use of bail, one in four accused were ultimately not convicted, whereas in Braid, the area with high remand, one in ten were not convicted. This implies that in Doon, any bail offences recorded prior to final disposal will overstate the level of proven bail abuse in that locality by up to twenty-five per cent.

Chapter 3 POLICE DECISIONS begins the exploration of the significance of the pattern identified in chapter two. It describes the sample of accused who were studied in detail, outlines their characteristics and looks at police options and responses to their cases. Accused at Doon were involved in less serious crime (as measured by victim harm) than accused in the other areas. Police in all areas generally disliked undertakings and rarely used them unless there was a local policy for their use in certain types of case. Police at Braid were more willing than police in either of the other areas to release those involved in serious crime. Though those arrested at Doon were more likely to be on bail than those arrested in the other areas, accused at Tweed and Braid were just as likely to have cases pending or to be in breach of another current court order (probation, community service) or to be on deferred sentence.

Analysis of police reasons for keeping accused in custody shows that the immediate circumstances of an incident was a prime police concern. Variation in police responses were explained by local policies and practices. Doon police gave more prominence to perceived risk to the community and considered criminal record to be an important gauge of this. Criminal record featured less prominently in police decisions in the other areas and accused were less likely to be thought as presently a risk to the public. Accused in Doon were more likely to have multiple bail orders than accused in the other areas and Doon was the only location where police had a policy and a frequent practice of keeping people with outstanding bail orders for custody court. Tweed police did not describe this as a policy but it was a frequent practice, and Braid police said that an outstanding bail order was of marginal importance in their custody decisions. Observation identified that when the police consider an individual case they consider both likely prosecution and court response - although likely prosecution response figures more prominently. In general, police who have been present in custody court will report back informally to colleagues on court responses to accused - the informal talk amongst police about what happened at court helps to generate a view of the local court as confirming the appropriateness of police custody decisions (when accused are remanded) or, for accused in certain cases about which police feel strongly and who are not remanded, as making incomprehensible bail decisions.

Chapter 4 PROSECUTION ATTITUDES TO BAIL notes that prosecutors' attitudes to bail in undertaking cases was tempered by their view of likely court response. The assessment of likely court outcome is an important way in which courtroom practices influence decision-making prior to court. In Braid, where the court made greatest use of remand, prosecutors were more likely to oppose bail. This pressure toward remand was absent in the other areas where the pressure for bail was such that , for example, in Tweed prosecutors would not oppose bail for people who had been released on undertaking. In contrast prosecutors opposed bail in over half the undertakings at Braid. Opposition to bail in undertaking cases was always an indication that prosecutors believed that accused should have been detained in police custody.

Police use of custody at Doon increased the chance that the prosecutor there would both look for the court to attach bail conditions to the release of more accused and that bail would be agreed more often. Since they viewed bail orders as placing a restriction on accused, Doon prosecutors responded to police use of custody and undertaking by being more likely to seek to have bail conditions attached to an accused's subsequent release by the court. In many instances where bail was agreed both in Doon and Tweed it was not necessarily agreed as an alternative to remand. For accused in custody cases, prosecutors at Doon and Tweed considered the age of bail convictions and bail orders, the similarity to the present offence and the seriousness of the offence for which the accused had been bailed, and would agree bail for those with recently granted bail orders if the new charges were seen as minor or non-analogous. The more frequent opposition to bail by Braid prosecutors was partly explained by the greater likelihood that accused at Braid would have a history of previous custodial sentences recorded, by the higher number of serious cases there (as measured by victim harm), but it was primarily linked to the greater likelihood that Braid prosecutors would consider that the existence of any Bail Act conviction or of an outstanding bail order would be grounds for opposing bail. Prosecutors at Doon were more likely than prosecutors elsewhere, to agree to the further release of those on multiple bails.

The implications of court pressure may have been a greater likelihood of prosecutors agreeing/opposing bail, however it did not necessarily produce acquiescence to court use of bail and remand. Whereas Braid prosecutors were more likely to consider the court as being too willing to remand, Tweed prosecutors were more likely to wish to see an increased use of remand and those at Doon to see a reduction in the use of bail and an increase in the use of ordaining.

Chapter 5 COURT BAIL DECISIONS In Doon and Tweed sheriffs rarely commented on prosecutors' attitudes to bail. In Braid prosecutors were regularly reproached in court for not opposing bail. Accused at Braid who did not apply for bail were more likely to be remanded than in the other areas. Only where a not guilty plea is entered is it possible for the prosecutor to present the grounds of opposition to bail to the court. For those accused pleading not guilty the focus of court discussion was usually the prosecution's interpretation of their criminal record. In the cases of younger accused (under 21), only where the prosecutor's interpretation of record was successfully challenged or where additional social information was given to the court by the defence, were accused granted bail. Where a plea of guilty is entered the prosecutor is precluded from agreeing or opposing bail in court. For those who were pleading guilty, there was no discussion of their criminal record in court and this had usually been the reason for fiscal opposition to bail having been marked. Offenders at Braid were more likely to be remanded during a deferred sentence than were offenders in other areas. Court responses to bail charges were tempered by their response to the substantive charges. Whereas courts did not always remand those with bail charges, in no area did the fact that someone had been released on bail preclude the court using custodial sentences. Those accused in Braid who were ultimately not convicted, were more likely to have spent time on remand than such accused in other areas. Further when accused in similar cases from the different areas were compared, those in Doon and Tweed were more likely to have been repeatedly released and to have received non-custodial sentences than accused in Braid who were more quickly brought into custody by the court.

Chapter 6 BAIL APPEALS The research found that the interpretation of bail legislation set down by Lord Wheatley in the judgement of a bail appeal (Smith V McC 1982 - see chapter 1) and sometimes referred to as the Wheatley guidelines, is no longer considered to be unambiguously authoritative. Although bail appeal judges maintained the continuing importance of theWheatley guidelines for bail decisions in the lower courts, they noted that the guidelines were not binding on the high court. Prosecutors in the high court (individually known as advocate depute, collectively referred to as crown counsel) had mixed views about the relevance of Wheatley, most sheriffs thought that the Wheatley guidelines were irrelevant to present bail decisions and many prosecutors showed only a vague knowledge of the guidelines. More prominent in their view were current high court decisions about bail appeals and most maintained that there was little evidence that the high court continued to adhere to the principles set out by Wheatley.

High court judges interviewed maintained that bail appeals are only successful where the high court considers that, in their application of law on bail, by granting or refusing bail in a particular case a sheriff has exercised their discretion wrongly. The high court will not grant an appeal if they consider that the law has been applied correctly even if, as individual judges, they themselves might have made a different initial bail decision. There were few bail appeals identified in the sample and none of these were prosecution appeals against the granting of bail. Such appeals are infrequent as crown counsel will not support prosecution bail appeals unless they believe that the sheriff has exercised their discretion wrongly. It is unusual for the high court to communicate reasons for rejecting or accepting the position on bail adopted by prosecutors and sheriffs in the lower courts. Those in the high court consider that, given existing resources in relation to the volume of high court business, this would be excessive for individual cases. The research was not designed to assess the extent to which high court decisions on bail appeals continue to adhere to the principles set out by Wheatley. However, the present level of communication between those working in the high court and those in the lower courts encourages the widely held view that decisions on bail appeals are generally unfathomable.

Chapter 7 BAIL ABUSE Recorded levels of bail abuse reflect the way in which bail is operated by the criminal justice system in particular localities. The current use of the Bail Act allows for the release of some who would otherwise be remanded, but many who are currently released on bail would not have been candidates for remand. Most people whether or not released on bail conditions were not alleged to have committed further offences. No evidence was found that in the areas with a propensity to grant bail the public were being placed at increased risk from large scale serious further offending. Those released on bail at Doon, where the use of bail by the court was high, were only slightly more likely to have further offences alleged than those at Braid, where there was a lower use of bail.

Returns from the court census had provided a different impression of the level of bail abuse in these areas, implying that Doon had the highest and Braid the lowest level of offending on bail. Most who breached their bail did so within the first twelve weeks of their bail order. In Doon over half of those who were recorded as having breached their bail had done so within its first four weeks. Most of this group were under 21. Many such accused at Braid are likely not to be detained by police there, but to be released for summons. The reports take several weeks to reach the fiscal from the police and, as these accused would not have been to court, they could not be on bail for the original matter. Any offending during that period would not be identified in official statistics in a way which would indicate that such accused had recently had contact with the criminal justice system.

Prior to the 1980 Act there was no information collected about the extent of offending on bail. The Bail Act has allowed the criminal justice system to make recidivism of bailees statistically visible in a way which was not previously possible and therefore, in areas with a culture of bail, there is likely to be increased awareness of this type of problem. However current concern about the level of recorded bail abuse is in part based on a misconception about the meaning of the statistics.

Levels of recorded bail abuse are often discussed as if they signified the level of repeat offending. Nevertheless, they are not a reliable measure of recidivism. The statistics record alleged breaches of the court's trust, with a high level of recorded bail abuse being associated with a high use of bail by the court. Offending on bail statistics are recorded by the police at the point of arrest and at that stage no account can be taken of whether accused will ultimately be convicted. The present study has found that guilt was not established for around ten percent of those in the sample who had bail charges in two of the areas, but that in the area where more people were on bail, thirty percent of bail offences in the sample there were not proved. Bail statistics give no indication of the significance of the breaches. The study has found that type and seriousness of either initial or subsequent offences as well as recency of bail orders were central to criminal justice responses to those breaches.

Figure A Criminal Justice Process for Study Sample at Doon

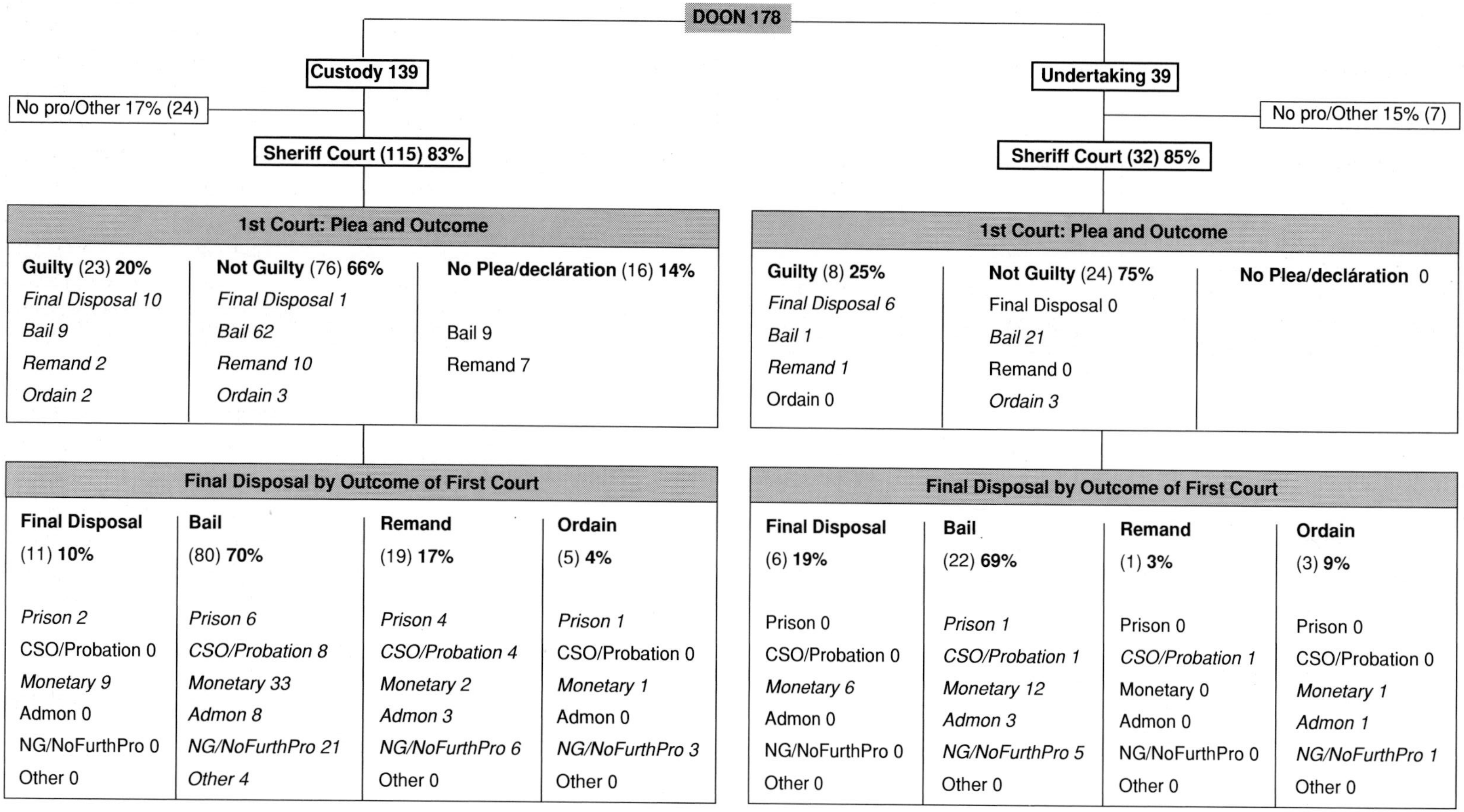

DOON 178

Custody 139

No pro/Other 17% (24)

Sheriff Court (115) 83%

1st Court: Plea and Outcome		
Guilty (23) **20%**	**Not Guilty** (76) **66%**	**No Plea/decláration** (16) **14%**
Final Disposal 10	*Final Disposal 1*	
Bail 9	*Bail 62*	Bail 9
Remand 2	*Remand 10*	Remand 7
Ordain 2	*Ordain 3*	

Final Disposal by Outcome of First Court			
Final Disposal	**Bail**	**Remand**	**Ordain**
(11) **10%**	(80) **70%**	(19) **17%**	(5) **4%**
Prison 2	*Prison 6*	*Prison 4*	*Prison 1*
CSO/Probation 0	*CSO/Probation 8*	*CSO/Probation 4*	CSO/Probation 0
Monetary 9	*Monetary 33*	*Monetary 2*	*Monetary 1*
Admon 0	*Admon 8*	*Admon 3*	Admon 0
NG/NoFurthPro 0	*NG/NoFurthPro 21*	*NG/NoFurthPro 6*	*NG/NoFurthPro 3*
Other 0	*Other 4*	Other 0	Other 0

Undertaking 39

No pro/Other 15% (7)

Sheriff Court (32) 85%

1st Court: Plea and Outcome		
Guilty (8) **25%**	**Not Guilty** (24) **75%**	**No Plea/decláration** 0
Final Disposal 6	Final Disposal 0	
Bail 1	*Bail 21*	
Remand 1	Remand 0	
Ordain 0	*Ordain 3*	

Final Disposal by Outcome of First Court			
Final Disposal	**Bail**	**Remand**	**Ordain**
(6) **19%**	(22) **69%**	(1) **3%**	(3) **9%**
Prison 0	*Prison 1*	Prison 0	Prison 0
CSO/Probation 0	*CSO/Probation 1*	*CSO/Probation 1*	CSO/Probation 0
Monetary 6	*Monetary 12*	Monetary 0	*Monetary 1*
Admon 0	*Admon 3*	Admon 0	*Admon 1*
NG/NoFurthPro 0	*NG/NoFurthPro 5*	NG/NoFurthPro 0	*NG/NoFurthPro 1*
Other 0	Other 0	Other 0	Other 0

Figure B Criminal Justice Process for Study Sample at Tweed

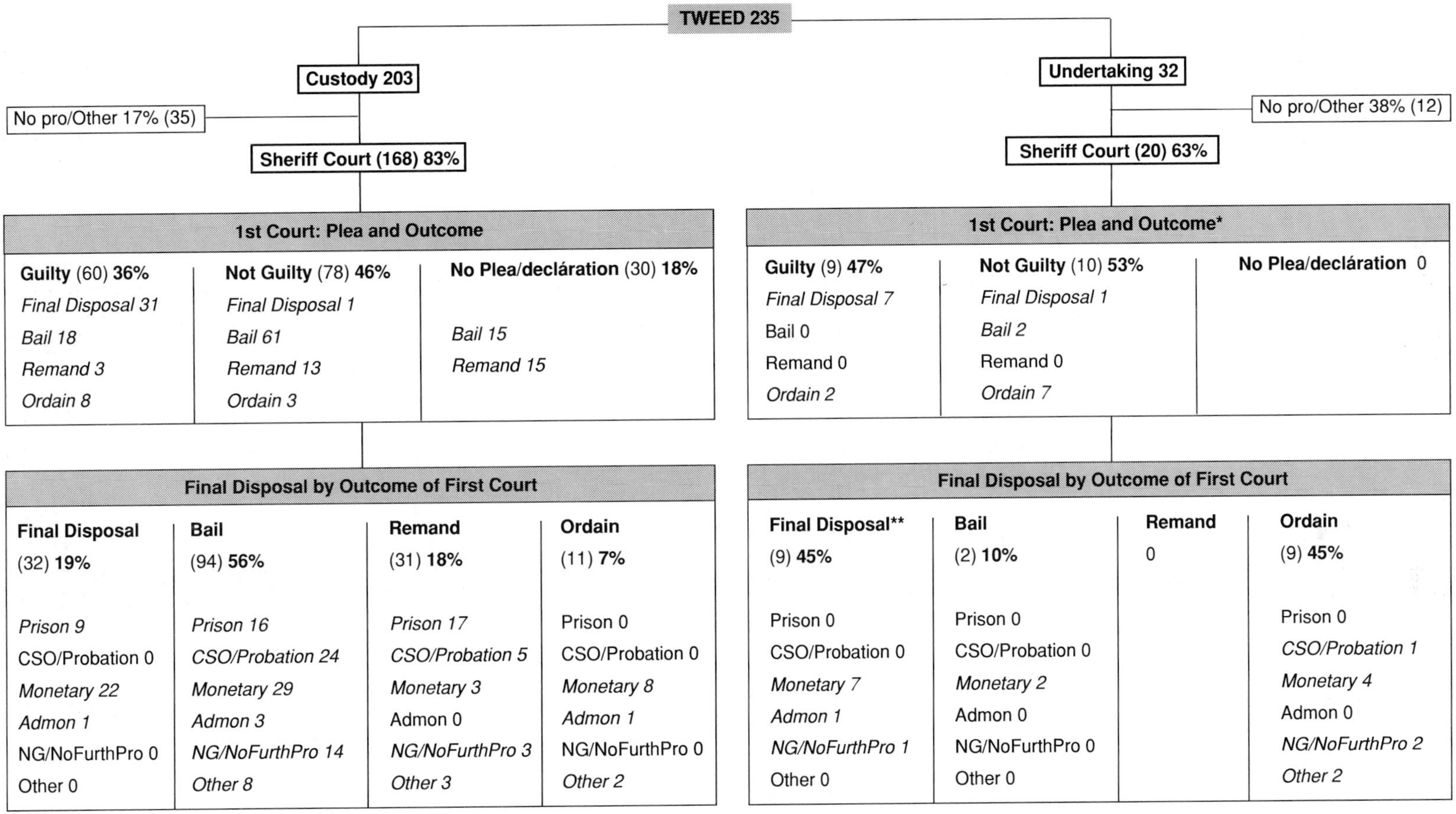

Custody — 1st Court: Plea and Outcome

Guilty (60) **36%**	**Not Guilty** (78) **46%**	**No Plea/declaration** (30) **18%**
Final Disposal 31	*Final Disposal 1*	
Bail 18	*Bail 61*	*Bail 15*
Remand 3	*Remand 13*	*Remand 15*
Ordain 8	*Ordain 3*	

Custody — Final Disposal by Outcome of First Court

Final Disposal (32) **19%**	**Bail** (94) **56%**	**Remand** (31) **18%**	**Ordain** (11) **7%**
Prison 9	*Prison 16*	*Prison 17*	Prison 0
CSO/Probation 0	*CSO/Probation 24*	*CSO/Probation 5*	CSO/Probation 0
Monetary 22	*Monetary 29*	*Monetary 3*	*Monetary 8*
Admon 1	*Admon 3*	Admon 0	*Admon 1*
NG/NoFurthPro 0	*NG/NoFurthPro 14*	*NG/NoFurthPro 3*	NG/NoFurthPro 0
Other 0	*Other 8*	*Other 3*	*Other 2*

Undertaking — 1st Court: Plea and Outcome*

Guilty (9) **47%**	**Not Guilty** (10) **53%**	**No Plea/declaration** 0
Final Disposal 7	*Final Disposal 1*	
Bail 0	*Bail 2*	
Remand 0	Remand 0	
Ordain 2	*Ordain 7*	

Undertaking — Final Disposal by Outcome of First Court

Final Disposal** (9) **45%**	**Bail** (2) **10%**	**Remand** 0	**Ordain** (9) **45%**
Prison 0	Prison 0		Prison 0
CSO/Probation 0	CSO/Probation 0		*CSO/Probation 1*
Monetary 7	*Monetary 2*		*Monetary 4*
Admon 1	Admon 0		Admon 0
NG/NoFurthPro 1	NG/NoFurthPro 0		*NG/NoFurthPro 2*
Other 0	Other 0		*Other 2*

***excludes 1 for whom a non-appearance warrant was issued**

****includes one with warrant from first court**

Figure C Criminal Justice Process for Study Sample at Braid

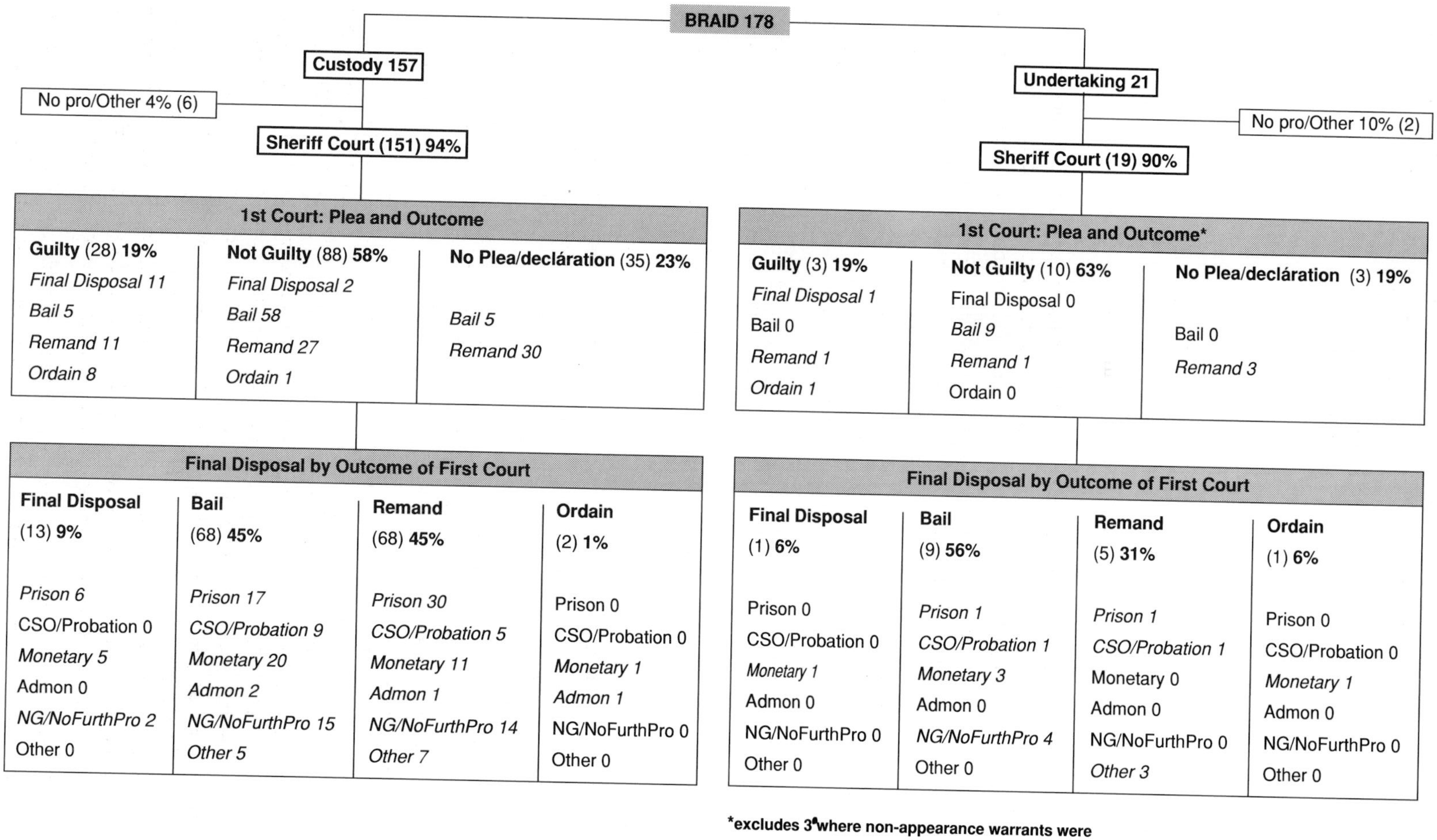

BRAID 178

Custody 157

No pro/Other 4% (6)

Sheriff Court (151) 94%

1st Court: Plea and Outcome		
Guilty (28) **19%**	**Not Guilty** (88) **58%**	**No Plea/decláration** (35) **23%**
Final Disposal 11	*Final Disposal 2*	
Bail 5	*Bail 58*	*Bail 5*
Remand 11	*Remand 27*	*Remand 30*
Ordain 8	*Ordain 1*	

Final Disposal by Outcome of First Court			
Final Disposal (13) **9%**	**Bail** (68) **45%**	**Remand** (68) **45%**	**Ordain** (2) **1%**
Prison 6	*Prison 17*	*Prison 30*	Prison 0
CSO/Probation 0	*CSO/Probation 9*	*CSO/Probation 5*	CSO/Probation 0
Monetary 5	*Monetary 20*	*Monetary 11*	*Monetary 1*
Admon 0	*Admon 2*	*Admon 1*	*Admon 1*
NG/NoFurthPro 2	*NG/NoFurthPro 15*	*NG/NoFurthPro 14*	NG/NoFurthPro 0
Other 0	*Other 5*	*Other 7*	Other 0

Undertaking 21

No pro/Other 10% (2)

Sheriff Court (19) 90%

1st Court: Plea and Outcome*		
Guilty (3) **19%**	**Not Guilty** (10) **63%**	**No Plea/decláration** (3) **19%**
Final Disposal 1	Final Disposal 0	
Bail 0	*Bail 9*	Bail 0
Remand 1	*Remand 1*	*Remand 3*
Ordain 1	Ordain 0	

Final Disposal by Outcome of First Court			
Final Disposal (1) **6%**	**Bail** (9) **56%**	**Remand** (5) **31%**	**Ordain** (1) **6%**
Prison 0	*Prison 1*	*Prison 1*	Prison 0
CSO/Probation 0	*CSO/Probation 1*	*CSO/Probation 1*	CSO/Probation 0
Monetary 1	*Monetary 3*	Monetary 0	*Monetary 1*
Admon 0	Admon 0	Admon 0	Admon 0
NG/NoFurthPro 0	*NG/NoFurthPro 4*	NG/NoFurthPro 0	NG/NoFurthPro 0
Other 0	Other 0	*Other 3*	Other 0

*excludes 3 where non-appearance warrants were

OPERATING BAIL: DISCUSSION OF THE IMPLICATIONS OF CRIMINAL JUSTICE CULTURES

INTRODUCTION

The purpose of this study has been to describe and to explain current criminal justice practice in relation to bail in Scotland, as well as to assess both the effectiveness of the Bail etc. (Scotland) Act 1980 as it is currently being operated and to consider the significance of bail abuse. Three criminal justice cultures have been identified, one characterised by a high use of bail, one by a high use of unconditional release and one by a high use of remand. Each illustrates a potential direction in which policy and practice on the operation of bail could move nationally. In terms of the Act's general aim to enable the release of untried and unsentenced prisoners, the research has found that the legislation is partially effective in that it does allow the release of some who would otherwise have been detained in custody and there is little evidence that such release is hindering the administration of justice or placing the public at increased risk from those who commit serious offences. The limits to the effectiveness of the Act are produced by the ways in which the legislation is operated within different criminal justice cultures. In this section we consider some implications of the criminal justice cultures which are described in the report in order to highlight the issues which are raised by each and we make some recommendations in relation to the consistency of bail decision making.

The findings of this study underline that it is misleading to conflate the level of recorded offending while on bail with the level of recidivism. This conflation has recently increased public anxiety that the criminal justice system is ineffective, since the rise in the recorded level of offending while on bail is often taken as a sign that the courts are increasingly releasing those who continue to offend and the public are thereby being placed at greater risk from repeat offenders. Offending on bail statistics recorded by the police are *reported breaches of bail* and are not adjusted to take account of the proportion of charges which are not ultimately proved. Police are improving their recording of offending while on bail and this, together with a high use of bail by the court, can increase the statistical visibility of some recidivism. This increased visibility does not necessarily indicate an increased risk to the public. This research has found that accused in the area with a lower use of bail (Braid) were just as likely to have pending cases on their criminal records as were accused in the area with a high use of bail (Doon). However, those in the area with a low use of bail were less likely to be on bail in respect of their pending cases than were accused in the high bail area. In short, the higher level of offending on bail which was recorded in Doon was associated with a high use of bail by the court but was not associated with the public in that area being placed at increased risk from those committing further offences. The lower level of offending on bail which was recorded in Braid was not associated with the public in that area being at reduced risk from those committing further offences.

It is important to stress that the purpose of bail is to enable the release from custody of untried and unsentenced prisoners until by due process of law their innocence or guilt has been established and, if necessary, sentence has been passed - it is not intended to stop crime and it cannot stop crime. However, release on bail can accord crime committed during that release with a particular significance and ensure that those who commit crime while released on the courts' trust will ultimately receive additional penalties for breaching that trust. This research has found that in all areas those convicted of breach of bail were given significant penalties by the courts including, under some circumstances, consecutive custodial sentences. The research has also found that for all areas those with a record of bail convictions were less likely to be granted bail in the future. There was, nevertheless, a lack of agreement across the areas about the circumstances under which someone's bail record would render them unbailable. The challenge for the criminal justice system is to operate bail legislation consistently in a way which minimises the risk to which the public are put by those who commit crime; which limits the extent to which those convicted and who do not ultimately receive a custodial sentence, will have spent time in custody prior to conviction ; and which minimises the likelihood that those who are accused of crime but who are not ultimately convicted will have spent time in prison.

BAIL DECISION MAKING

This study has found that in making decisions about bail there are changing priorities given to aspects of cases by police, prosecutors and courts. Police usually focus on the incident, prosecutors focus on the evidence in the case and the accused's record whereas, for those pleading not guilty, the focus of discussion at court is the record. When asked about their custody/release decisions, police were more likely to mention factors associated with process (such as the need to get cases to court quickly) as an explanation for their action in undertaking cases. In custodies, the demeanour of the accused to police in the immediate circumstances of the incident was important. Police did not often consider accused to be a risk to the community and therefore this was only infrequently given as a reason for detention in custody. The differing weight given by the fiscals to record in relation to incident explained the frequent disjuncture between police, prosecution and court views about the appropriate response to an accused pre-trial. For prosecutors, both at the sheriff court and the appeal stage, protection of the public featured more prominently, and this was a function of the greater prominence given to criminal record in prosecutor decision making and in particular to prosecutors' interpretation of a continuing pattern of behaviour. Sheriffs, in contrast, in the main indicated that their prime concern was with likelihood of absconding as they considered that instances in which the public was at risk were rare.

CRIMINAL JUSTICE CULTURES: OVERVIEW

In this report we argue that to understand the operation of bail it is necessary to understand the structure of the criminal justice system (that is, *which practitioners and agencies* - police, prosecutors, courts - *can do what*), the content of criminal justice relationships (that is, *what they are actually doing*) and the features of the cases experienced locally (that is, *what they are doing it about*). We have examined the way in which these elements interact and found that they produce particular cultures which encourage the making of some types of decision and discourage others. In Doon which had a culture of bail and in Tweed which had a culture of liberation, bail was rarely, if ever, opposed for those who the police had not kept in custody and the courts there took active steps to encourage the timing of bail applications to minimise the extent to which people were remanded. In Braid, where there was a culture of remand, prosecutors regularly opposed bail for accused who had not been kept in custody by the police, and they were regularly criticised in court for not opposing bail as frequently as the court would have wished.

Table A summarises the characteristics of each culture and table B summarises the implications of the cultures.

For many in the criminal justice system bail is valued because a bail order provides a written statement of the conditions under which the court is prepared to trust

Table A Criminal Justice Cultures: Summary of Features

Culture Type	*Police*	*Prosecution*	*Court*
Bail (Doon)	policy & practice of detaining those on bail; high use of custody and undertaking	*presumption of bail* for police custodies and undertakings; bail history interpreted relative to other elements of record	Most cases to *court within 24 hours; high use of* conditional release *(ie bail);* low use of custodial sentences
Liberation (Tweed)	practice of detaining those on bail; medium use of custody and undertaking	*presumption of ordain* unless police custody; bail history interpreted relative to other elements of record	*high use of unconditional release (ie ordain);* low use of custodial sentences
Remand (Braid)	bail irrelevant to custody decision; low use of custody high use of release for summons	*regular opposition to bail* for cases released by police; any bail history likely to lead to bail opposition	*high use of remand release tended to be conditional;* high use of custodial sentences

someone sufficiently to permit their release. These conditions are usually read to the accused in court and they have to confirm their agreement to them. There was a consensus among criminal justice practitioners that breaching the court's trust by failing to comply with bail should be regarded seriously, nevertheless in practice the implications of breaching bail were variable and police, prosecutors, sheriffs and high court judges did not attach the same weight to different breaches of bail. Whereas police, prosecutors and the high court all maintained they gave greater weight to breaches which involved further offences, most sheriffs were more likely to consider failure to appear at court to be the more serious breach. In addition, though in practice prosecutors had variable responses to breaches of bail involving further offences, they all opposed bail for accused who had previously failed to appear at court.

CULTURE OF BAIL

The situation in Doon illustrates a culture which promotes the routine widening of the use of bail to those who would not otherwise be candidates for remand. Police there were highly sceptical about bail because of the frequency of its use. Because of police policy and the practice of generally detaining in custody those found on arrest to be on bail, people were brought into custody for relatively minor matters for which neither the prosecutors nor the court would have wished them to have been further detained.

The high use of police custody and undertaking at Doon contributed to the high use

Table B Implications of Criminal Justice Cultures

Culture Type	*Positive Implications*	*Negative Implications*
Bail (Doon)	1. Court and prosecutor have early review of police action in most cases 2. More recidivism is identified as bail abuse 3. Those not ultimately convicted less likely to have spent time in prison	1. Police see more people with bail orders and use custody more often because of bail orders 2. Release by court more likely to be conditional, even when remand would not have been a consideration 3. More repeat bail orders issued 4. Generates anxiety about effectiveness of the criminal justice system and risk to the public from recidivism 5. Police generally highly sceptical of usefulness of bail 6. Longer term - likely to increase the use of remand as young people more quickly develop records which decrease their chances of bail in the future
Liberation (Tweed)	1. Prosecutor and court have early review of police action in many cases 2. Tendency to use unconditional release for more minor cases 3. Therefore those in such cases not later candidates for police custody because of bail 4. Recidivism identified as bail abuse includes fewer minor matters 5. Fewer repeat bail orders issued 6. Those not ultimately convicted less likely to have spent time in prison	1. Less recidivism is identified as bail abuse 2. Police dissatisfied, though dissatisfaction focused on particular cases 3. Prosecutors dissatisfied with court pressure for low use of remand
Remand (Braid)	1. Police satisfied with use of bail, as more custody decisions confirmed by court 2. Repeat bail orders rare 3. System can deal with a high volume of cases	1. Most cases not subject to oversight by prosecutor and court till several weeks after arrest 2. Police more likely to release accused for whom prosecutors would have preferred custody 3. Prosecutors dissatisfied with court pressure for high use of remand 4. Tendency for release to be conditional 5. Those not ultimately convicted more likely to have spent time in prison 6. Recidivism less visible as bail abuse

of bail by the court since prosecutors and sheriffs there indicated a preference for those accused who had appeared from police custody or undertaking to have bail conditions attached to their release. The reason for this was that they thought that because police had not simply released these accused for summons, it was necessary to use bail conditions, since these make certain injunctions to people about their behaviour, (that they should not commit offences, interfere with witnesses or otherwise obstruct the course of justice) as well as ordering them to appear at court at an appointed date and time. Should these accused abuse their release by breaching their bail, the court could then exact a further penalty for this breach of trust and this would be recorded so that, in the future, release for those who breached their bail would be less likely.

A culture of bail implies a closer monitoring by the court of the behaviour of those who come into contact with the criminal justice system, especially if, as in Doon, Scottish Criminal Records Office records are accurate to within 24 hours. However it can generate serious disquiet about the effectiveness of bail and, to the extent that bail is thought to be equated with recidivism, can contribute to anxiety that the criminal justice system is ineffective since, by releasing perpetrators of crime it is placing the public at risk, rather than protecting them. Ultimately, criminal justice practices in Doon may be self-defeating

> "... I know that the Chief Constable....has said in public...that he is very concerned at the very weak lenient attitude shown by judges ..towards allowing too many people, and he says its only the hard core who commit crimes and they are allowed bail time after time after time and they go out and they commit further offences....he was referring..to the repeated pattern of housebreakings in this area..and he said that they ought not to be allowed out on bail until they have stood trial."
>
> "What is your response to that?"
>
> "...I have a lot of sympathy with that point of view...because I see weak young men who appear before me in breach of bail, not in respect of one set of bail conditions, but perhaps in respect of a set of 3 or 4 previous appearances when they have been put on bail .... there is something wrong with an administration which allows someone to breach so many bail conditions and yet be allowed out on bail...." (sheriff at Doon).

The more people the police detain for minor matters, the higher the proportion which will be released by the court; the more minor the case in which bail has been granted, the more likely it is that prosecutors and the court will agree to further bail; the more people on bail, the more minor recidivism will be recorded as bail abuse - and the greater will be the impression of an ineffective system. Paradoxically, what is being operated is a system which processes cases more quickly in their initial stages and which monitors people's behaviour more closely.

CULTURE OF LIBERATION

A culture of liberation implies a more sparing use of bail by courts, a tendency to use unconditional release for more minor cases, and therefore for there to be fewer people on bail. For this reason, as well as because prosecutors at Tweed would not oppose bail for those who police had not kept in custody, though police had a practice of detaining those already on bail, the cycle inflating the use of bail and which characterised Doon was absent from Tweed. Prosecutor and court had an early review of police action in fewer cases than at Doon, nevertheless, over 40% of accused in that area had their case seen by prosecutor and court within one week of arrest and charge. Though Tweed police did express dissatisfaction with the use of bail, they were less likely to express the view that current use of bail made their efforts to control crime futile, and in practice their concerns tended to be focused on the release on bail of particular accused in the sample. In this area the release of some accused by the court was contentious, though often the explanation for a different action to that which the police would have preferred lay in the prosecutor or court according greater priority than the police to aspects of an accused's record, to different definitions of what was considered to be a serious record (for example, the extent to which pending cases or children's panel disposals were considered), to additional information coming to light in court, or simply to the extent to which the prosecutor or court thought that accused should be given further opportunity to demonstrate their ability to behave within the law.

CULTURE OF REMAND

Decisions about releasing or detaining accused are in part decisions about regulating the flow of cases through the criminal justice system. A culture of remand implies that a higher volume of cases can be processed but that more of them will take longer to get to court and that therefore those who commit offences within a short period of their release by police will not have these offences identified as bail abuse. Criminal justice agencies in Braid were processing a much higher volume of accused than were those in the other areas. For example, Braid police processed a higher volume of accused than did police in Tweed which was an urban area. Braid police gave current bail orders a low priority in considering their response to accused. They were nearly twice as likely to release people for summons - that meant that for more cases it would be several weeks before the fiscal or the court could review police action. Records in that area were less up to date than were records in the other study areas because the high volume of cases for that police force meant that there were delays in updating, so both new cases and court results were slower to be recorded (although recording of new bail orders, because this was given a priority, appeared to be as accurate in Braid as elsewhere).

Therefore whereas in a bail culture those who committed offences within the first four weeks of their release were highly likely to be on bail at the time, such people in a remand culture may not even have had the report of the initial incident sent to the prosecutor - as such, because they would not have been to court they could not be on bail, and any subsequent offending alleged would not be identifiable statistically as it would, had they been on bail. Yet the findings of our research are that the sample in this area was just as likely to have pending cases on arrest and were only slightly less likely to be alleged to be in breach of bail as the sample in the other areas. This implies that the public were no better protected from recidivism by criminal justice bail practices in a remand culture than they were elsewhere. The higher the use of remand by the court, the lower the visibility of recidivism, the less problematic that bail legislation appeared to the police. Police often take a court decision to remand as an endorsement of their original custody decision. In a culture of remand police will interpret more of their decisions as being confirmed by the court and will see fewer signs that the court released people who the police would have preferred to have been detained.

BAIL ABUSE - AN INDICATOR OF RECIDIVISM OR A BREACH OF TRUST?

What this set of relationships implies is that any difference between Doon and Braid in the level of recorded bail abuse does not reflect a difference in the level of recidivism but rather a difference in the extent to which the courts in these areas were prepared to release people on trust and a difference in the extent to which that trust was breached. Criminal justice practice means that Doon police deal with more people on bail orders and because they are dealt with as custodies they have a higher profile in police consciousness than if they were dealt with as summons.

Police reports in custody cases have to be completed before the end of a police shift as accused will be in court within twenty-four hours. For those released for summons, a court appearance may be several weeks away as it can take between two and five weeks for police to report these cases to the prosecutor. Such accused, if they offend in the interim may face further charges but these can not be recorded as being breaches of bail. Such offences will therefore not be recognised in official statistics as being associated with people who had recent contact with the criminal justice system. Most of those in Doon who were alleged to have breached their bail, did so within four weeks of their initial release by the court. The combination of criminal justice responses to those thought to be involved in repeat offending at Doon was therefore contributing to the production of a high level of recorded bail abuse; whereas the response of the criminal justice system to repeat offending at Braid was an important explanation for the lower level of bail abuse recorded there.

The counter argument would be that a slightly lower level of bail abuse at Braid implies lower incidence of recidivism because of the local court's propensity to remand. If this were the case, it would imply that the system at Braid was marginally better than that at Doon in identifying potential recidivists. However, for this to be accurate, we would expect that fewer in the sample at Braid would have had pending cases on arrest and fewer would be found to be subject to other types of court order, because it would imply that police and courts there were more accurate at targeting those accused who needed to be detained in custody. As we show in chapter three, this was not the case and a culture of remand does not imply that criminal justice practices in that area are responding to those likely to commit further offences any more effectively.

In short, we are arguing that

- **a high level of recorded bail abuse does not necessarily equate with a high level of recidivism**
- **a low level of recorded bail abuse does not necessarily equate with a low level of recidivism**

Rather

- **a high use of police custody + a high propensity of prosecutors to seek bail conditions + a high use of court bail —> a high level of recorded bail abuse**
- **a low level of police custody + a high propensity of prosecutors to oppose bail + a high use of remand by court —> a low level of recorded bail abuse**

Offending on bail statistics are recorded by the police at the point of arrest and at that stage no account can be taken of whether accused will ultimately be convicted. The present study has found that guilt was not established for around ten percent of those in the sample at Tweed and Braid who had bail charges, but that in Doon, where more people were on bail, thirty percent of bail offences in the sample there were not proved.

In none of the areas is level of bail abuse an accurate and reliable measure of recidivism. Rather breach of bail is a signal to the court that particular people have a history of having abused the court's trust and it is responded to as such by prosecutors and courts. Crimes and offences committed while on bail are accorded a particular significance by virtue of this. The seriousness of the breach is dependent on the circumstances of particular incidents and at present there is sufficient flexibility for courts to deal differently with someone who, for example, has been granted bail on housebreaking charges and who has breached bail by becoming drunk and incapable, from someone who has been bailed on robbery charges and who has breached their bail by committing a robbery. Bail abuse statistics cannot distinguish between these - criminal justice practitioners responding to cases can and do. *The present research has found that type and seriousness of either initial or subsequent offences as well as recency of bail orders were central to criminal justice responses to those breaches. The range of disposals used by courts in their response to breach of bail is indicative of the significance accorded to particular breaches in the context of the other criminal matters for which an offender is being sentenced.*

Many criminal justice practitioners who had worked under the previous bail legislation felt that the strength of the present Act is that it enables a record of breaches of trust to be kept for individuals. Prior to the 1980 Act this had not been the case and there was no mechanism for monitoring the behaviour of those released on bail by the court, and no statistical information collected about the extent of offending on bail. Many accused were released on condition that they lodge a sum of money with the court. Only their subsequent failure to appear would be monitored by the criminal justice system. There would be no permanent record of any problematic behaviour associated with their release on bail. The penalty for failure to appear would be the loss of the money and many criminal justice practitioners who also had experience prior to the 1980 Act, have pointed out that this penalty was minor as it was often regarded by accused as a fine.

The current implications of failing to comply with bail are more serious. Police have a power of arrest for anyone thought to be in breach of a bail order and any convictions for failing to comply with bail are permanently recorded. In all areas bail convictions were seen as a contra-indicator for further release on bail and in some areas the existence of any bail conviction was sufficient grounds for the fiscal to oppose bail. Ultimately, those who are convicted of breaching bail will, under the present legislation, not only receive an additional penalty from the court, but will be less likely to be granted the court's trust in the future. Present prosecution practice is to libel a bail charge automatically if someone is on bail. Though a few prosecutors mentioned that they would not libel bail charges if the breach were a minor matter, in practice bail charges were libelled even in those cases which prosecutors themselves described as minor. An important implication of this in a culture of bail is that those who are coming into contact with the criminal justice system and being given bail for more minor matters can quickly build up a record which in the future may preclude them from being granted bail even if the new offences alleged would not otherwise imply a need for custody. The long term implications of a culture of bail may well be a rise in the numbers of people who, because of their bail history, are more likely to be remanded. As one advocate depute stated in interview . . . . .

> "I think more people get kept in custody because of the Bail Act now than probably prior to the Bail Act, because the Act's a relevant

consideration in whether to grant bail or not which it wasn't before."

RISK AND PREDICTION

The findings of our research imply that there may be issues of targeting decisions - does the lack of difference between Braid and Doon in the level of recidivism imply that neither area could target their use of release appropriately and that we should consider some kind of exercise to improve the prediction of those likely to abuse bail? Although bail decisions are about risk, from our observation of criminal justice practice we have found that it is unusual for bail decisions solely to be based on this. This was because, for the police, the risk issue generally concerned immediate risk because of the circumstances of an incident and therefore this did not prevail as a factor for decisions at a later stage in processing accused. Despite the fact that protection of the public featured more prominently in prosecutor decision making, it was unusual for accused to be considered to present a serious risk to the public. Therefore though occasionally police and prosecutors were concerned that the release of particular accused would pose a sufficiently serious risk to the public to outweigh other factors, such cases were unusual. Sheriffs as well as prosecutors and judges in the high court confirmed that it was rare for sheriff court cases to involve accused who posed a threat to public safety.

In practice, therefore, the question of risk of breaching bail is generally subsumed within other considerations when criminal justice practitioners form their views on bail. In other words, when considering the question of bail for individual accused, unless there is strong evidence of risk to public safety, the question which criminal justice practitioners ask is less like 'Is this person likely to breach their bail?' and more akin to, 'Does this person need to be in custody?'

> "We accept that bail should be allowed unless there is good reason for opposing it. We only oppose it if we don't have much alternative." (prosecutor at Tweed)

> "If someone is released on bail and told not to commit another offence I fail to see why there is a problem for anyone to be released on bail. They are presumed innocent ....only special conditions affect liberty and tend to be used in crimes against the person where that factor is a prime consideration." (prosecutor at Tweed)

The question as to whether someone needs to be in custody, while subsuming within it an assessment of the potential of breach of bail, requires a wider range of factors to be considered and is more compatible with a presumption in favour of bail than is the simpler question about likelihood of breach. This last question, to the extent to which it was based on any general characteristics (such as case type etc.) of those thought to be at high risk of breaching bail, would in effect remove the presumption in favour of bail for that group. If current concerns about the effectiveness of bail decisions are to be addressed by giving this factor greater priority in bail decisions, then in the interests of consistency it is important that guidance on this should be given to decision makers. Such guidance would be more effective if it were to be based on an agreed formulation about the relative weights which should be attached to different features of cases.

BAIL - LIBERATION FROM CUSTODY OR RESTRICTION OF LIBERTY?

Prosecutors in all areas indicated that they were sometimes seeking the extra constraint of bail for those who would not otherwise be candidates for remand. Usually, prosecutors felt that the public interest would be better served by these accused having conditional rather than unconditional release. This was more frequently the case in Doon and Tweed where bail tended to be described by prosecutors as a way of constraining accused than in Braid, where bail operated more often as a liberation from custody. In all areas defence agents rarely asked for their clients to be ordained, yet prosecutors indicated that there were occasions when they would have been prepared to accept this unconditional release if it had been sought[1]. In general, the practice of defence agents tended to imply that, for them, often the key aspect of the court decision was whether or not their client was released. However, in view of the significance of bail history in criminal justice responses to individual accused, this approach may not be in the longer term interests of their clients who, if they have further contact with the criminal justice system in an area with a culture of bail, are likely to be detained in custody because of the existence of a bail order, even if any new alleged incident would not otherwise have been thought by police to merit custody.

The perception of bail as a restriction of liberty is an important explanation for the reluctance of many criminal justice practitioners to make greater use of special conditions. Though many practitioners were concerned about the enforceability of special bail conditions and were reluctant to make wider use of them primarily for this reason, there was also a strong reluctance to consider more use of these because of the additional constraint which such conditions place on liberty. In Braid, where there was a greater tendency to operate bail as a liberation from custody, greater use was made of special conditions.

BAIL HISTORY - SIGNIFICANCE

Criminal record, especially in relation to bail convictions and current bail orders, has been shown to be central to criminal justice liberation/custody decisions. This centrality underlines the limits of policies directed towards impacting on bail decisions through the provision of social and other information about accused. Although such information could occasionally affect criminal justice views in particular cases, in general it was marginal to deliberations.

In all areas prosecutors opposed bail for accused with a record of analogous previous convictions or of convictions for failure to appear. However, definitions of what constituted a bailable record were variable in respect of what was considered to be a short or long time-gap between offences as well as in relation to bail history (i.e. bail convictions and current bail orders). In this respect, greater consistency in interpretation of bail history could be encouraged if more guidance were to be given to prosecutors about the circumstances under which bail convictions may carry more or less weight (e.g. the point, if any, at which some bail convictions may no longer be considered; the circumstances under which bail should be further agreed for those already on bail, and the circumstances under which it should not be further agreed).

We have explained that in all areas, if an accused was on bail at the time of arrest, then a breach of bail charge would routinely be libelled. However, there was wide disparity

[1] Those released without bail conditions would still be subject to a penalty if they failed to appear at court without reasonable excuse.

in views amongst police and prosecutors about the numbers of bail charges which should be libelled for accused who were facing multiple charges or who had more than one bail order. Doon police often libelled multiple bail charges if there were multiple bail orders, though prosecution practice was to alter this when marking a case. In Doon and Tweed the prosecution practice was usually to libel one bail charge per case and, if an accused was subject of more than one bail order, to state that within the narrative of the charge. In Braid there were few cases where there was more than one bail order and though usually one bail charge would be libelled per case, occasionally prosecutors would libel a bail charge for each substantive charge on a complaint. Sheriffs in each area indicated that the method of libelling charges did not impact on their practice in that if faced with multiple bail charges they would generally give the most serious sentence on the first and admonish on the rest.

Nevertheless, without a consistent and well-understood practice in relation to charging, it is difficult to see how the significance of bail convictions in a criminal record can be clearly understood. (For example, 2 bail convictions recorded in a case which consisted of 2 charges might relate to the number of charges in the case or the number of bail orders which were breached - the first situation would imply that the person had been released on the court's trust once and had breached it, the second that they had been given two opportunities by the court and had abused these). Given the importance of bail history in criminal justice considerations of custody/release, the lack of an agreed charging practice, understood by those who operate it and consistently applied, is problematic. Across the three areas, there was no consistent view about appropriate charging practice in relation to multiple breaches of a single order, or breaches of multiple orders. Some thought that they should consider only the most recent bail order, others thought that multiple charges should be libelled if the bail orders were some time apart, or if the incidents leading to the charges on a complaint were some time apart, while others thought that the key distinction was whether they were from the same court or a court in another area. Though there is SOHHD guidance on how breaches of bail should be counted for statistical purposes, there appears to be no guidance for police or prosecutors about appropriate charging practice.

BAIL HISTORY - RECORD OF RELIABILITY OR OF UNRELIABILITY?

Bail history was interpreted by many criminal justice practitioners as being a record of someone's reliability. We maintain, however, that it is rather a record of unreliability and that to recognise this is to recognise a key change which could be made, if the criminal justice system does in fact require a record of reliability in order to assess someone's suitability for release. For though the pending chapter of someone's criminal record contains information about any bail orders which are current, as soon as a case is disposed of by the court, the fact that the person was released on bail is removed. The only permanent indicator which a record has that someone has ever been on bail is if they have a conviction for having breached their bail order. It is therefore not possible to judge, from looking at someone's convictions, whether they were given bail at any time and did not breach the order, or whether they have breached every bail order that they have been granted. A genuine record of reliability could be provided if the convictions chapter of criminal records were to contain information about whether bail had been granted during a particular case and whether that bail order had been breached.

THE WHEATLEY GUIDELINES, CONSISTENCY AND COMMUNICATION: THE IMPACT OF APPEALS

We explain in chapter one that the power relations embedded in the criminal justice system means that the views of the court, especially the high court, are crucial to understanding the operation of bail. In chapter five we illustrate the ways in which sheriffs' courtroom practice could encourage or discourage release on bail. The high court, having the authority to define sheriff court bail decisions as having been correct or incorrect, has the potential to constrain localised cultures and to help promote consistency in bail decisions nationally. There was a generally held view amongst those working in the sheriff courts that high court decisions about bail appeals were unfathomable and that the principles for interpreting the Bail Act which were set out in 1982 by Lord Wheatley were no longer being applied. There was disagreement about the extent to which this was beneficial.

Bail decisions in the lower courts are about particular cases in the context of law; appeals are about the application of law in the context of the case. This difference in concern helps to explain the discrepancies which can occur between attitudes to bail in the lower courts and those in the high court. The guidance which would assist those in the lower courts to have a better understanding of high court views on bail and which would encourage a consistency of approach, is felt by many criminal justice practitioners to be presently lacking. It was found that there was little communication between those working in the high court and those in the sheriff court about the explanation for the outcome of bail appeals. Results of appeals are not communicated to the sheriffs who made the original decision, and if advocate deputes decide not to support a prosecution bail appeal, or not to oppose bail when the defence appeals a remand decision, the reasons for this are not communicated to procurator fiscals. As the research did not include a systematic study of bail appeals, we cannot comment on whether or not the high court is judging bail appeals consistently and in relation to Wheatley's guidelines. It is unequivocal, however, that there is presently a gap in understanding about bail between the high court and those in the lower courts and a lack of communication about the reasons for high court decisions is contributing to this. If more consistency in approach to bail is considered to be desirable then a pre-condition of this would be the formulation of an interpretation of the legislation to which both the higher and lower courts could operate, together with provision for the feedback of more information about high court decisions to those working in the lower courts.

CONCLUSIONS

Criminal justice decisions in particular cases not only have an immediate impact on what happens to the accused but also have a long term impact on how criminal justice practitioners will respond to that person in the future. The research has found that experience of imprisonment and bail convictions contribute to the production of criminal records which in the future will make people more likely to be candidates for custody than for release. Those coming into contact with criminal justice agencies in an area with a high use of bail are likely in the longer term to have bail convictions on their records and such convictions are understood by police, prosecutors and courts as signifiers of poor bail risks. Many of these accused are involved in offences for which, in other areas, they would be ordained. Court sentence is used as a measure of seriousness of offending when practitioners interpret records. Those coming into contact with the system in an area with a high use of custodial sentences will more quickly develop records which will be taken to indicate serious offending.

At their core, current anxieties about bail and its abuse are anxieties about the effectiveness of the criminal justice system both in its administration of justice and its protection of the public. Our findings suggest that *the choice that needs to be made in considering bail is not a simple choice - between protecting the public from recidivism or reducing the level of custodial remand - but rather a choice about the extent to which those accused of having committed crime should, during the course of their case, have their release subject to conditions which facilitate the monitoring of their behaviour and the extent to which we are prepared to risk those who are ultimately not convicted having spent time on remand in prison.* Each culture has specific implications which we have explained although we would emphasise that these cultures are not immutable but rather are dynamic and capable of modification. In this chapter we have restricted recommendations to action which would promote more consistency in current practice and which would improve understanding of practice both for those within the criminal justice system and those outwith it. The findings of the research nevertheless raise more fundamental questions about the way in which bail is used. The *answers to the questions of how bail should* be used and about which cultures *should* be promoted and which inhibited, lie outwith the bounds of the research, since they depend on social, moral and political visions of how the criminal justice system ought to operate in order to operate in the public interest. The information provided in this research, while not providing final answers as to what should be done about bail, will, we hope, have provided sufficient understanding of the implications of different courses of action to encourage informed debate about the way in which bail should be operated in the future.

PART II

FINDINGS OF THE RESEARCH

CHAPTER 1

BAIL IN SCOTLAND

INTRODUCTION

This chapter presents the background to the research and explains the purpose of the study. An interpretive framework for understanding bail decision-making is outlined. When police arrest and charge someone they can detain them in custody to appear the next day at court or they can release them, in which case if they appear at court this will be at a later date. Prosecutors have the discretion to decide whether or not a case will be prosecuted and they can reverse police decisions by releasing people who police have kept in custody or by issuing a warrant for the arrest of someone who the police have released. If a case goes to court prosecutors can decide to oppose the court's release of anyone who pleads not guilty, or, if they are agreeing to release, they can ask for this to be subject to bail conditions. For all accused prior to sentence, the court decides whether bail will be granted, refused or whether a person will be released unconditionally. An understanding of bail decision-making therefore requires a recognition of the criminal justice system's institutional structure and the ways in which the parts of that structure (police, prosecutors and courts) interact. This sets the form and helps to shape the content of professional relationships which criminal justice practitioners develop in individual localities. This interaction produces a localised criminal justice culture which sets the assumptions within which practitioners work to interpret the law in particular cases. For this reason an understanding of criminal justice responses in dealing with particular cases requires an understanding of the significance of the features of the cases within the localised criminal justice culture. In this chapter we describe the legal and institutional structure (police, prosecution and courts) in relation to the operation of bail.

AIMS AND DESCRIPTION OF THE STUDY

The study was designed to provide a detailed description of how bail operates and the circumstances which affect its operation. It involved examining the variability of priorities given to aspects of bail risk at police, prosecution and court stages of processing cases through the criminal justice system; the implications which this variability has for communication between officials at each stage; and the ways in which these affect bail decisions.

The research aimed to

1. examine the information available to decision-makers at different stages in the process, to look at how this was used and the relative priorities given to criteria for decision-making at each stage.
2. follow through cases detained in custody or released on undertaking by the police and to look in detail at factors affecting procurator fiscal (prosecutor) attitude to bail and at circumstances in which accused are remanded by courts, are liberated on bail, or ordained for a subsequent court appearance.

3. look at stages in the process and circumstances under which accused already on remand are considered for liberation.
4. examine the nature and significance of bail abuse.

In order to do this a sample was collected from all arrests about which the police in three study areas (Doon, Tweed and Braid)[1] made a decision to detain in custody or release on an undertaking to appear in the sheriff court.[2] Though some of the sample cases ended up in the district or high courts, for reasons which will be explained in the course of the report, the focus of the study is those cases about which a bail decision was made in the sheriff court. Detailed information was collected about these cases and decision-makers were interviewed about their decisions as they made them or as soon as practicable thereafter. So far as possible, cases were followed through to final disposal and information about bail appeals was collected where relevant. [Full details are in the methodology section at annex1]

THE STRUCTURE OF BAIL DECISION-MAKING: AN OVERVIEW

In Scotland crimes and offences which are uncovered or reported to the police are reported to the procurator fiscal who decides on whether and how to proceed with prosecution in court. Figure 1.1 summarises the custody/release decision options at each stage of the criminal justice process and Figure 1.2 shows the points at which bail applications may be made during the course of a case. When police arrest an accused person, they must consider whether that person should be released and the case reported to the fiscal for possible summons to court; whether the person should be released on signing an undertaking that they will appear in court on a particular date, which is within 7 days of the undertaking, or whether the person should be kept in custody until the fiscal decides whether they should appear in court, which will be on the next lawful day.

When the procurator fiscal looks at the police report of a case where the accused has been released on undertaking or detained in custody, they have to decide whether to proceed against the accused and, if so, whether to have them brought before the court immediately or to release them from the undertaking or from custody and, if the case is to be proceeded through court, to summon them there at a later date (by way of

1 To anonymise the study areas names of Scottish rivers have been used. There is no geographic link between the areas studied and the river names chosen.

2 There are four types of criminal court in Scotland: District Courts - presided over by lay justices or stipendiary magistrates. All district court cases are dealt with under summary procedure (see note to figure 1.1). All common law crime may be prosecuted in the district court excluding murder, culpable homicide, robbery, rape, fire-raising, theft by housebreaking, housebreaking with intent to steal, theft, reset, fraud, embezzlement exceeding £1000, assault involving fracture of a limb, assault with intent to rape, assault to the danger of life, assault by stabbing, uttering forged documents or bank notes, offences relating to coinage. Statutory offences may be tried in the district court if the maximum penalty does not exceed 60 days' imprisonment or a fine of £1000 or both. Only one district court in Scotland has a stipendiary magistrate and this court has the same powers as a sheriff court sitting summarily.

Sheriff Courts - presided over by a sheriff and jury (for cases being dealt with under solemn procedure) or a sheriff alone (for cases being dealt with under summary procedure). Any common law crime or statutory offence can be prosecuted summarily in the sheriff court except for those for which the high court has exclusive jurisdiction or unless statute specifies that they may only be tried under solemn procedure. Maximum powers of a sheriff court are fine not exceeding £2000 or imprisonment of not more than 3 months. Maximum period of imprisonment is extended to 6 months for a second or subsequent dishonesty or offence involving personal violence.

High Court - presided over by a Lord Commissioner of Justiciary (high court judge) is both a court of first instance and a court of appeal. It can try any crime triable under solemn procedure unless excluded by statute.

Source: A. L. Stewart, The Scottish Criminal Courts in Action; 1990; Edinburgh; Butterworths.

In 1989 53% of cases proceeding to court were called to the Sheriff Court, 46% to the District or the Stipendiary Magistrates' Court, and 0.5% to the High Court (Criminal Procedure in Scottish Courts; Statistical Bulletin; December 1991).

Figure 1.1 Criminal Justice Decision Options Under The Act

	Options	*Implications*
Police	Release the accused person and report them to the prosecutor for summons to court	*Police reports to the prosecutor with 2 to 3 weeks - though can take around 5 weeks. If case is proceeded with then accused will be served with a complaint (statement of charges) and a citation which names the court and date at which they must appear. Failure to appear is a contempt of court.*
	Release the accused person on undertaking	*The court date is set for within one week of the date of arrest and is stated on the undertaking form which the accused has to sign before their release. Failure to appear is a contempt of court.*
	Detain the accused person in custody	*Must be brought before the court on the next lawful day.*
Procurator Fiscal	If the plea is not guilty: Agree to accept that the court ordain an accused for a further court appearance	*No reasons need be given to court.*
	Agree to accept that the court release an accused on bail (with either standard or special conditions)	*Reasons are not usually given for agreement to bail though a request for special conditions will usually have to be justified to the court.*
	Oppose the granting of bail	*Reasons must be given, and before court the fiscal must decide whether or not they will appeal if the court decides to grant bail.*
	If the plea is guilty the prosecution has no authority to comment on their attitude to bail	
Court	If the plea is not guilty or sentence is being deferred Ordain an accused for a further court *appearance*	*No conditions attach to release of an accused/offender other than that they attend court on the date set. Failure to appear is a contempt of court.*
	Release on bail	*Standard Conditions are: to appear at court on the appointed date; not to commit an offence while on bail; not to interfere with witnesses or otherwise obstruct the course of justice; accused/offender to make themself available to enable enquiries or a report to be made to assist the court in dealing with them. Any special conditions which the court deems necessary may be added. Failure to appear is a contempt of court or may be dealt with as an offence under Section 3(1)(a) of the Bail Act. Breach of any other condition is an offence under Section 3(1)(b).*
	Remand in custody	*Trial must be within 110 days for cases dealt with under solemn *procedure or 40 days for summary **cases.*

*Solemn procedure: The trial of criminal cases with a jury either before a sheriff in the sheriff court or a Lord Commissioner of Justiciary in the high court.
**Summary procedure. The trial of criminal cases without a jury before either a single sheriff in the sheriff court (who could impose a maximum custodial sentence of 3 years) or lay justices in the district court. (S.R. Moody & J. Tombs; Prosecution in the Public Interest; 1982; Scottish Academic Press)

Figure 1.2 Criminal Process: Stages Where A Bail Application Can Be Made[1]

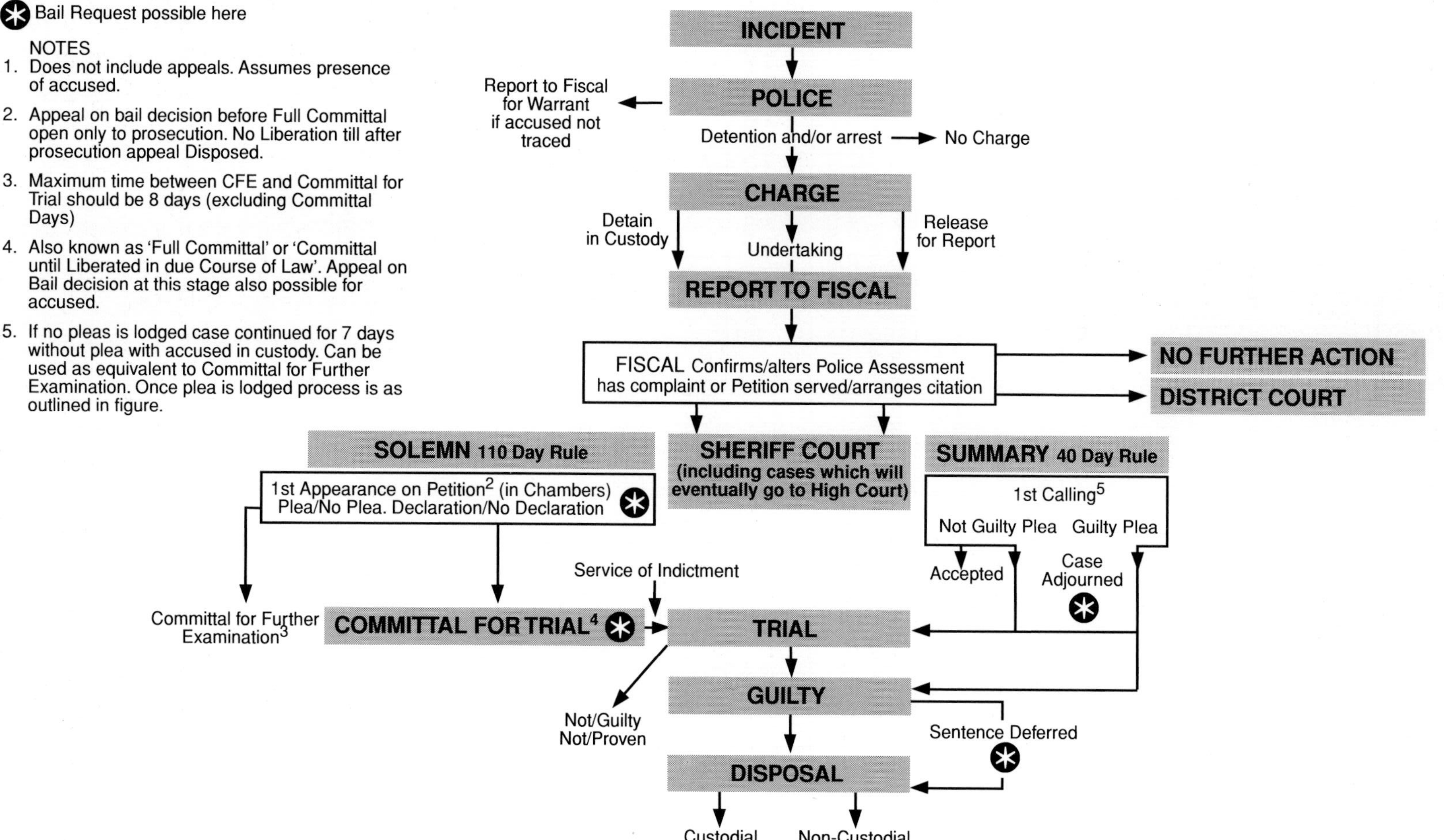

✱ Bail Request possible here

NOTES

1. Does not include appeals. Assumes presence of accused.
2. Appeal on bail decision before Full Committal open only to prosecution. No Liberation till after prosecution appeal Disposed.
3. Maximum time between CFE and Committal for Trial should be 8 days (excluding Committal Days)
4. Also known as 'Full Committal' or 'Committal until Liberated in due Course of Law'. Appeal on Bail decision at this stage also possible for accused.
5. If no pleas is lodged case continued for 7 days without plea with accused in custody. Can be used as equivalent to Committal for Further Examination. Once plea is lodged process is as outlined in figure.

summons or warrant). If the fiscal does not release the person then they must decide whether, if the accused pleads not guilty in court, they should oppose that person's release prior to trial, ask for the release to be subject to the conditions of a bail order, or agree that the person should be released unconditionally prior to trial. At this stage the accused is the prisoner of the procurator fiscal and, as such, the attitude of the fiscal to release or detention is crucial.

Less serious cases are dealt with under summary procedure and serious cases are dealt with under solemn procedure (see footnote to figure 1.1). Once a summary case comes before a sheriff for consideration at the first court (pleading diet), the sheriff must consider, if the plea is one of not guilty, whether the person should be detained in custody till trial, released on bail conditions or released unconditionally. If the plea is guilty, and the sheriff decides to defer sentence, then the same custody/release decisions must be considered, prior to the sentence. Prior to conviction the court can only remand an accused if such a remand is sought by the procurator fiscal (Maxwell & Sillars v McGlennan 1989, SCCR 117). If the court were to remand without this having been sought by the fiscal, then the fiscal could release an accused, although they could not attach conditions to that release. Once guilt has been established, an offender becomes the court's prisoner and the fiscal no longer has any authority to agree or oppose bail.

CONCERNS ABOUT BAIL

The purpose of the Bail Etc (Scotland) Act 1980 is to minimise the number of people held in custody for first court appearance, for trial or for sentence. The Bail Act removed the need to lodge money as a standard condition of bail. At that time it was anticipated that a reduction in the remand population would follow. However, between 1981 and 1985 annual figures for remand receptions rose by just over 40% from 13,500 to 18,985. It was during this period that the Lord Wheatley, in judging a bail appeal (Smith v McCallum, 1982), set out principles (sometimes referred to as the Wheatley guidelines) for interpreting bail legislation and which set out exceptions to the presumption in favour of bail. After 1985 a downward trend in remand receptions began, though historically numbers still remained high. This trend continued (there were 15,000 receptions in 1988-89) till 1992 when figures started to rise again.

In a report on custodial remand (Wozniak et al, 1988) it was argued that, compared with England and Wales, Scotland stood out as receiving a higher number of prisoners (299) on pre-trial remand per 100,000 inhabitants (the England and Wales figure was 111). For post trial receptions in Scotland the figure was 55 and for England and Wales 32 prisoners per 100,000 of the population. The high incidence of remand receptions was coupled with a comparatively short average period spent on remand.

Accompanying this there have been increases in the recorded levels of offending while on bail. This rose from 2,765 offences in 1983 to 19,853 in 1991. Police argue that such figures reflect significant levels of bail abuse and that in consequence the Bail Act has fallen into disrepute. In early 1992, fuelled by findings of police research in England and Wales (Brookes, 1991; Ennis & Nichols, 1991; Northumbria Police, 1991) that people on bail were responsible for a significant proportion of recorded crime in certain areas, considerable press attention was given both there and in Scotland to the threat posed to the public by those released on bail. The police, it was maintained, were being impeded in their protection of the public by an inappropriate use of bail.

An assessment of the significance of these issues raised about bail has been hampered by a lack of systematic information in Scotland. At the time of the research, statistics were not collected on the number of bail orders issued by courts each year. It was not therefore possible to assess the extent to which courts may be making greater use of bail, whether there has been a change in the proportion of bail orders breached, or whether there has been a change in the proportion of those granted bail who breach their bail conditions. On the other hand, it is known that the police have been working to improve their recording practices for these offences. In short, there was no regularly collected reliable information against which assertions about the operation of bail could be assessed[3].

UNDERSTANDING/PREDICTING BAIL RISK: PREVIOUS RESEARCH

Questions about the extent to which there is an unduly high number of remand receptions and an unacceptable level of bail abuse are questions about the appropriateness of bail decisions. These decisions are about the nature of a risk. Opposing views on these questions are in effect arguing that there has been a failure in accurate prediction. The first view implies that people unlikely to abuse their bail are being inappropriately assessed as unsuitable bail risks. The second view sees inaccurate prediction as resulting in the release of too many people who go on to breach their bail conditions.

Previous research on bail and remand in Scotland (Melvin & Didcott, 1976) attempted to identify characteristics of those found to abuse their bail and then used these to test the predictability of bail abuse. They found that being unemployed, having no fixed address and factors relating to criminal history - such as similar previous convictions, charges of theft and multiple charges, were the best distinguishers of those identified as having abused their bail from those not so identified. However, overall, these factors were still poor distinguishers of bad bail risks as most (69%) of the apparently worst bail risks were not identified as having abused their bail. The researchers commented

> "....even people who seemed to be the worst risks were mostly not - as far as was known - bail abusers. To select people for bail and custody simply on the basis of these 'high risk' factors would not therefore be very efficient: one third of the bail abusers were not identifiable in this way, while almost half of the non-abusers would be wrongly identified by using them." (1976: 51)

In recent years there has been growing interest in prediction studies in social science, some of which have resulted in the development of prediction scales (Mair,1989). It is beyond the remit of the present discussion to provide a comprehensive overview of prediction in social science, nevertheless a few points are relevant here. The most successful prediction scales in criminology, risk of custody scales, have been directed towards the prediction of behaviour of criminal justice personnel. Such scales are developed in relation to the legal/policy constraints on sentencers' decisions and are based on the study of local practice. They are valid for the population on which they are based, they presuppose the ability to feed back information about outcomes and, as dynamic policy tools, require routine monitoring of practice as well as periodic re-validation. At their most useful, these scales can be used as screening devices to help practitioners such as social workers and probation officers to target their activities, to monitor their effectiveness in targeting, to assist managerial decision making, especially

---

3 Since 1992 there has been a Scottish Office Working Group on offending while on bail. This group has a statistical sub-group which has investigated the need for improved bail statistics. Collection of additional statistical information began at the start of 1993.

about resource allocation and can assist practitioners in formulating responses to 'difficult cases' (Roberts 1989).

Widening the use of prediction to assess risk of re-offending raises a number of problems. The most serious problems are posed by the difference between re-offending and re-conviction - it is generally not possible to measure re-offending and often only re-conviction information is used; the difficulty of developing models sensitive to seriousness and frequency of re-offending. There are difficulties in identifying the behavioural rules adopted by people, such as offenders, whose circumstances may be only partially understood by those trying to identify relevant behavioural rules; and, even if such 'rules' could be identified, the extent of their generalisability would be problematic. This contrasts with legal practitioners who are operating within recognised legal and organisational constraints. In addition there are ethical problems, since it is one thing to develop screening devices to aid organisational responses, it is quite another to make a decision about someone's future based on these. How far should differences in non-legal factors, such as race and gender be considered within such scales? Would it be discriminatory to have a separate scale for men and for women, or would it be discriminatory not to have separate scales? Prediction research in criminology has shown the dangers of 'false positives' - Melvin and Didcott's (1976) work provides a clear example of the high proportion of false positives (i.e. accused identified as poor bail risks who did not subsequently abuse their bail) which it is possible to generate from the use of such methods.

These questions are raised here to illustrate some of the limits and difficulties of prediction research. More pragmatically, the results of such work, especially in relation to bail, are no more encouraging than the findings of Melvin and Didcott. In an experiment in Philadelphia Municipal Court in the early 1980's bail guidelines were developed on this basis. When the guidelines were operated, within 90 days of the first court appearance 12% of the control cases (i.e. those for whom guidelines weren't used) had failed to appear for a subsequent court and 11% had been arrested for allegedly committing crimes in this period as compared with the failure to appear of 13% and an alleged further offending of 10% of experimental cases (i.e. those where the guidelines were used)(Goldkamp and Gottfredson, 1985: 182).

A review of prediction research in other areas (Murray, 1989) has concluded that such results are typical of prediction research. Critics of this type of work maintain that such results reflect fundamental difficulties which are inherent in prediction research. Whether problems are viewed as inherent or whether they are seen as temporary and resolvable by increased sophistication, it is undisputed that this work is time-consuming (the pilot stage for the Philadelphia project lasted 2 years) and, particularly in relation to bail, results have been disappointing. Compare, for example, the 10% failure of experimental cases in Philadelphia with the information from a survey carried out by the Association of Chief Police Officers (Scotland) between January and March 1988 which suggested that, extrapolating from figures for three police forces for which the information was available, about 11% of people granted bail in that period went on to abuse their release by committing further offences.

Nevertheless an adequate understanding of the operation of bail does require an understanding of how bail risk is presently assessed. This implies a focus on the organisational contexts and the situations in which risk decisions are made. Such an approach recognises that risk is neither static nor is it uniformly perceived. Rather it changes at different stages in a case being processed through the criminal justice system and the varying immediate concerns of different parts of that system will affect how risk is viewed at any given time.

BAIL DECISION-MAKING: INTERPRETIVE FRAMEWORK

The results of research aimed at discovering how people understand and make use of information need to be presented in a form which is understandable as both a *description of practitioner accounts* of their practice, and an *explanation* of that practice and its wider significance. That is the purpose of the interpretive framework developed here. Practitioners are, of course, people who operate within the criminal justice system's institutional structure and this sets the form and helps to shape the content of the professional relationships which are developed in individual localities. A description of that structure in relation to bail is given later in this chapter.

The focus of the report, however, is the content of professional relationships - how practitioners work and understand their work within the criminal justice system; and the constituent features of cases - the incident; the evidence; the accused; the victim.

These three elements - the *structure* and *content* of relationships and the *features of cases* - interact to produce (among other things) bail decisions. At one level the statistical information which has been collected in the course of this study is simply a prosaic description of the results of the interaction in the study areas during the period of the research. But this interaction produces more than outcomes which can be measured statistically. The research findings indicate that the results of the interaction produce what are referred to in this report as *criminal justice cultures* which operate to encourage some types of decision and to discourage others.

MODELS OF DECISION MAKING

In analysing the data for the study we considered what we would describe as the "traditional model" of criminal justice decision making and we found that it cannot help us understand bail practices. The traditional model presupposes that differences in pattern between localities can be explained by differences in cases and in the practices of individual decision makers. It assumes that to understand criminal justice decisions, it is sufficient to understand that legitimate responses of criminal justice practitioners to pre-given facts of cases can only vary within the legally defined limits of individual practitioner discretion.

Figure 1.3 Traditional Model of Criminal Justice Decision Making

FACTS OF CASE + INDIVIDUAL DISCRETION + LAW → DECISIONS

However, we found that this model prevented us understanding the way in which the law on bail is being used, since within this model individual discretion is taken to be an explanation for decisions. We argue that *the operation of discretion is not an explanation, rather it is a topic of enquiry.* Individual discretion operates within the constraints of the law, organisational policy and local policy and practice. To understand the use of bail therefore we need to understand how that discretion is structured as well as the ways in which it is facilitated or constrained. We are arguing here that a more satisfactory explanatory model of the way in which the law on bail is being applied - that is, one which can help us account for the type of systematic variation which we have identified, and one through which we can consider the way in which alternative policies may impact on the use of discretion in bail practice and outcome - needs to consider the dynamics of criminal justice relationships. Figure 1.4 illustrates this by showing the elements which interact in the construction of a criminal case in response to an incident.

Figure 1.4 Cultural Model of Criminal Justice Decision Making

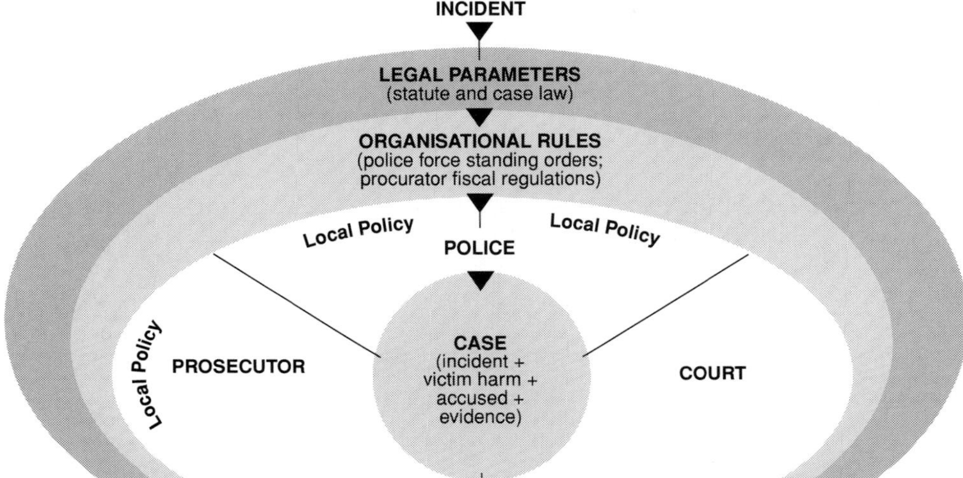

Bail decisions are made daily by criminal justice practitioners. They are an aspect of the routine practice of police, prosecutors and courts in responding to cases which are dealt with through the criminal justice system. Often these decisions must be made in only a few minutes. Although all decision makers must, in theory, be able to give an explanation for their decision, they are not routinely required to articulate this explanation. A decision to keep an accused person in custody is the decision about which explanation is most likely to be required. Often it is recorded, although this recording generally takes the form of one or two words noted on a detention sheet, a case minute sheet or court record sheet. A more elaborate account of a decision to detain or any account of a decision to release is only required where the decision has been contentious.

Social scientists have pointed out that the more that an understanding of a situation is shared between people the fewer words they require to communicate about it. This shared understanding is sometimes referred to as 'common sense' and embedded in 'common sense' are the cultural assumptions which people make as they develop their understanding of the situations they experience. It is particularly notable in situations where decisions are made regularly and quickly, since under these circumstances practices tend to become routinised. For practitioners, many bail decisions are understood as being 'common sense'.

We argue that criminal justice cultures are produced by the interaction of all parts of the system, they are not simply the result of the wishes of one part, such as the court, although the impact of pressure from one part of the system on another will be affected by authority relations within the system. For this reason courts are of particular significance. Those elements of criminal justice culture which are less visible are nevertheless important since, as we have argued, local criminal justice culture is produced and reproduced by the interaction and experience of all criminal justice agencies within different localities. The patterns we have described are therefore the results of these interactions.

We have developed a typology of the criminal justice cultures which we studied.

Figure 1.5 Typology of Criminal Justice Cultures

Culture Type	*Police*	*Prosecution*	*Court*
Bail (Doon)	*high use of custody*	*presumption of bail* for police custodies and undertakings;	*high use of bail;* low use of remand and ordain; low use of custodial sentences
Liberation (Tweed)	*medium use of custody and undertaking*	*presumption of ordain* unless police custody;	*high use of ordain;* medium use of bail low use of remand; low use of custodial sentences
Remand (Braid)	*low use of custody*	*regular opposition to bail* for cases released by police;	*high use of remand;* medium use of bail low use of ordain; high use of custodial sentences

It is the particular localised culture which sets the basic assumptions from which people work when they operationalise the formal rules for considering cases. In other words, criminal justice responses in dealing with particular cases need to be understood by understanding the significance of the features of the cases within the localised criminal justice culture. This report will show how this operates in the areas studied.

During the research practitioners were asked to explain the reasons for their bail decisions and it was often the case, in the early stages of work in each area, for practitioners to express some surprise at being asked for the reasons for some of their decisions. These were cases where, to the decision-maker, their decision was seen as being self-evident. The researcher, as stranger, was turning a decision which was assumed to be unproblematic 'common sense' into a problem requiring explanation. For example, in Tweed some fiscal deputes were puzzled at being asked about their attitude to bail in cases where accused had been released by the police on an undertaking to appear at court. Bail was never opposed for such accused in that area and it was taken to be a mistaken understanding of the researcher that these cases should be included in the study. In contrast, in Braid, where bail was regularly opposed by the fiscal in undertaking cases, no one remarked upon the inclusion of this category of case in the research. The importance of what and how much it is necessary for people to say to each other in order to communicate is at the heart of understanding criminal justice responses to the question of bail. This is most clearly evident if we consider the 'case'.

THE FOCUS OF BAIL DECISIONS: THE CASE

The case is the means through which criminal justice agents activate the system. It has two purposes: firstly, to convey to those within the criminal justice system an account of an incident, and secondly to stimulate an appropriate criminal justice response. Both these aspects of a case need to be recognised when considering decision-making.

When they deal with an incident in which they believe the law to have been breached, police officers know the kind and amount of information which they will have to provide to the fiscal and the way in which it must be provided in order for the fiscal to be able to consider taking action. It is this construction of events and those involved in them which is referred to as the case. The key document in the initiation of a case is the police report. The report is not simply a direct reflection of 'what happened' but is an account, based on the reporting officer's understanding of what occurred and what it is relevant for the prosecutor and, ultimately the court, to know. This understanding is structured by legal procedure, the law relating to the particular incident type, the law of evidence and the rules for their application. The police construction is directed towards eliciting the recognition from the prosecutor that there is a case against an accused which should be answered. Liberation/custody decisions are part of the criminal justice response to police characterisations of incidents and are an integral part of the account which is compiled. Sometimes, when setting out the case, police will suggest to the prosecutor that it is more appropriate for the accused to remain in custody during the course of any proceedings.

LEGAL AND REGULATORY PARAMETERS

Custody/release decisions are made under the Criminal Procedure (Scotland) Act 1975 as modified by the Bail etc. (Scotland) Act 1980. This provides the framework which sets the outer parameters for what constitute legally acceptable bail decisions in Scotland. Guidance for the criminal justice system in operationalising the Bail Act comes in the form of High Court decisions on bail appeals, although particular organisations within the system have their own regulations for interpreting the Act. For police there are Force Standing Orders derived from the Lord Advocate's Guidelines to Chief Constables; for the prosecution (procurator fiscal service) there are Crown Office Regulations which are modified by means of circulars issued from Crown Office to procurator fiscal offices throughout the country. From time to time procurators fiscal may issue instructions to the local police about policy matters such as the ways in which they want certain types of case to be reported to them.

FORMAL FUNCTIONS OF BAIL

The formal function of the Bail Act is to provide for the release of untried and unsentenced prisoners while securing the protection of the public and the administration of justice. With the exclusion of treason and murder, case law has established a presumption in favour of bail, although there are certain exceptions to this which are set out in the case of Smith v McCallum (1982, SCCR 115), often referred to as the Wheatley guidelines. The main grounds for not releasing an accused on bail are where: the identity of an accused is in doubt, the continued presence of the accused is necessary for further enquiry, the accused's liberation might impede continuing enquiries, the accused has no fixed abode, the police have reason to believe that the accused may interfere with witnesses, commit another offence, or abscond and not turn up for trial; and the accused appears to be unable to understand the terms of a bail undertaking which they might be required to give.

The Act fulfils its function by aiming to ensure that an accused appears in court at the appointed time, does not commit any offence while on bail, does not interfere with witnesses or otherwise obstruct the course of justice, makes themself available to enable enquiries or a report to be made in order to assist the court in dealing with them. To this end the 1980 Act created a new offence whereby anyone failing to comply with the bail order or undertaking is considered to have committed a further offence.

THE STRUCTURE OF BAIL DECISION-MAKING: COURT

Since the 1980 Act came into force it has been the subject of interpretation and comment through a number of key High Court decisions. The most famous of these was the result of the consideration of a Crown appeal against a Sheriff's granting of bail and has become known as the Wheatley Guidelines (Smith v McCallum 1982). These were directed to those in the lower courts and were set out because of what Wheatley described as 'divergent attitudes to bail' there.

In introducing the guidelines Wheatley said,

> "In the light of a fairly extensive experience of the Bail etc (Scotland) Act 1980 I consider it desirable to set down certain guidelines in relation to the allowance or refusal of bail in the present state of the law. This is a field in which no absolute classifications can be made, as each case has to be dealt with on its own facts. But it seems to me that there are certain considerations which should generally regulate the decision on allowance of bail, and adherence to such general considerations while having regard to the facts of the individual case could, I am sure, save a lot of needless appeals, thus saving a deal of judicial time and public expense."

Stating, as a point of principle, that

> "an accused should be granted a bail order unless it can be shown that there are good grounds for not granting it"

He set out two broad categories of ground on which bail could be refused:

1. the protection of the public
2. the administration of justice.

The grounds specified in the judgement were: significance within an accused's record as well as the nature of charges which might imply a need to protect the public. The example given was of a persistent record over years, particularly for dishonesty; and recent discharge from prison for dishonesty; and being charged with a similar offence. Additional grounds were also given such as, the nature of an offence in 'very special circumstances' (although this was not elaborated); alleged intimidation of witnesses; an accused having no fixed abode; or there being 'reasonable grounds' for suspecting that they will not turn up for trial.

The guidelines generated some controversy at the time particularly because Wheatley identified exceptions to the presumption in favour of bail, stating that bail should be refused in such cases unless there was good reason for the decision to be otherwise. These were cases where an accused was in a position of trust such as: being already on bail; having been ordained to appear for trial on another matter; being on probation or having a community service order; being on licence or parole; being on deferred sentence. Finally, the judgement also identified grounds which were not considered to be a good basis for refusal of bail. These were firstly, after full committal, bail being opposed on the grounds of police making unspecified further inquiries. At this stage it was stated that such inquiries would need to be specified if they were to be considered as grounds for refusing bail. Secondly, detention for a social enquiry report, this not being, of itself, an adequate reason not to release on bail. It would have to be shown that the report could not be prepared without detention of the accused.

The Wheatley guidelines, which were once an unambiguously authoritative interpretation of the Bail Act, no longer have this status. Remaining, in theory, of the same status as when they were first set down, it has been found during the study that in practice, their authority is questioned with some practitioners going as far as to deny their continuing relevance to bail decisions. The extent of their relevance for contemporary decisions is therefore a matter of debate which will be examined more fully in chapters five and six when court responses to bail are discussed. At present it is simply noted that the Wheatley guidelines form the framework within which police and prosecution bail decisions are made since they are the basis of police and prosecution guidelines for operating bail.

THE STRUCTURE OF BAIL DECISION-MAKING: POLICE

The Bail Act strengthened police powers to deal with those suspected of breaching bail conditions by actions which would not otherwise constitute arrestable offences, since it gives police the power of arrest without warrant where they have 'reasonable grounds for suspecting that the accused has broken, is breaking or is likely to break any condition imposed on his bail' [Section 3(7)]. Police procedures for bail decisions are operated within the interpretive space permitted by the policies set out within Force Standing Orders. Standing Orders on bail in the study areas tended to have been established in the early 1980's with only minimal updating. As such they reflect interpretations of the Bail Act which were current at that time. Though each police force has its own standing orders, the core features for those on bail in the three study areas were the same. In all the areas it was stipulated that an accused should not be detained unnecessarily and that if a decision is made not to release an accused, then this information and the reason need to be included in the report for the procurator fiscal. There is generally a statement of the circumstances under which liberation of accused is held to be inappropriate, for example, cases which must be dealt with under solemn procedure, such as treason, rape, murder, incest; or which are likely to be dealt with under solemn procedure (unless the procurator fiscal has been consulted and assents to release). In general the circumstances reflect those outlined earlier under the heading of Formal Functions of Bail.

The standing orders do not indicate that breach of bail is, of itself, automatically a reason for detaining someone in custody. If anyone is found on arrest to be subject to an existing bail order then standing orders generally indicate that such accused should be detained in custody where the offence for which they have been arrested in itself justifies custody or where the bail order relates to a serious crime or offence and the nature of the breach of conditions necessitates their detention, such as when the breach involves a similar offence.

Within these stated official limits there is therefore a considerable area of discretion. In the three study areas this was operated differently, for example, in interpretations of what were acceptable fixed addresses, in the extent to which those already on bail for other matters could be released again, as well as in the types of charge which, because of particular local circumstances, result in custody. Particular differences are often the result of local procurator fiscal's instructions.

THE STRUCTURE OF BAIL DECISION-MAKING: PROSECUTION

Guidance for procurator fiscal (prosecutor) responses to bail is provided in the Procurator Fiscal Service Regulations. The original guidance was set out in March 1980 (Crown Office Circular 1671) and has been modified by subsequent Crown Office circulars. The instructions are drafted in relation to the expectation that the court will consider the likelihood of the accused absconding, the character of the offence charged, previous record and attitude of the Crown towards bail.

In Scotland custody cases dealt with under summary procedure must be dealt with within 40 days and will, if they go to trial, be tried without a jury and before a sheriff, if they are to go to sheriff court.[4] In general, for summary cases procurators fiscal are instructed only to oppose bail in exceptional circumstances and that bail should not normally be opposed where imprisonment is an unlikely outcome of a case. Custody cases dealt with under solemn procedure must be dealt with within 110 days and, if they go to trial, be tried with a jury before a sheriff, in the sheriff court or before a Lord Commissioner of Justiciary in the high court. The first appearance is in private and, if the accused is remanded, then the second court appearance will be within eight days, when they will again have an opportunity to apply for bail. For solemn cases the instruction is that bail should not normally be opposed at first court appearance unless it is intended to oppose bail at full committal. If opposition to bail has been because of the need for further enquiries, then the length of remand should be minimised so as to last only for the length of time necessary for the enquiries to be completed. Whatever the procedure being used for a case, fiscals are instructed to consider any conditions which might be necessary to enable them to agree bail. As with the police and courts, the stress is on custody being the exception to the normal rule of accused being released.

A comparison of the general principles on which bail should be opposed which are set out in the original circular with those currently in use is illustrative of the shift in attitudes towards the use of bail which has occurred over the past 10 or so years. The original guidance stated six specific principles which were the basis for opposition to bail, this compares with nine principles which currently form the basis of opposition. Three of the original reasons can be classified as being primarily concerned with the administration of justice. These relate to having a fixed address, the need for further enquiries, and the likelihood of an accused absconding. In all these cases the current principles have been elaborated in such a way as to restrict the circumstances under which bail should be opposed. For example, whereas having no fixed address was originally a principle of opposition, current guidance refers to the situation where an address at which an accused can be contacted is not offered. This implies that residence at the address is not necessary for an address to be acceptable to the prosecution.

A fourth principle, linked to cases involving serious assault or sexual offences against related children or close associates, was originally specified in relation to the administration of justice, in that the grounds for opposition were that it was against the public interest for an accused to be in contact with witnesses. As currently drafted,

4 More minor summary cases are also heard in the district courts before a lay justice or a stipendiary magistrate (see earlier explanation of courts).

however, this ground of opposition is no longer explicitly stated, making the principle no longer unambiguously about the administration of justice and appearing to be more closely concerned with the protection of the public. The final two original principles (where the accused is on bail and is alleged to have committed a similar or more serious offence; where someone's record indicates that they are involved in a career of crime and they have recently been released from prison or convicted) relate to the protection of the public and all of the current additional principles fall within this classification. In contrast to the limitation of circumstances under which bail would be opposed for the purposes of the administration of justice, the protection of the public principles have increased the circumstances under which bail could be opposed. So, for example, current guidance contains the generic principle of opposition to bail where the nature of the offence is such that it is in the public interest that accused be remanded.

Although current guidance to procurators fiscal is more detailed than that which was originally issued at the time of the Bail Act, the inclusion of the generic principle that an accused should have bail opposed if the nature of the offence suggests that this is in the public interest, underlines that there still remains considerable scope for local interpretation. A person's record is central to decision-makers' interpretations of an accused's likely conduct. Particularly under circumstances where there are broad categories of reason for opposing bail (such as "public interest"), prosecution definitions of what constitute a serious record become particularly important for understanding attitude to bail. These will be examined in chapter four where there is discussion of the range of interpretations of what constitutes a 'serious record' or a 'reasonable period' since an accused's last conviction.

CONCLUSION

The operation of the Bail Etc. (Scotland) Act 1980 is a subject about which there is much speculation and little systematic information. The study was designed to provide an illumination of present bail decision making practices. An interpretive framework has been outlined in order to describe the form of bail decisions. The rest of the report is concerned with the decisions made in the study areas during the research, the significance of their features within localised criminal justice cultures and the significance of those cultures for the use of bail and remand in Scotland.

CHAPTER 2

CRIMINAL JUSTICE DECISIONS IN DOON, TWEED AND BRAID

INTRODUCTION

In the first chapter it was pointed out that information about the use of bail is not routinely available. Official statistics in Scotland make little reference to the criminal justice process and are primarily concerned with the types of cases which pass through the courts and the outcomes of these cases. The information necessary to design a study of statistically representative bail decisions is not available. The study areas were chosen because access could be agreed for the research with all criminal justice agencies in these localities. The areas are therefore illustrative of working practices for different types of locality and of the implications of pursuing particular policies in relation to bail. In order to identify the population of decisions from which the main sample for detailed study was drawn, information was collected from police detention sheets and from a census of bail decisions which was carried out in the sheriff courts studied during the period of the research. This allows for both an assessment of the representativeness of the decisions studied and a check on any impact on police and court patterns of decisions which the presence of researchers might have had during the observation fieldwork.[1] This chapter describes the study areas and their use of bail which was recorded in the research. Patterns of local police and court decisions are presented and outcomes are given for a sample of accused whose court cases were followed through to final disposal. These figures give a broad picture which describes the results of criminal justice interactions recorded in the study areas during the period of the research.

MAIN FINDINGS

The results of the census show that there was marked variation in criminal justice decision making though there were few differences between the areas in the incidence of accused being involved in particular types of case. Police at Doon kept a high proportion of people in custody and the court census there recorded a high use of bail, low use of remand and a low use of custodial sentences. A high proportion at Doon, especially those accused of dishonesty were ultimately not convicted. In Braid, where

---

1 **Scope and Limitations of the Census:** Information on methodology is provided at annex 1. The bail census was used to generate a picture of court decisions for the population for which a bail decision might be relevant in the study areas. The exercise was conducted over a nine month period in each area and included decisions about all accused who appeared at court in person at the first calling of their case and those whose failure to appear resulted in a warrant being issued for their arrest. This included all cases from the police divisions to be studied in detail where the accused appeared from police custody or to answer an undertaking as well as those accused answering summons who chose to appear in person. A pilot study conducted in 1988 identified that if an accused did not appear at the first calling and no warrant was sought as the result of the non-appearance, a bail decision was unlikely to be considered during the course of that case. Preliminary work in setting up this study did not indicate that this had changed. Nevertheless, as it is possible that bail can become an issue at a subsequent diet in cases where the accused was not present in person at the first calling (e.g. if the accused failed to appear at a subsequent court date), the census cannot be presumed to include all court bail decisions.

police kept fewest accused in custody and where the court census recorded a high use of custodial remand, accused were less likely to apply for bail than in the other areas. In contrast, in Tweed, where the rate of police use of custody fell midway between the other areas, the court census recorded a similar level of use of remand and of custodial sentence to Doon. Of the three areas, Tweed made greatest use of the option to ordain accused. The high level of not guilty outcomes at Doon suggests that statistics collected for offending on bail in that area and which are recorded by police prior to court outcome will significantly overstate the level of proven bail abuse.

SOCIAL AND CRIMINAL PROFILE OF THE STUDY AREAS

The study was conducted in areas involving different police forces, procurator fiscal regions and sheriff courts, which were chosen because access could be agreed for the research with all criminal justice agencies in the locality. The areas were therefore illustrative of working practices for different types of locality but were not chosen because they were known to represent different patterns of use of bail. The need to question decision makers directly and the need to ensure a sufficient sample size of cases in order to examine outcomes, dictated the choice of cases being collected from one police sub-division in Doon[2] which focused on a small relatively prosperous town with light service industry. Tweed cases were collected from one police force division which covered the half of a city with a large commercial area. The crime problems characteristic of Tweed were shoplifting and late night, week-end street disorder in the city centre. Because dishonesty cases were infrequent and tended to be shoplifting rather than other types of dishonesty, the sample in this area was boosted by including dishonesty cases from the neighbouring division in the city which contained more industrial developments and a greater area of housing. In Braid, cases were also collected from a full division. This locality covers a large, mainly rural area in the hinterland of a major conurbation and centring for police administrative purposes on three small towns. Although the number of incidents reported to the police are regularly amongst the highest in that force area, during the first week of main fieldwork one sub-division was producing too few cases for the study to be viable. It was therefore extended from the originally planned coverage of one sub-division to encompass the full division. Crimes of particular concern in that area were crimes of violence - serious assault, carrying offensive weapons, robbery, assault with intent to robbery and crimes of dishonesty, housebreaking and theft by opening a lockfast place.

POLICE DECISIONS

The police are the first point of criminal justice contact for accused and, as such, police decisions help to define the input to the rest of the criminal justice system. In order to examine police decision making, information was collected in each area about all accused processed by the police during the three month period of the study.

If seriousness of case is considered as a likely criterion for the police decision to keep accused in custody then figure 2.1 could be taken to imply that Doon had a greater proportion of accused in serious cases than either of the other areas. Custody there was used at double the rate at which it was used at Braid and there was a greater use of undertakings there.

2 Decisions in other sub-divisions were taken in different locations.

Figure 2.1 Decisions for all* Arrested and Charged During the 12 Study Weeks

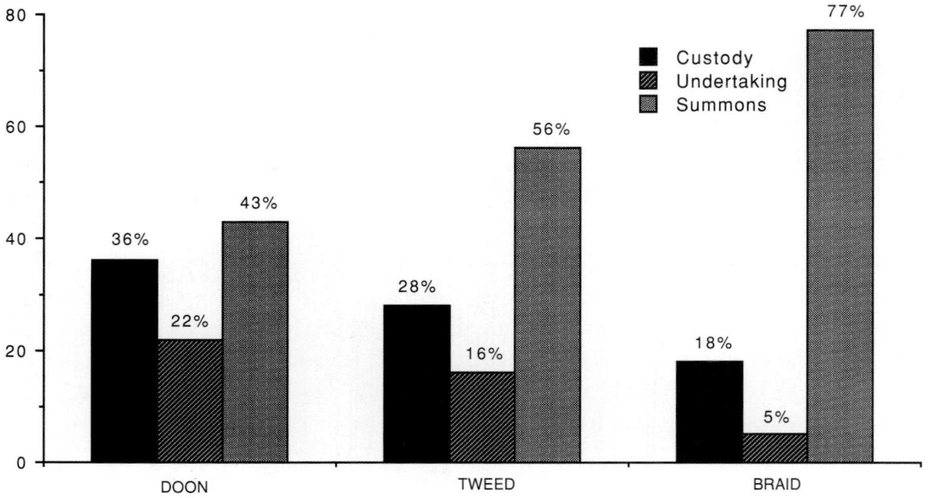

*Doon n=511; Tweed n=900; Braid n=1193

POLICE DECISIONS: OFFENDING ON BAIL

Most accused were not already on bail though more at Doon were on bail (12%, compared with 3% in Tweed and 8% in Braid). However, these figures need to be treated with caution since the "Not Known" figure for Doon is high (21% of cases) and the low figure for Tweed (3%) may be a result of recording practice as the fact that the accused was on bail was not routinely recorded on the police detention sheet in that area.

Figure 2.2 compares police action for those with and those without bail orders. In all areas accused already subject to bail orders when arrested were more likely to be detained in custody than accused without bail orders. Doon and Tweed detained similar proportions of accused without bail orders while in Braid a smaller proportion of accused not subject to a bail order were detained in custody.

Comparing the three areas, the difference in the action taken by police where the accused was subject to a bail order suggests that for police the existence of a bail order had varying significance. In Braid the bail order had least influence on decision outcomes since over half of those with bail orders were reported for summons. This is in marked contrast to Tweed and Doon where fewer of such accused were reported for summons. In areas where police keep more people with outstanding bail orders for custody court, the sample can be expected to contain more people with outstanding bail orders than will the sample drawn from elsewhere.

COURT DECISIONS: BAIL CENSUS - MAIN CHARGES

Information was collected over a nine month period on around 1,000 accused at Doon, 2,500 at Tweed and 1,500 at Braid. The census was not a comprehensive survey of all the decisions made by the study courts as it was designed to focus on the types of cases where a bail decision was relevant. Figures presented in this chapter are therefore patterns reflecting court action on accused recorded in the census and cannot be taken

Figure 2.2 All Accused Arrested by Police During the 12 Study Weeks: Police Action on Cases With and Without Bail Orders*

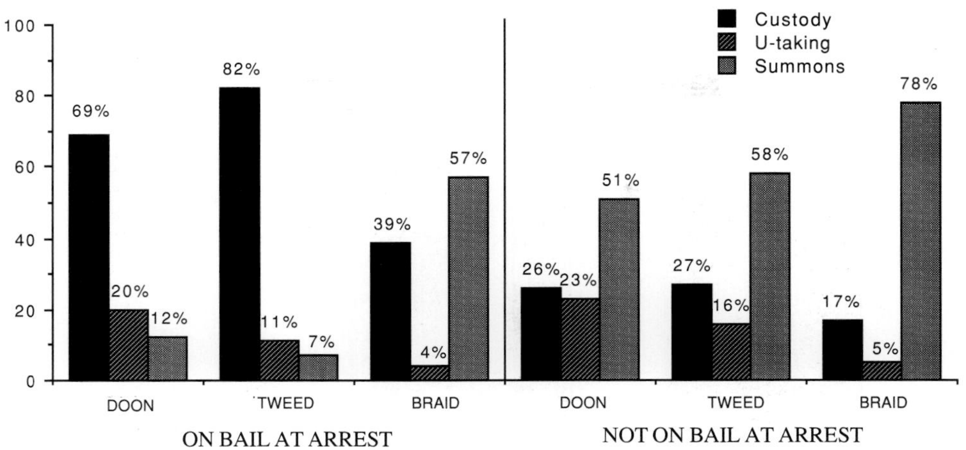

* Doon excludes 70 cases where it was not stated whether the accused was on bail. On Bail Doon n=61;Tweed n=28;Braid n=91; Not on Bail Doon n=380;Tweed n=872;Braid n=1102

as a complete description of court action for all cases which were dealt with in these courts. (See footnote 1 - Scope and Limitations of the Census). There was little difference between the courts in the types of cases for which accused appeared. Around a third of accused were facing dishonesty charges, between 15% and 20% were accused of violence and around 15% were accused of breach of the peace. (See annex 2)

ACTION AT FIRST COURT

Of those accused in summary[3] cases who entered a plea at the first calling of their case, over half in Tweed and Braid pled guilty whereas this was the plea for only 42% in Doon. Each criminal justice decision forecloses on some options for responding to cases and opens up others. Plea is an important example of this since it shapes the potential for prosecution and court response to an accused. A plea of guilty removes the right of the prosecution to oppose bail as well as removing any presumption of innocence. Therefore in Tweed and Braid the fiscal had the possibility of opposing bail for fewer than half of accused in summary cases.

APPLICATIONS FOR BAIL

Because accused are technically considered to have returned to custody when they appear in court, an application for bail has to be made. In theory, an application for bail can be made in any case which is not disposed of at the first court appearance. However, bail was not recorded as having been a consideration for any accused who were ordained for a subsequent court date.[4] These accused are therefore excluded from the present discussion.

3 This discussion excludes accused in solemn cases since their standard response at first calling is that of no plea and no declaration. Fuller information is presented at Annex 2.
4 Care must be taken with this as there is a high rate of missing information in Doon (see methodological annex).

Table 2.1 Census - Accused in Summary Cases: Court Bail Decision Where a Verbal Application Was Not Made*

	Doon	*Tweed*	*Braid*
Not guilty plea			
Bail	50%(5)	23%(7)	18%(6)
Bail (special)	20%(2)	7%(2)	0
Remand	30%(3)	70%(21)	82%(28)
Total	100%(10)	100%(30)	100%(34)
Guilty plea			
Bail	50%(5)	17%(4)	11%(4)
Remand	50%(5)	83%(20)	89%(31)
Total	100%(10)	100%(24)	100%(35)
All Accused	7%(20)	8%(54)	14%(69)

* In Doon information was incomplete for 225 accused, in Tweed 12 accused and Braid 41 accused. Doon excludes 3 accused, Tweed 3 accused, and Braid 7 accused who appeared from prison or remand on other charges.

An application for bail was made by over 90% of accused in Doon and Tweed and by over 80% in Braid. A failure to make a verbal application did not always result in an accused being remanded as there were a small number of cases where no bail application was made and bail was granted. Of those who did not make a formal application for bail, 60% at Doon, 24% at Tweed and 14% at Braid were granted bail.[5] This suggests that the absence of a formal application for bail varied in significance between courts. For no application could be taken by those in court to imply that there is no need for a discussion of an application, since there is a tacit understanding that bail is an appropriate measure in a particular case. But it could also be possible for it to be understood by those in court that there is no point to making an application since there is a tacit understanding that bail would definitely not be granted in a particular case.

FISCAL OPPOSITION TO BAIL IN COURT

The greater tendency not to apply for bail at Braid was accompanied by a greater likelihood of fiscal opposition to bail there. The procurator fiscal can oppose bail for any accused not entering a guilty plea, although prior to conviction the court can only remand an accused if the fiscal opposes bail (see chapters 1 and 4).

Table 2.2 also shows that the fiscal opposed bail in court in a greater proportion of cases where the accused was granted bail with special conditions, than in cases where the accused was liberated on standard bail. Special conditions, as the procurator fiscal guidelines imply, are directed towards enabling the release on bail of those who would otherwise have been remanded. Although these figures show that those whose bail had special conditions attached are more likely to have their bail opposed, most had bail agreed.

5 Further information is presented at annex 2.

Table 2.2 Census - Accused in Summary Cases: %age of Court Bail Decisions Where Fiscal Opposed Bail in Court* (excludes guilty pleas)

	Doon	*Tweed*	*Braid*
Bail	6%(13)	5%(20)	15%(43)
Bail (special)	14%(3)	18%(7)	24%(6)
Remand	100%(34)	100%(81)	100%(151)
All Accused	19%(50)	21%(108)	43%(200)

*Care should again be taken with these figures as the level of information missing was high in Doon. Doon 166 accused not known (39% of total); Tweed 6 accused not known; Braid 14 accused not known. Excludes accused who were ordained and 3 accused who appeared from custody at Doon, 3 at Tweed and 9 at Braid.

FIRST COURT OUTCOMES - ALL ACCUSED

Figure 2.3 shows the court decision patterns recorded for accused in both summary and solemn cases.

Braid and Tweed sheriff courts respectively liberated just under 50% of accused on bail but Braid remanded in custody twice the proportion of accused as were remanded at Tweed and nearly three times the proportion at Doon. In Tweed 37% of accused were ordained to appear again whereas in Braid and Doon only 20% were ordained to appear. This raises the question of whether those involved in similar types of cases which are remanded in Braid are granted bail in Tweed and further whether bail is used by Doon and Braid sheriff courts in circumstances for which accused would have been ordained by the court in Tweed.

FINAL OUTCOMES

The discussion of the total census population has so far given an indication of the input of accused which was made to each court. A short look at the outcomes for a sample of these accused will provide an overview of the output pattern of each court.

Figure 2.3 Census: All Accused - Outcome of First Court
(Solemn and summary cases, excluding final disposals)

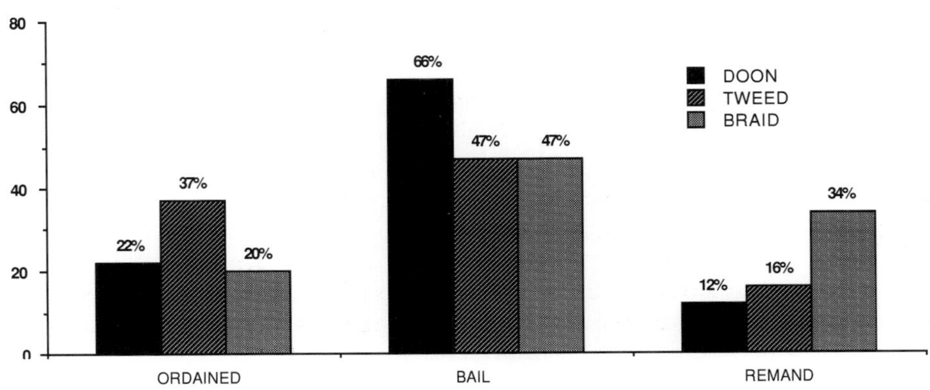

Doon n = 814; Tweed n = 1620; Braid n = 1073

All accused whose cases occurred in the first twelve weeks of the census were followed through to disposal (Figure 2.4).

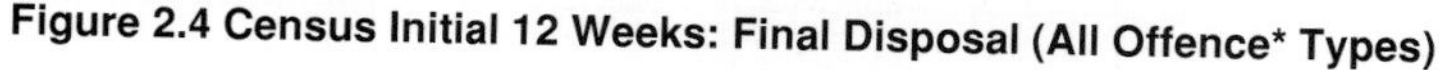

Figure 2.4 Census Initial 12 Weeks: Final Disposal (All Offence* Types)

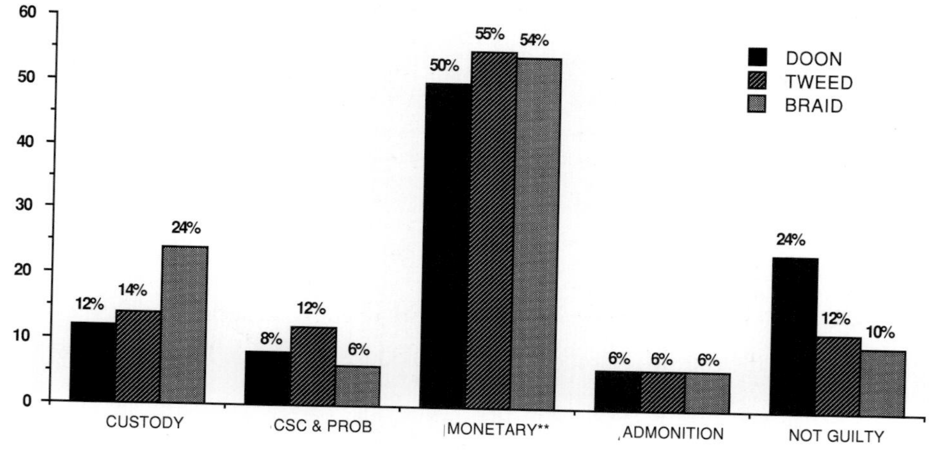

* Accused were recorded by main charge which, for the purposes of the study, was decided at the start of processing a case. Excluded from the calculations for this figure were: those accused for whom sentence was deferred (Doon 11, Tweed 33 and Braid 21 accused) or where a warrant was still outstanding after the accused had failed to appear at Court (Doon 5, Tweed 10 and Braid 1 accused). Doon n= 396; Tweed n= 798; Braid n= 418

In each area 1% of outcomes were classified as 'Other'. These were - referred to the children's panel, hospital order - and have been excluded from figure 2.5.

** Monetary includes monetary penalties combined with disqualification.

***Not guilty = cases where a plea of not guilty was accepted by the procurator fiscal, the accused was found not guilty or the case was deserted.

There were marked differences in the outcomes of the cases with the two key differences being the level of not guilty outcomes at Doon and the use of custodial sentences for offenders in Braid. Nearly a quarter of accused in Doon, compared with around 10% at Tweed and Braid were not convicted. A third of dishonesties in Doon were not convicted, compared with about 10% of dishonesties in the other areas.

Offenders at Braid were more likely to receive custodial sentences than offenders at other courts. Custody was an outcome for over half convicted of serious/sexual assault, forty per cent of dishonesties and over a quarter of breaches of the peace in that area. This compares with a custodial sentence being given for a quarter of serious/sexual assaults and dishonesties and for one in ten breaches of the peace at Tweed. Doon made least use of custodial sentences with only a fifth of serious/sexual assaults and dishonesties and only one per cent of breaches of the peace resulting in prison.

CONCLUSION

The analysis of police detention sheets and the results of the census have provided an outline of criminal justice decisions recorded during the research in the study areas and have enabled us to identify significant differences between the areas in police decision making and court use of bail and remand as well as in their use of imprisonment. Police at Doon detained people in custody at twice the rate of police in Braid. The court census, while not providing a rate for court action in all cases, showed that for accused who appeared personally, there was a greater use of bail by the court at Doon, of ordaining by the court at Tweed and remand by the court at Braid.

In brief, Doon had a high use of police custody; a high level of not guilty outcome; and low use of custodial sentence for those appearing personally. A high proportion of accused appearing personally at Doon (nearly a quarter) ultimately had a not guilty outcome. Braid had a low use of police custody, though for accused recorded in the census it had a high use of solemn procedure, low level of not guilty outcome and a high use of custodial disposal. The high use of remand recorded at Braid was linked to a high use of custodial disposal there, nearly a quarter of accused recorded in the census at Braid, and whose cases were followed to final disposal, received a custodial sentence. The very high levels of not guilty outcomes at Doon suggest that any statistics for offences committed on bail in that area and which are recorded prior to court outcome will significantly overstate the level of bail offending. The extent to which the high level of remand recorded at Braid can be explained by accused in more serious cases being detained by police there, together with the implications of the court use of bail and remand which has been identified by the census will be examined through the detailed study of a sample of cases from each area.

CHAPTER 3

POLICE DECISIONS

INTRODUCTION

This chapter looks at the contribution of the police to the pattern of local criminal justice response to cases through a detailed study of a sample of accused for whom bail decisions were made in the study areas. It was argued in chapter one that understanding bail decisions requires an understanding of the particular cases occurring locally. Before looking at the contributions of individual agencies to local criminal justice response, it is necessary therefore to consider the features of local cases. These are explored through an examination of a sample of accused from police detention sheets and whose cases were recorded in the court census. In each area the number of accused detained in custody in the sample represented around three-quarters of all custodies recorded on police detention sheets. In Doon and Braid those in the sample released on undertaking represented 35% of all accused released on undertaking and in Tweed 23%.

Criminal justice personnel in all areas operate within the framework of national legislation and rules of guidance. This implies that it is practices which must be examined to understand the different local patterns which have been identified. The parameters within which police operate bail are outlined in this chapter together with a description of the types of decisions made. A comparison is made of the types of reason given for the decisions in each area and the chapter concludes with a discussion of the police contribution to criminal justice responses to local cases.

MAIN FINDINGS

The pattern of police decisions outlined in chapter two were reflected in the composition of the sample. Differences in response to accused were not accounted for by record in general, although bail history was important in Doon. Accused at Braid had more problematic records than accused in the other areas in that they were more likely to have a history of custodial sentences. Although more accused at Doon were found to be on bail at arrest and to have bail convictions, accused in the other areas were just as likely as those at Doon to have pending cases. Those released on undertaking at Braid were more likely than those released on undertaking at Doon to have analogous pending cases. When information about victim harm was analysed it was found that, Doon police were more likely to detain in custody those accused of minor dishonesty whereas Braid police were more prepared to release on undertaking those involved in serious dishonesties (cases where the loss was valued at over £1000).

When police reasons were examined it was found that the major reason for releasing the accused on undertaking related to local policies which had been agreed with the procurator fiscal in each area. Accused in dishonesty cases were released on undertaking if the police thought that it would assist them with clearing up crime. The most frequently given reasons for detaining people in custody in Tweed and Braid were to facilitate justice and then the risk to the community. Doon police gave more prominence to the risk to the community and record was more often given as a reason for decisions there. Doon and Tweed gave a higher prominence to the existence of outstanding bail orders in their consideration of custody. The lower prominence given to existing bail orders in police explanations for detaining in custody at Braid, and the increased likelihood that those on bail would be released there contributes to the explanation of the lower use of police custody in that locality.

Accused at Doon, by being more likely to be kept in custody or released on undertaking, are more likely to be seen quickly by the court than those in Tweed and Braid. Although they were no more likely to have been involved in alleged repeat offending, this police use of custody would increase the likelihood that such accused would be on bail at the time of any further alleged incidents. Such police practices render alleged recidivism statistically visible and for this reason could impact on bail abuse statistics.

THE FOCUS OF DECISIONS

The focus of decisions is the case - the accused; the incident in which they are alleged to have been involved; the victim and the identified harm which they have experienced; and finally, that which links the other elements together, the evidence. As explained in chapter one, the case is constructed by criminal justice personnel and the police provide the key document which initiates a case - the police report - which explains who is accused of what; the witnesses available; the details of what they witnessed; information about other evidence; the response of the accused to having been charged. This report is accompanied by a computer print-out of the accused's criminal record which includes both convictions and pending cases. The information which the police provide is treated as both a basis and a justification for their response to the accused. It is important to recognise, when considering the comparison of cases between the areas, that the research has been designed to enable an examination of differences in criminal justice responses to cases. It cannot look at differences in criminal justice responses to incidents which become the subject of cases. For example, there may be differences between areas in criteria used to define incidents as serious assault or simply assault. The research was not designed to assess these. The decisions made locally about charge type convey localised police constructions of the seriousness of a given incident and this is an important part of the criminal justice response to a case.

SAMPLE

During the observation fieldwork[1] detailed information was collected over 12 weeks about all arrests made in the study areas and which resulted in an accused being detained in custody for court. This resulted in a sample of 139 custodies at Doon, 203 in Tweed and 157 in Braid. In addition, for the initial 4 weeks in Doon and Tweed information was collected about all cases which police released on undertaking (39 undertakings were recorded at Doon and 32 at Tweed). In Braid it was found that few accused were released on undertaking and in the initial 4 weeks information was collected on only 7 cases. Therefore information was taken over 12 weeks and this resulted in 21 accused in this category being included in the sample.

1 Observation fieldwork was carried out at Doon during the initial period and at Tweed during the third quarter of the census. Fieldwork in Braid was planned for the final quarter of the census there.

POLICE DECISIONS

In chapter 2 it was shown that police at Doon made the greatest use of undertakings and used custody at double the rate at which it was used by police at Braid. Braid police made the lowest use of custody and undertaking. It could be taken from this that Braid police are better at targeting custody on those involved in more serious cases. In order to examine differences in seriousness of cases occurring within the study areas, the features of sample cases were examined. The elements of the cases which will be described here are the nature of the charges, the characteristics of accused and measurable aspects of victim harm. This last will be used as a gauge of incident seriousness. The final element of a case, the evidence, will only be considered here in so far as it is pertinent to bail decisions.

THE CASE

INCIDENT TYPES

Figure 3.1 shows the types of incident for which accused in the sample were arrested. In each area the largest category of crime with which accused in the sample were charged was dishonesty, (see methodological annex for a full description of the types of cases in the sample). This reflects the pattern identified from police detention sheets (see annex 3).

Figure 3.1 Types of Offences: Comparison of Sample: and Police Detention Sheet Data on all Accused (%ages)

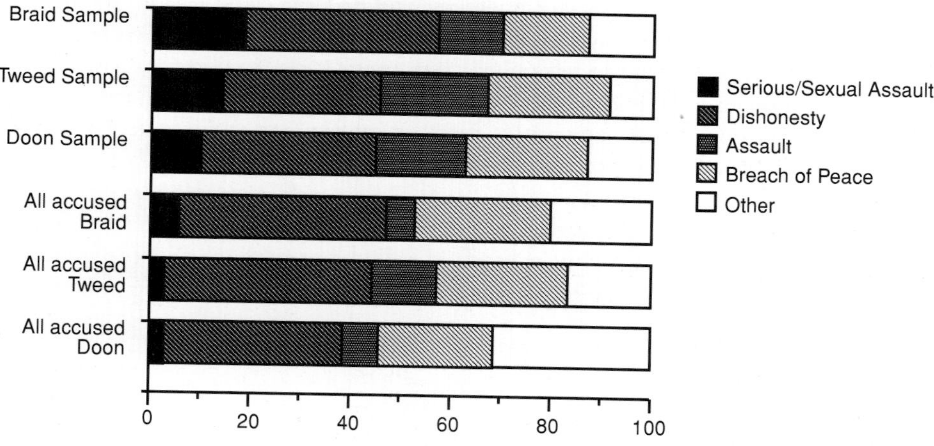

Serious and sexual assault and assault are over-represented in the sample reflecting the likelihood that accused charged with violence will be detained in custody or released on undertaking. In Doon and Braid the proportion of dishonesty in the sample is similar to that for all accused whereas in Tweed the proportion is less. This suggests that the police in Tweed are less likely to detain in custody or release on undertaking accused who are charged with dishonesty and implies that dishonesty cases in Tweed tended to be dealt with as less serious than those in the other areas. Over a quarter of the dishonesty cases in the sample at Tweed were charged with shoplifting compared with 11% at Doon and Braid.

SOCIAL CHARACTERISTICS OF ACCUSED - SEX, RACE AND AGE

There was no significant difference in the sex and race characteristics of the sample in different areas. Over 90% of the sample in each area was male and most were classified as white[2].

Most accused were under 30, with the 16 to 30 age group being over-represented in the sample[3], reflecting an increased likelihood of those in these age groups being detained in custody or released on undertaking. The sample in Tweed tended to be older than the sample in the other areas. (In Doon 44% and in Braid 43% of the sample were under 21 as compared with 28% of the sample in Tweed). Accused released on undertaking in Tweed and Braid were younger than accused detained in custody: 41% at Tweed and 62% at Braid who were released on undertaking were aged under 21 compared with 25% of custodies at Tweed and 40% at Braid. In Doon the situation was reversed with 37% of those released on undertaking being under 21 compared to 46% of accused detained in custody.

SOCIAL CHARACTERISTICS OF ACCUSED - ADDRESS

Most accused were able to give police an acceptable address. Accused who can give no fixed address (NFA) are detained in custody and there were no exceptions to this amongst those in the sample whom police defined as NFA (14% of the sample in Doon, 19% in Tweed and 15% in Braid)[4]. Generally addresses were local and permanent (64% of the sample at Doon; 62% at Tweed; 72% at Braid). In addition, a small proportion of accused in each area had local addresses which were classed by police as temporary (9% at Doon; 8% at Tweed; 3% at Braid). Police were generally willing to accept temporary addresses although occasionally they would not if the accused had only stayed at the address briefly, or if their permanent address was outside of Scotland. In each area around one-tenth of the sample gave addresses which were outwith the jurisdiction of the court. This was the case for a high proportion of accused released on undertaking at Doon(41%) and was a reflection of the local policy to use undertakings for those accused of football related incidents.[5]

CRIMINAL RECORD CHARACTERISTICS OF ACCUSED

When cases are processed by the police after the accused has been charged, information on their previous offending histories is obtained from the Scottish Criminal Records Office (SCRO). This record of pending cases and previous convictions is appended to the police report for the current case. Previous convictions, their seriousness (assessed on the basis of the recorded sentence) and pending cases are all taken into account by decision makers. Information was collected on the criminal record of accused in the sample and the sample characteristics are summarised in table 3.1.[6]

---

2 Under one per cent were classified as being from other racial groupings.
3 Annex 3 gives details of the age of main sample accused as compared with the age of all accused arrested by police during the study.
4 The figures for all cases which were collected from police detention sheets indicate that there were few such accused in any of the areas: 4% of all accused in Doon; 6% of all accused in Tweed and 3% of all accused in Braid. Logically, the number of cases of no fixed address in the sample should be less than or equal to the numbers recorded for all accused from a locality. That the number of NFA's in the sample at Doon is larger than the number recorded for all cases is an artefact of police recording practices and reflects that a number of addresses which were initially offered by accused were later checked out by the police and found not to be acceptable. This included a small number of accused who refused to give an address.
5 Many of these were away supporters.
6 More detailed tables are provided in annex 3

Table 3.1 Summary of Record: %age of Sample With Particular Characteristics

	Doon Custody	U-taking	Tweed Custody	U-taking	Braid Custody	U-taking
Convictions in last 3 yrs	82%	51%	70%	44%	78%	71%
% with convictions who'd served custodial sentence	31%	11%	41%	7%	49%	40%
Analogous pending case	46%	21%	38%	3%	42%	38%
Non-analag. pending case	16%	16%	11%	6%	17%	19%
Subject to current court order (excluding bail)	27%	16%	32%	6%	27%	33%
Currently on bail	33%	5%	28%	0	18%	24%

Though most accused had convictions within the previous three years and most had a pending case, fewer than half had served a custodial sentence or were subject of a current court order. The criminal record profile of the sample at Doon and Braid was similar, with the exception that those in Braid were more likely to have served a custodial sentence and those in Doon were more likely already to be on bail. The sample at Tweed were least likely to have previous convictions or to have pending cases. Police not only consider past convictions but also take into account pending cases, indeed, for some police officers pending cases are viewed no differently to convictions. In all areas pending cases tended to be for matters analogous to the current charges which accused were facing. The record characteristics of those released on undertaking by police at Braid were similar to those of accused detained in custody by police at Doon and Tweed. This suggests that record was less of a factor in police decisions in Braid.

CRIMINAL RECORD CHARACTERISTICS OF ACCUSED - PREVIOUS CONVICTIONS

It was indicated in the outline of formal rules for considering bail presented in chapter one that having a recent history of previous convictions for similar offences is a contra-indication for the granting of bail. Of those with previous convictions in the three years prior to their arrest, 54% of those detained in custody at Doon, 39% at Tweed and 40% at Braid had analogous previous convictions within the last year. This was the case for 50% of those released on undertaking in Doon, 57% in Tweed and 53% in Braid.

Seriousness of record was also measured by the most serious sentence as this is a gauge generally used by criminal justice practitioners. Less detailed attention was paid to previous court sentences by police than by prosecutors who regularly considered it. It was nevertheless occasionally mentioned by police. In Braid around half of the accused detained in custody, and who had convictions in the previous three years, had served a custodial sentence while this was the case for 31% of accused detained in custody in Doon and 41% in Tweed. This could imply that accused at Braid had been involved in more serious offences or that they were appearing in courts where greater use is made of custody. This last possibility is important in the context of the high proportion of sample accused who were local to the sheriff court area and the identification from the census of Braid court as making a higher use of custodial disposals than the other study courts.

CRIMINAL RECORD CHARACTERISTICS OF ACCUSED - CURRENT BAIL

Most of the sample were not currently on bail. As suggested in chapter two, this aspect of the sample profile was significantly affected by local police policies in relation to those accused who were on bail at the time of their arrest. In Doon, operational policy was to detain all such accused in custody, in Tweed police were also more likely to consider the existence of a bail order as being an adequate justification for custody whereas in Braid, bail was not, of itself, thought to be sufficient to justify custody. A greater proportion of accused detained in custody in the sample in Doon had previous contraventions of the Bail Act in the past 3 years and a higher proportion were on bail when they were charged. In Doon 50% of accused had contravened the Bail Act within the last three years compared to 35% in Tweed and 28% in Braid. A higher proportion (33%) of accused released on undertaking in Braid had previous contraventions of the Bail Act compared with 8% in Doon and 6% in Tweed. Accused in the sample at Braid were least likely to be on bail although they were as likely as accused in the other areas to be subject to other current court orders (such as community service or probation) and to have cases pending. This indicates that though those in the sample at Doon were contributing more to the level of local bail abuse statistics than were the sample elsewhere, there was little difference between the areas in the level of alleged further offending from these accused.

In summary, accused detained in custody in Braid were more likely to have served a custodial sentence in the past than accused in Doon. Though Braid custodies were just as likely to have pending cases as custodies at Doon, they were less likely to be on bail. Those on undertaking in each area were less likely to have served a custodial sentence or to have pending cases than were those detained in custody. In Doon and Tweed they were less likely to be on bail.

DEGREE OF VICTIM HARM

An important measure of seriousness and a contributory factor to police responses is the degree of harm suffered by victims. This has been used to assess the level of seriousness of the sample crimes and offences. Though there may be differences in criteria used by police in different areas to define incidents as more or less serious, the decision made about the type of charge conveys the localised police construction of that incident's gravity and is an important constituent of the criminal justice response to a case. Victim harm is difficult to measure since some elements, such as emotional trauma are not easily recorded. The way in which it was recorded for the research reflects a requirement for accessible, reliable and classifiable information to be collected about the types of harm most regularly recorded on police reports. It was not intended to produce, and does not produce, a sensitive measure of harm suffered as a result of crime. For example, in this section, analysis of serious assault cases does not include sexual assaults because of the insensitivity of the harm measures which have had to be adopted. (Charges of serious assault accounted for 87% of the serious/sexual assault classification in the sample at Doon, 89% in Tweed and in Braid 100%). The information used here is that which is available to decision makers at the time of their decisions, it therefore reflects one basis on which both they and the research could consider seriousness of crime.

Some types of offence, such as breach of the peace, do not always have a clearly identifiable victim, therefore analysis here is restricted to the three main categories which always involved victims. Table 3.2 shows offence type by degree of victim harm for serious assault, assault and dishonesty cases. The classification of serious assault used in the research also includes charges of possessing an offensive weapon, assault and robbery, and other serious violence.

Table 3.2 Offence Type by Degree of Victim Harm

	Doon		*Tweed*		*Braid*	
	Custody	U-taking	Custody	U-taking	Custody	U-taking
Serious assault						
Serious injury*	*57%*	*0*	*23%*	*0*	*20%*	*0*
Slight injury**	*7%*	*0*	*31%*	*0*	*20%*	*67%*
No harm	*36%*	*0*	*46%*	*100%*	*60%*	*33%*
Total	*100%*	*0*	*100%*	*100%*	*100%*	*100%*
N=	*14*	*0*	*26*	*1*	*25*	*3*
Assault						
Serious injury	*20%*	*0*	*9%*	*17%*	*9%*	*0*
Slight injury	*65%*	*42%*	*42%*	*33%*	*41%*	*0*
No harm	*15%*	*58%*	*49%*	*50%*	*50%*	*100%*
Total	*100%*	*100%*	*100%*	*100%*	*100%*	*100%*
N=	*20*	*12*	*43*	*6*	*22*	*1*
Dishonesty* **						
No fin loss	*6%*	*0*	*11%*	*0*	*12%*	*0*
£0.5-10	*8%*	*0*	*6%*	*0*	*0*	*0*
£11-50	*20%*	*11%*	*23%*	*100%*	*13%*	*33%*
£51-100	*14%*	*11%*	*14%*	*0*	*5%*	*0*
£101-250	*16%*	*11%*	*9%*	*0*	*13%*	*17%*
£250-1000	*12%*	*67%*	*17%*	*0*	*20%*	*17%*
£1001 +	*22%*	*0*	*19%*	*0*	*38%*	*33%*
Total	*100%*	*100%*	*100%*	*100%*	*100%*	*100%*
N=	*49*	*9*	*64*	*2*	*56*	*6*

*Serious injury = injury which requires attending hospital as an in-patient or a fracture of a bone.
**Slight injury = injury which requires no treatment or treatment attending a general practitioner or hospital as an out-patient.
***Excludes accused in cases where the value of the loss was unknown.

DEGREE OF VICTIM HARM - SERIOUS ASSAULT

Doon had (both absolutely and proportionately) fewer serious assault cases but had the greatest proportion of cases which resulted in serious injury. Over half of serious assault victims at Braid, and just under half of those at Tweed were uninjured. The wider definition of this offence category outlined above helps to explain the high proportion of cases with no injury, as well as underlining the difficulty in discussing seriousness of crime. However it does not account for the difference between the areas in response to accused in these cases. In Doon 42% of the serious assault cases involved possession of an offensive weapon, in Tweed the figure was 28% and in Braid 14%.

DEGREE OF VICTIM HARM - ASSAULT

The assaults which resulted in injury classified as serious are explained by cases which, although the injury ultimately turned out not to be serious, resulted in an overnight stay in hospital for the victim and also by cases where the victim had received a fracture but this was not classed as a serious assault. The pattern of most of the Braid cases not resulting in injury is repeated for the assault figures. Again, victims at Doon were more likely to be injured than were those at Tweed and Braid. Whether police at Doon were reluctant and Braid were more willing to define cases as serious assaults rather than simply assaults, whether the nature and timing of intervention in incidents at Braid resulted in fewer victim injuries, or whether there are other explanations for these findings is beyond the remit of this study.

DEGREE OF VICTIM HARM - DISHONESTY

Table 3.2 shows that the seriousness of dishonesty cases was markedly different between the areas. Doon and Tweed had less serious dishonesty offences with cases for around a half of custodies involving loss of less than £100. In comparison, Braid had more serious dishonesty, over a half of custodies in Braid were involved in cases with over £250 loss as compared with around one-third in Doon and Tweed. Only in Braid did police release on undertaking any accused involved in cases with loss of more than £1000.

CASE TYPES, SERIOUSNESS AND POLICE DECISIONS

Using victim harm data as a measure of seriousness of case, it could be expected that the sample at Braid would have a higher level of custody for dishonesty than Doon and Tweed; that Doon would have most custody for assaults in the sample; that Tweed would have a higher level of custody for serious assault than Braid. However in practice[7] Tweed had the highest (97%) and Doon the lowest (83%) use of custody for those sample accused involved in dishonesty. Braid had the highest use of custody for the sample who were involved in assault cases (96%) and Doon the lowest (63%). Decisions about serious assault cases were closer to the pattern which could have been anticipated from the victim harm data, with Tweed having a higher use of custody for those alleged to have been involved in serious assault than Braid, although the disparity between the level of victim harm and police responses to accused makes it clear that other factors are involved in considering action.

While seriousness of record or of incident are factors considered in criminal justice decisions about accused, they did not account for the pattern of restriction of liberty identified for the sample. Although more accused at Doon were on bail at arrest, accused in the other areas were just as likely to have pending cases. The different police responses to these accused need therefore to be assessed in relation to police accounts of their practices in the study areas.

LOCALISED POLICIES

At the initial stage of police involvement, albeit within the parameters set by the legislation as well as any local policies agreed by the procurator fiscal, the liberation/custody decision rests entirely with the police who are accountable to the

7 It should be stressed that this section simply compares outcomes anticipated on the basis of victim harm with actual decisions made for these accused. It is not a rate at which custody and undertaking decisions were used for these categories of offence in the study areas.

procurator fiscal and, ultimately to the court, for their decisions. As could be expected, there were broad similarities between the Force Standing Orders on bail in each of the study areas, although there were some differences in localised policies. In all the areas drunk drivers were released on undertaking (for this reason such accused were not picked up for the sample unless there were other charges as well). Unlike the other two areas, in Braid there were no additional policies about the use of release on undertaking. In Doon those accused of being involved in football related incidents were released on undertaking and disqualified drivers were detained in custody. In Tweed, the policy was to release on undertaking those accused of involvement in week-end street disorder in the city centre.

DECISION-MAKERS

The responsibility for police decisions about cases in Doon and Tweed lay with the officer in charge of the shift who was the duty inspector or the deputising sergeant. Generally they would be contacted by an arresting officer and would base their decision on that officer's verbal report. In Braid, the decision officer was duty bar sergeant, or a duty sergeant at sub-divisional headquarters. Although the need to detain accused was reviewed every 24 hours, in practice during the research very few of these reviews resulted in a change of the initial decision.

CID cases were dealt with differently in all areas in that it was the officer in charge of a case (detective inspector; detective sergeant) who would make the custody/liberation decisions. (In both Tweed and Braid their cases were sent directly to the fiscal. In Doon, for convenience, CID cases were collected and taken to the fiscal along with uniform cases). In Braid, custody decisions for CID cases were also formally made by the uniform custody sergeant though the case papers went directly from CID to the fiscal. To clarify the apparent anomaly that a more junior officer might override a more senior officer's decisions, police in Braid were asked to explain what would occur in the event of disagreement with a duty inspector's decision - all stated that this rarely happened but were confident that a discussion of the case would ultimately result in agreement.

Procedures for checking written reports differed in each locality. In Doon the duty inspector checked written reports, in Tweed the duty inspector did not see written reports as all paperwork was checked by the station sergeant and then by uniformed administration staff before going to the fiscal. A similar procedure to Tweed was operated in Braid.

DECISION OPTIONS

Police choice is delineated by the Criminal Procedure (Scotland) Act 1975 and the Bail etc (Scotland) Act 1980. There are three options for police if a case is likely to be dealt with under summary procedure. (For cases which may be either summary or potentially solemn, accused are detained in custody and the case discussed with the procurator fiscal.) The accused can be released for summons or citation to court, they can be released on an undertaking to appear at a specified court on a specified date (usually within the next 7 days); or they can be detained in custody to appear at court on the next lawful day.

Releasing an accused and reporting them for summons. Processing accused for this type of case takes a brief period and, though it generally takes place within the police office, it can, if necessary, be done at the scene of an incident since names, addresses and other details of accused can be checked with headquarters over the radio. The accused are usually released immediately after these details are confirmed. In cases considered to be straightforward, the duty inspector may only be informed after a decision to use this option has been made. Officers have on average 2 to 3 weeks in which to complete their written report in these cases in Doon and Tweed, although on occasion they may take longer (around 5 weeks) in Braid.

Release on Undertaking. Processing accused to be released on undertaking needs to be carried out in a police station. Theoretically officers have to complete these reports before the ends of their shift - in Tweed the report had to be with the fiscal the next day and the case would call in court that week; in Doon undertakings were called in court on 2 days a week (Tuesdays and Thursdays) and the case had to be with the fiscal by 3 pm on the day before the accused was due to appear in court; in Braid undertakings were called to court once a week and the case had to be with the fiscal 2 days prior to court. Court dates are set and are stated on the undertaking forms which the accused has to sign. If there are co-accused some of whom have been detained in custody, then the dates are set so that the co-accused should appear together.

Detention in Custody. Processing these accused can take some time and may remove officers from the streets for an hour or two. The accused has to be brought into an office with cell accommodation and processed there. This can involve photographing, finger printing, record checks and bail checks as well as compiling a written report. All of this has to be completed before the end of the shift.

PATTERN OF DECISIONS

The outcomes of decision making have been outlined and it has been suggested that police policies, especially in relation to bail, may explain the difference in decision patterns between the areas better than case type or seriousness of record. This section will look in more detail at the process of decision making which resulted in the pattern of outcomes described above. Decision making was explored through observation of case decisions and interviews with decision making officers.

The formal guidelines are that decision making should reflect the seriousness of an offence; the previous convictions of an accused and their attitude to the police at the time of arrest. Age and other social factors are less important in considering how to deal with a case than are more immediate concerns such as that of the likelihood of an accused committing further crime.

REASONS FOR RELEASE ON UNDERTAKING

The varying policies in the study locations are reflected in different decision patterns. As already noted, all areas had a policy of releasing drunk drivers on undertaking. Those who only had drunk driving charges were therefore excluded from the sample.

Table 3.3 indicates that the most frequently mentioned reasons for releasing accused on undertaking were local policy, with the lack of a local policy in Braid contributing to the low level of undertaking usage in that area. In Braid there was little difference in the frequency with which 'facilitating justice' and 'risk to the community' were mentioned and only a slight difference between the frequency of these types of reasons in Tweed, with 'risk to the community' being mentioned slightly more often. The biggest disparity was at Doon, the area with the highest use of undertaking, where 'facilitating justice' was mentioned more frequently than any other non-policy considerations.

Table 3.3 Police Reasons for Use of Undertakings (%age of Mentions)

	Doon	*Tweed*	*Braid*
FACILITATING JUSTICE	**39%**	**15%**	**40%**
Need to get quickly to court	13%	4%	13%
Co-operated with police	13%	9%	9%
Further enquiries necessary	13%	0	9%
Time of arrest	0	0	3%
Go to court with co-accused	0	2%	6%
RISK TO COMMUNITY	**17%**	**22%**	**38%**
Seriousness of offence	0	4%	3%
Nature of victim harm	11%	7%	0
Likelihood of recurrence	4%	2%	16%
Previous convictions	2%	9%	19%
POLICY	**37%**	**52%**	**6%**
Football related	37%	2%	0
Week-end city centre incident	0	48%	0
Road traffic offence*	0	2%	6%
OTHER	**8%**	**11%**	**15%**
Holiday weekend	6%	0	3%
Health/family	2%	7%	6%
Drunk (released U/T when sober)	0	4%	6%
N	54	46	32

1 in Braid not stated.
Numbers total higher than sample as more than 1 factor was mentioned in some decisions.
% ages do not add to 100 because of rounding.

POLICY

Policy undertakings were more likely to have one reason only and were primarily used with accused in breach of the peace and assault cases. Five of those in such cases in Doon were accused of police assaults in football related incidents. While in this area police assaults would normally be kept as custodies, in football related incidents the policy of releasing on undertaking those accused involved in such incidents, overrode the usual practice. There were no examples where policy overrode normal practice in Tweed and there was no local policy for use of undertakings at Braid.

RISK TO COMMUNITY

The most serious of the cases at Doon, an indecent assault, had the most factors mentioned (nature of victim harm, that there had been a long gap between offence and arrest, and that the accused was undergoing treatment). This was also true of the most serious undertaking case at Tweed which was an assault and robbery. The accused in this case was released on undertaking because they had no previous convictions but the nature of the offence meant that police wanted to get it to court quickly. This was a borderline case where, had the accused been involved in a more minor incident they might have been released for summons. (Braid had no comparable cases in this category.) Three further accused at Tweed had no previous convictions and a further three were released on undertaking since they had had previous contact with the children's panel for analogous offences.

FACILITATING JUSTICE

In Doon and Braid all those where co-operation with the police was mentioned were involved in dishonesty cases in one of which, at Braid, police stated that they expected this release to enable them to get property back. This was not the case at Tweed where accused released for facilitating justice reasons were charged with breach of the peace or with assault. Although just immediately prior to the fieldwork period the Chief Constable responsible for Doon had publicly complained about the level of recorded offending on bail, and although in general discussions police in Doon expressed strong disapproval of releasing accused who on arrest were found to have outstanding bail orders, two accused who were released on undertaking because of their co-operation with police were on bail at the time of arrest (one of the cases was ultimately deserted and the other ended in an admonition). There was some variation in view about interpretation of appropriate practice expressed in this locality between CID officers interviewed and uniformed officers. Uniformed officers were not willing to release those who were found on arrest to have been on bail, whereas CID were more likely to believe that those already on bail could be released if they co-operated with the police. In this, CID views at Doon were closer to uniform and CID views in the other study areas.

The explanation for the release of bail cases as facilitating justice can be illustrated by a discussion which took place in Doon with the officer responsible for the release on undertaking of a man accused of dishonesty and who was on bail at the time of his arrest. Officer B indicated that the accused was involved in sneak-in thefts from houses and shops, that they were minor crimes and that he was a 'habitual thief'. B stated that if people were habitually involved in dishonesty that he would detain them in custody only if it was absolutely necessary otherwise he preferred to release them on undertaking. He maintained that most of the accused with whom he dealt were people with whom he had fairly regular contact and that 'If I lock them up then they won't speak to me next time'. In other words, the possibility of release was an encouragement to accused to co-operate by providing police with information which might lead to solving crimes or getting property returned. B continued that unless a person were awkward, involved in a large crime or were likely to be dealt with under solemn procedure, then he would release them on undertaking. When asked to clarify this view in relation to this accused whom he had already described as a 'habitual thief' yet who had been released on undertaking, he responded that 'bail is a toothless tiger' in which he could see no point since he did not believe that courts took a serious view of it. B argued that locking people up did not help to clear up crime. Since it had been observed by the researcher during the study that when police are considering record they look at the pattern and incidence of crime displayed there, B was asked why, while maintaining that he would lock up habitual housebreakers, he had felt this accused should be released, B argued that this accused was a 'nuisance' rather than a major problem. This illustrates that 'clearing up crime', which was how this officer saw his work, was viewed as not necessarily compatible with detaining people in custody.

In those instances where further enquiries were mentioned at Doon co-accused were involved in a group assault and a neighbour dispute; with one person being released because of a computer malfunction. In Braid all accused for whom 'further enquiries' was given as a reason were involved in cases of dishonesty. In one, there were numerous charges and the police needed time to compile a full report, in the other two the police thought that release might enable them to get property back.

OTHER

Age was not a factor mentioned specifically in decisions in any of the areas. Social factors had an important part to play in decision making in only a small number of cases overall. In two cases in Tweed women on charges of petty assault and breach of the peace were said to have been released because they had young children at home. For two accused, one at Doon and one at Tweed, considerations mentioned in the discussion of the decision involved health grounds. One of these at Tweed, a man who was charged with an assault on his wife, suffered from a chronic heart condition and the duty inspector was extremely concerned that he should not be detained in custody.

DISCUSSION

Doon made the greatest use of undertakings, even allowing for an exceptional incident which occurred during the fieldwork and which inflated the figures. In this locality, although reports were encouraged to be quick, paperwork for undertaking cases was not treated in the same way as paperwork for custodies. There were two undertaking courts each week (Tuesday and Thursday) and the deadline for cases to be received by the fiscal was 3 pm on the day prior to court. This meant that there was less reluctance to use undertakings. There was a tendency at Doon often to assume that release would be undertaking rather than for summons. This was explained by officer C who argued that reporting someone for summons takes an unduly long time, especially in dishonesty cases where accused were regularly being picked up by the police for similar offences. He continued that any significant wait before a case was heard in court would mean that there would be further pending charges as it was expected that accused would continue to offend. Under these circumstances C thought that pending charges would be 'rolled up', a practice which police felt was unsatisfactory since it was believed that the end result was that the cases would overall be dealt with more leniently than if they had each come to court on a separate occasion. It was argued that if such accused were dealt with regularly through the court then, because each case would be dealt with separately, the court would be more likely to place more weight on the offences which were libelled. In this area some officers maintained that additional information was more likely to be collected at this early stage, prior to the case being seen by the fiscal, rather than for police to ask the fiscal to seek a remand to allow them to make further enquiries.

This last argument was also echoed in Tweed where, as with Doon, a high proportion of accused given undertakings were released for policy reasons, - in the case of Tweed, if they were alleged to have been involved in incidents occurring in the city centre at week-ends. However, because there were no advantages to operational police in using undertakings, in that in this area paperwork was treated with the same priority as paperwork for custody cases, when under pressure, some inspectors felt that the policy was not justified and would therefore report such accused for summons.

In Braid, there was little use of undertakings for other than drunk driving cases. Although there was not the same pressure from the fiscal's office to deal with undertaking paperwork as for custodies since there was only one undertaking court per week (on a Wednesday) and the deadline for the fiscal to receive papers was by the Monday prior to court, cases in this area were either custody or report. Use of undertakings for other types of cases was not encouraged by the local procurator fiscal office. There were mixed views about this amongst local police, though most had little preference for undertakings since they maintained that an undertaking report placed additional pressure on them, yet they had no corresponding control over the accused. The fact that the criminal record profile for undertakings at Braid was similar to that for custodies elsewhere, suggests that accused who would be released on undertaking in other areas may be being released for summons in Braid. In other areas similar questions provoked responses implying that those for whom undertaking might have been considered and rejected were being released for summons as this would also allow time for completion of report.

For those who would have preferred to see more use of undertakings, it was the potential bargaining position which this gave them with accused which most attracted them to it. This was reflected in some of the sample outcomes for Braid. Operational sergeants at sub-divisional headquarters who were more likely to feel their shift staff fully stretched if any were taken off the streets, preferred to avoid undertakings for operational reasons.

REASONS FOR POLICE CUSTODIES

When the figures for decisions were examined at the start of this chapter, Doon was found to use more custody, have more accused with outstanding bail orders and victims of physical violence were more likely to sustain injuries than other areas. Braid police used less custody although similar proportions of accused as at Doon had analogous pending cases and victims in dishonesty cases were likely to have experienced greater financial loss. Tweed fell between the other areas in the frequency of use of custody, in the likelihood of victims of physical violence sustaining injury though more of the accused there had analogous pending cases.

Although at the start of this report it was indicated that police, when discussing bail generally, give a high profile to risk to the community, when police in the study areas were considering cases, only in Doon were reasons of this type more frequently mentioned than others when police discussed the reasons for releasing or detaining individual accused in custody. Even there, at a time when that police force were publicly expressing high concern about offending on bail, there was only a marginal difference between the frequency of mention of risk to the community and of 'facilitating justice', which was the next most frequently given type of reason. In Braid 'facilitating justice' reasons were more often mentioned.

Record characteristics ranked third in frequency of mention in each of the areas. There was, however, variation in police understanding of seriousness of record across the areas. More accused in Braid had serious previous convictions recorded than the other areas (as measured by most serious sentence) and there was a lower prominence given to existing bail orders in police explanations for detaining in custody there. However, record was mentioned as frequently in Doon as it was in Braid as a reason for detaining accused. The increased likelihood that the police at Doon would define a record as 'serious' is an important contributory factor to the high use of custody there.

Table 3.4 Police Reasons for Use of Custody

REASON TYPE	*NO. OF MENTIONS* Doon	*Tweed*	*Braid*
FACILITATING JUSTICE	**28%**	**36%**	**35%**
Timing of court (speed & with co-accused)	2%	1%	3%
Co-accused on bail	<1%	1%	0
Uncooperative with police (refuse desist, resist arrest etc)	7%	14%	13%
Further enquiries necessary	8%	10%	7%
Likely Abscond	1%	1%	5%
NFA	10%	9%	7%
RISK TO COMMUNITY	**29%**	**34%**	**27%**
Nature of victim harm	7%	12%	5%
Nature of crime	17%	16%	14%
Likely recurrence	5%	6%	8%
RECORD CHARACTERISTICS	**24%**	**18%**	**24%**
Nature/No. of previous convictions	12%	6%	12%
Previous convictions include bail	<1%	0	<1%
Time since previous convictions	0	0	2%
Nature/No. of pending cases	2%	0	4%
Time since last pending case	0	0	0
On bail	10%	12%	5%
On probation/CSO/SD/Licence	<1%	<1%	1%
PERSONAL CHARACTERISTICS	**12%**	**6%**	**3%**
Uncertain mental health	4%	2%	2%
Violent/aggressive	<1%	3%	1%
At personal risk (includes drunk etc)	8%	1%	<1%
PROCESS CONSTRAINTS	**6%**	**4%**	**9%**
Interdict	0	<1%	0
Likely custodial sentence	0	0	<1%
Warrant in existence	6%	4%	9%
DETERRENCE	**0**	**<1%**	**0**
N	251	275	273

Numbers total higher than sample as more than 1 factor was mentioned in some decisions.
% ages do not add to 100 because of rounding.

FACILITATING JUSTICE

Facilitating justice as a reason for custody was more frequently mentioned as a category of reasons in Tweed and Braid. The most frequently given single reason in that category (and the second most frequently given single reason in those areas overall) was accuseds' lack of co-operation with the police. In contrast, the biggest single reason in this category at Doon was that accused were of no fixed abode. The figure in Doon was inflated by one individual who was of no fixed abode and who was arrested ten times in three weeks, charged with minor offences such as drunk and incapable and breach of the peace. The accused was well known to the police who on one occasion said that he was being detained in custody because he was 'obnoxious to everybody' when he was drunk and that it was for his own benefit as he would get a meal and may be at risk of harm while he was drunk.

The other main reason for custody was that an accused was 'uncooperative with the police'. This mainly involved a physical or verbal assault upon police. (In Doon 61% of this category involved a police assault, in Tweed 83% and in Braid 39%). Other reasons included refusing to desist from problem behaviour, refusing information, refusing to give samples of breath, urine or blood, giving a false address or trying to avoid arrest. In Tweed one inspector had a 'personal policy' of detaining accused charged with police assault although this was not policy throughout the division.

Those where further enquiries were mentioned were mainly dishonesty cases. Although there were some serious or sexual assaults and drugs offences.

RISK TO COMMUNITY

Of risk to the community reasons for custody decisions in all areas, the nature of the crime was mentioned most frequently, with the nature of victim harm and likely recurrence accounting for fewer than half the mentions in the group. In Tweed and Braid the main type of case in which the nature of the crime was mentioned was serious or sexual assault cases. However, in Doon risk to the community reasons were evenly divided across serious or sexual assault, dishonesty and assault charges. This is partially a reflection of the fact that, at Doon, those accused of police assault or resisting arrest were routinely detained in custody. Although 'nature of crime' has been classified as implying 'risk to the community' for the purposes of this research, it should be noted that 'nature of the crime' in Doon often included police assault charges. This was not the case in other areas, where accused with this type of charge were sometimes released, although lack of co-operation with police which fell short of such charges was sometimes given as an additional ('facilitate justice') reason for detaining accused.

In each area over half of the cases where 'the nature of harm to the victim' was mentioned were crimes of violence (serious and sexual assault and assault). There were several instances in each area where the ongoing risk to the victim was mentioned. In one example of these in Braid, the accused was charged with an assault upon his wife. Police explained that they did not consider it appropriate to release the accused on undertaking as this was not sufficient to guarantee the victim's safety and prevent the accused returning to the house. The police officer commented, "I can't set bail conditions but the court can".

RECORD CHARACTERISTICS

Of record characteristic reasons for custody decisions, the nature and number of previous convictions and the fact that an accused was on bail were mentioned more than other aspects of records. Only in Tweed was bail mentioned more frequently than other features of record. This is likely to be linked to the fact that the decision inspectors in Tweed rarely saw the paperwork associated with cases, and, given that there was a local practice of detaining accused if they were on bail, then it is likely that where accused were found to have a bail order then this would be considered to be the salient piece of information which the arresting officer needed to convey about the accused's record to enable a decision to be made. Where time since previous convictions was mentioned it tended to be within a short time span, usually within the previous week.

PERSONAL CHARACTERISTICS

In general personal characteristics were less frequently mentioned as reasons for custody decisions than any others. Doon had a much higher number of mentions of personal risk factors such as drink or uncertain mental health. This is explained in part by a few accused who were repeatedly arrested while drunk and who therefore inflated these figures. Given the number of accused involved in serious assault at Braid it is perhaps surprising that violence and aggression were not often mentioned there.

RESPONSES TO EXISTING BAIL ORDERS

The formal policy of police in Doon is to detain an accused in custody if, when they are apprehended, they are found already to be on bail. The figures given earlier in the report show that this policy is generally followed. This was not the policy at Tweed and some decision makers expressed ambivalence about such a policy. Nevertheless those accused who were already on bail were in practice generally detained in custody in Tweed. As one officer commented, 'a bail order can be very handy if you want to keep someone - that's being honest'. Discussions with CID and uniform officers revealed a divergence of opinion about use in Doon, although less of a divergence in Tweed. The CID in Doon saw bail as a 'bargaining counter' which they would use to obtain information from an accused in exchange for the release of that accused on undertaking instead of their detention for custody court. Such a view was also expressed by uniformed officers in Tweed, though not those in Doon. In Braid police would not detain someone solely on the grounds that they had an outstanding bail order. It was explained that, when considering release, the important factor was whether the bail order was for an analogous matter. If the charges for which the accused was on bail were not analogous to the current offence, then Braid police said that there was no need to keep an accused in custody. However, they stated that if an accused was on bail on a petition charge they would be kept in custody.

CONCLUSIONS

Individual factors which contribute to police decision making have been examined in this chapter. However, it is not simply a question of aggregating factors but rather their complex interplay in any particular situation which explains the decisions made. In the locality with a court tendency to remand (Braid), police were more willing to release people and less concerned about considering bail as a reason for detaining accused in custody. In contrast, in Doon and Tweed, where the court made greater use of release options (bail and ordain), bail was the third most frequent reason given for detaining accused in police custody.

The higher police use of custody at Doon is primarily accounted for by the greater tendency to define a record as serious and by the prominence police there gave in their decisions to police assault charges and the existence of a bail order. Yet the record profile of accused at Doon was similar to that for accused who were released in Braid. Although accused at Doon were more likely already to be on bail, they were no more likely to have pending cases. Accused at Doon, by being more likely to be kept in custody or released on undertaking, are more likely to be seen quickly by the court than those in Tweed and Braid. Although, as measured by pending cases, they were no more likely to be alleged to be involved in repeat offending, this police use of custody would increase the likelihood that accused would be on bail at the time of alleged further offending. Such police practices will therefore impact on bail abuse for this reason alone. Nevertheless, how far this is the case is dependent on the response of the rest of the criminal justice system to local police practices.

After cases leave the police, there are two types of feedback which are generally received about what happens with accused in the early stages of their case. The first type is from the procurator fiscal's office and occurs on those occasions where the fiscal is commenting on police handling of a case. This feedback is generally about the adequacy of the information which police have provided in their report and the way in which this impacts on the initial stages of prosecution. The second type of feedback is about those cases which are taken to court for a plea. The information here is of a different order; it comes in the form of feedback from court police officers and from court sheets which are examined at the end of the day. Results collected by police from the court sheets are a basis for criminal justice statistics. However they also provide feedback which is not a comment on police action but is used by local police as a basis for informal comment on court action. If a case has been taken to court, police believe that they have discharged their responsibility in solving crime but whether the court is viewed by police as having appropriately discharged its responsibility in this is dependent on the decisions made and this forms part of informal talk within the police office. It is in and through this process that the local court reputation is established amongst operational police. But this reputation, while linked with the particular court in question, is also taken to be indicative of the behaviour of all courts. A remand decision is often taken as a confirmation of the police custody decision. However, a court bail decision for accused whom local police believe should be kept in custody, is taken, informally, as being indicative not only of the failure of the local court to recognise the need for custody, but of a generalised failure of courts and, of the generalised failure of bail legislation to secure the detention of those accused who police feel should be detained.

Police in Doon were more cynical about bail and expressed more dissatisfaction with the legislation than police in either of the other study areas. This area, which had a high use of court bail and a high level of police custody gave the existence of outstanding bail orders prominence in considering how to deal with accused. In Tweed police views were more mixed, with some dissatisfaction being expressed occasionally. This area had a level of use of court bail which fell midway between that of Doon and Braid as did its use of police custody. Here too, the existence of bail orders was given prominence in police consideration of whether or not to detain accused in custody. In Braid, the locality with the culture of remand, there were few expressions of dissatisfaction with bail legislation. The court had a high use of remand, police had a low use of custody and police gave little consideration to the existence of current bail orders in their accounts of reasons for detaining accused in custody.

CHAPTER 4

PROSECUTION ATTITUDES TO BAIL

INTRODUCTION

When police report cases it is the procurator fiscal who decides whether there is a case to be answered and to which court an accused will be called for this purpose. The prosecutor therefore has a pivotal role in both the structure and operation of interaction between different elements within the criminal justice system. When the fiscal considers a case they are looking at and responding to police decision making; when they think about the potential implications of their attitude to bail they are looking to sheriff and high court decision making. It is therefore at this stage of processing cases that criminal justice agencies operate most visibly as a *system.*

It was earlier argued that police reports should not be understood as direct reflections of the incidents to which they refer but as *accounts* which form a key part in the construction of particular legal cases. Police interpretation of an incident will lead them to characterise the case and respond to it in a particular way. Liberation/custody decisions are part of that response and form an integral part of the account which is compiled. In its compilation, care will be taken to provide information about the available evidence for the charge which the reporting officer believes will be appropriate, along with the description of the incident and explanation of any related circumstances. That the construction in the police report does not necessarily produce the same response from the prosecutor, is clear both from deputes' actions and from their explanations of action in particular cases.

MAIN FINDINGS

Fiscals gave more priority to criminal record in their considerations than police and this was an important explanation for disagreement with some police decisions. Variation in prosecutor decision making between the areas was primarily accounted for by the extent of flexibility in interpretation of significance of bail history in individual criminal records. Regular references to court views were made by deputes during the study and it was clear that the anticipation of court wishing to release, especially those kept on undertaking, was an important factor in depute attitude to bail.

In all areas bail history (i.e. having an outstanding bail order or bail convictions) was important in fiscal understandings of whether release on bail conditions was appropriate. However, deputes at Braid were more likely to consider any previous bail convictions as a reason for opposing bail whereas for deputes in other areas, their response to bail convictions was more dependent on their recency. In all areas being on bail was an important reason for opposing bail, but it was rarely the sole reason. Accused at Doon were more likely to have multiple bail orders and prosecutors there were more likely to agree to the further release of those on multiple bails. In contrast to the other areas where, if the present charge was less serious than that for which bail was originally granted, bail was more likely to be agreed, in Braid it was more likely to be opposed by deputes on the grounds of the seriousness of the charge since the accused had already been released on bail.

We have seen from the previous chapter that overall, the sample at Braid were involved in more serious incidents, nevertheless this did not, of itself, account for differences in decision-making between the areas. This chapter shows that when solemn and summary cases in the sample were analysed and case types were distinguished, in each category of case deputes at Braid were more likely to oppose bail than were deputes elsewhere. Police in Braid were flexible, not considering bail to have more weight than other factors in their decisions. The result of this was that they regularly released those who, because of their bail history, the fiscal would have preferred to have been detained in custody. Police at Doon, by routinely keeping people because they were on bail, detained in custody those whom the fiscals there, because of fiscal flexibility about approach to bail, did not wish to be further detained.

Fiscals tended to view bail orders as placing a restriction on accused. Observation of fiscal decision making identified that in many instances where bail is agreed it is not necessarily being agreed as an alternative to remand. Prosecutors responded to police use of custody and undertaking at Doon by being more likely to seek bail conditions being attached to an accused's subsequent release by the court than fiscals in the other study areas. Deputes' attitude to bail in undertaking cases was tempered by their view of likely court response. This meant that deputes at Tweed would not oppose bail in undertakings, in contrast bail was opposed in over half the undertakings at Braid.

Opposition to bail in undertaking cases was always an indication that deputes believed that accused should have been detained in police custody. For accused in custody cases deputes at Doon and Tweed would agree bail for those with recently granted bail orders if the new charges were seen as minor or non-analogous. Deputes at Braid opposed bail more frequently than deputes in the other areas. This was partly explained by the higher proportion of serious cases in Braid, but it was also linked to the greater likelihood that deputes at Braid would consider that the existence of any Bail Act conviction or of an outstanding bail order would be grounds for opposing bail.

Police use of custody at Doon increased the chance that the fiscal there would both look for the court to attach bail conditions to the release of more accused and that bail would be agreed more often. The impact of this on the potential for court response is significant since unless the fiscal opposes bail it must be granted. Fiscals were not only responding to the police, they were also responding to anticipated court action which acted to inhibit or encourage a presumption that cases would be ordained, bailed or remanded. This assessment of likely court outcome is an important way in which court practices influence decision-making prior to court. In Braid, where the court made greatest use of remand, deputes were more likely to oppose bail. This pressure toward remand was absent in the other areas.

FORMAL POLICIES

Localised liberation/custody policies operated by the police would have to have the prior agreement of the procurator fiscal. If police were not enthusiastic about undertakings because they placed extra pressure on them to produce reports with no tangible gain, procurator fiscal depute attitudes to undertakings were also often unenthusiastic with the exception of prosecutors in Doon where undertakings were viewed positively, and their use for football related cases in particular was seen as a mechanism for getting problematic cases to court quickly while obviating the need for custody. Deputes who disliked undertakings tended to view them as alternatives to release for summons and, if they believed that an undertaking had been unnecessary, they would sometimes cancel it. Deputes at Tweed and Braid tended to associate increased use of undertakings with increased pressure on fiscal workloads brought about by a reduced use of citation rather than seeing them as a mechanism for reducing pressure on prosecutors by enabling a reduced use of police custody. This was strongly stated at Braid, where deputes, when asked about the low use of undertakings in the area and whether they saw any scope for increased use, stated unequivocally, in the words of one depute that:

> "You are asking do I want the courts loaded on a particular day?...At present I feel that cited cases are used instead - I would not consider an undertaking being used as an alternative to custody". (depute at Braid)

The parameters set by the procurator fiscal service regulations which specify conditions under which bail should be opposed were outlined in chapter one. Accused who are in custody are technically prisoners of the procurator fiscal and remain so until guilt or innocence has been established, either by an acceptable plea or as the outcome of a trial. At this stage in the process the procurator fiscal controls what happens with cases, although that control is ultimately overseen by the court.

MARKING ARRANGEMENTS

How a case first comes to the attention of the procurator fiscal is the initial signal as to the seriousness with which it is viewed by the police. That signal affects the speed with which a case is initially examined by the marking depute. Custody cases are looked at as soon as they are received from the police. Undertaking cases are dealt with in the same way if the volume of custody cases permits, while cases which have simply been reported will be examined after the urgent business is complete. Although police will sometimes consult with the procurator fiscal before deciding whether or not a case should be reported as a custody, the first point at which the fiscal is generally aware of a case is when the police report arrives for consideration.

Initial decisions are made about cases by procurator fiscal deputes (marking deputes) who assess reports of alleged offences, decide whether, on what charges and in which court to proceed with cases. This process is known as marking.

> 'The origin of the expression probably lies in the fiscal's practice of underlining the important words or phrases in the report which will be regarded as crucial in presenting and establishing the prosecution case in court. Marking may also refer to the notes made on the minute sheet attached to the back of the report which record, in a kind of fiscal shorthand, the processing of the case. For example, the note *Sh Smy Cite* (Sheriff Summary Cite) is both a record of the fiscal's decision to prosecute an accused in the sheriff court by means of a summary complaint and an instruction to fiscal support staff to arrange for the issuing of such a complaint'. (Moody and Tombs, 1982)

In Doon and Braid marking was organised according to the type described by Moody and Tombs as Marking Depute, which is that all cases were marked by deputes allocated to marking for a specific period. In Doon the marking depute was also the depute who appeared in court. In Braid, cases were marked by two deputes together, one of whom would be appearing in court, this arrangement was changed part way through the fieldwork period and the new arrangements mirrored those of Doon. In Tweed there was a Marking Team with all cases being marked under a senior depute's supervision by a summary team of deputes with a team leader. The summary team leader marked most of the cases although the court depute was a member of the summary team and would occasionally be involved in marking.

MARKING: CUSTODIES AND UNDERTAKINGS

The marking process has been described in detail by Moody and Tombs (1982). For present purposes, therefore, the process will be summarised and the discussion will focus on custody and undertaking cases. When the procurator fiscal depute receives a police report they will consider the sufficiency and strength of the evidence; whether and how to proceed; the charges to be libelled; and their attitude to bail at the first calling of the case. Police reports for custody cases usually arrive in the procurator fiscal's office by 9 am on the day of court (usually the day following arrest). In Doon and Tweed deputes had only a short time to mark cases before court since the daily custody court began at 10 am; in Braid there was more time available for marking custodies as the daily custody court began at 2pm. There is more flexibility with reports for undertaking cases, which are expected a day or two before court. Marking generally takes place very quickly, with it being exceptional for more than about 5 minutes to be spent on a custody case at this stage. Often much less time than that is spent though occasionally consultation may be necessary, either with the senior depute or with other colleagues, and in such cases marking may take longer.

In all areas deputes argued that it was not in their interest to keep accused in custody since as soon as someone is detained this increases the pressure on the fiscal to process cases more speedily. However, they maintained that they would argue in court for custody if it was unequivocal that this was necessary, but that in borderline cases the benefit of the doubt tended to be given to the accused.

> "You've got to consider what the offence is; whether they are on bail; whether it is analogous; how often they have been on bail in the past; recency; persistence of offending; and when you're trying to fit the date within 40 days its got to be a consideration. Custody trials: you have to mark the cases as full statements within 7 days; cite the witnesses and compile the list immediately; BF (mark the papers to be brought out) for 8 or 9 days; take papers (to be checked and married up with associated papers). There are always worries about clearing papers through...."
> (depute at Tweed)

For summary cases there tends to be an assumption that even at first appearance the case is ready for trial, although there would always be a few cases for which additional information needed to be sought. For such cases, if accused are held in custody, there are 40 days to complete the case and have it tried in court. On petition matters the time necessary to prepare for trial varies according to the complexity of the case. Although if the accused is in custody there are 110 days in total to have the case completed, in practice there are generally 50 days to prepare the case and 80 days within which the indictment must be served. This restricts the number of petition custodies that can be dealt with at any one time.

SAMPLE

Table 4.1 shows details of the main sample collected from the police together with the initial action taken by the procurator fiscal. The area where the police detained more accused in custody was also the area where cases were more likely not to be proceeded with or were proceeded in the district court. This is likely to contribute to police dissatisfaction in that area. In contrast, the low level of police dissatisfaction expressed at Braid is likely to be linked to the high percentage of cases which were proceeded in the sheriff court.

Table 4.1 Initial Procurator Fiscal Action by Police Reporting of Case

	Doon Custody	U-T	*Tweed*** Custody	U-T	*Braid* Custody	U-T
Sheriff Court	*83%*	*85%*	*83%*	*63%*	*97%*	*90%*
No proceedings	*5%*	*10%*	*1%*	*0*	*1%*	*5 %*
Other*	*12%*	*5%*	*16%*	*38%*	*2%*	*5%*
Total	139	39	203	32	157	21

*Other = proceed in District Court, liberate for citation, liberate for further enquiries, diverted, fiscal fine.
** It was important to ensure a sufficient representation of dishonesties since previous research has shown that accused in this type of case may be more likely to be involved in offending on bail. The sample at Tweed was boosted to improve the representation by taking details of custodies with dishonesty charges from a neighbouring police division (together the two divisions covered the whole city of Tweed). This resulted in the addition of 13 accused. Sensitivity checks were carried out on the data to control for the possibility that these additional cases might bias the sample. The additional cases were not included in the discussion of police decisions since information was not collected on these police decisions as they were made in a different police office to that in which the research was located.

Accused whose cases were to be proceeded with in the sheriff court were retained in the sample, others were removed from the sample at this stage[1]. The overall pattern of cases in the sample remained the same after these accused had been removed (see annex 4). Despite having had the number accused of dishonesty boosted at Tweed, the sample there had still a smaller percentage accused of dishonesty than the other areas. All accused remaining in the sample represent 28% of all accused who appeared personally at Doon sheriff court during this time. At Tweed it represents 22% of all accused who appeared personally and 28% in Braid.

PATTERN OF DECISIONS

The difference in pattern of responding to accused on undertaking in each of the areas was stark (Figure 4.1), with bail not being opposed in any of these in Tweed, but being opposed in over half of the Braid accused. It is worth noting that in Doon, when fieldwork started some deputes expressed surprise at the inclusion of undertakings in the study since they rarely opposed bail in such cases; in Tweed deputes were mystified at the inclusion of undertakings, in Braid their inclusion went unremarked.

Prosecution opposition to bail in undertakings was in all instances a mark of prosecution disagreement with the police decision to release and the figures above

1 Over a third of undertakings were removed from the sample in Tweed, a much higher proportion than elsewhere. The high proportion of such cases being removed is partly attributable to the fact that there was a daily district court, so that more cases could be dealt with there than in the other areas. A much smaller proportion of custodies were excluded from the sample in Braid (3%) than in Doon or Tweed. It is notable that a higher proportion of sample cases were not proceeded with in Doon than the other areas.

Figure 4.1 Procurator Fiscal Attitude to Bail by Police Decision

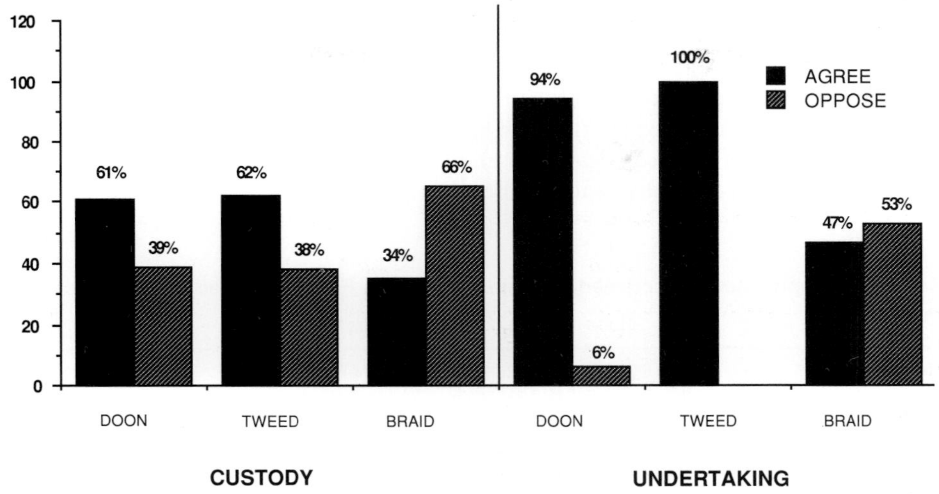

*Tweed 1 case outstanding; Braid 1 accused excluded: PF expected a guilty plea as accused 'institutionalised' - a guilty plea was in fact given in court. Custody Doon n=115; Tweed n=167; Braid n=151. Undertaking Doon n=32; Tweed n=20; Braid n=19

suggest that in Braid for undertaking cases at least, many of police release decisions were contentious. This was confirmed in discussion with deputes during observation

> "...often looking through reported cases I feel either that they should have been custody cases or that it would have been in the public interest to get an early report .....The police do not like to keep people in custody, sometimes reported cases should have been custody cases. Also there is some wheeling being done to get accused released. But this I think is in the public interest. Perhaps for the recovery of property for example, or further information about other crimes." (depute at Braid)

For custody cases, the converse was not true. That is, prosecution agreement to bail was not a signal that deputes believed that cases should have been released by the police. The pattern of prosecution responses in Braid again differed markedly from the other areas in that in Braid bail was opposed at the marking stage in nearly two thirds of accused detained in custody, whereas in the other areas the proportion was closer to one third.

SERIOUSNESS OF CASE

The prosecution response to police decisions is likely to be at least in part explained by the seriousness of the cases. Police decisions were more clearly explained by consideration of other factors and it is possible that in the prosecution offices a different significance was attached to seriousness of offence as measured by nature of offence; victim harm; criminal history. Braid had most custodies whose cases were proceeded as solemn, 23% (35) of accused, compared with 14%(16) of the sample in Doon and 16% (30) in Tweed. More accused in violence cases were proceeded as solemn in Braid. Even though there were more serious dishonesty cases there than in the other areas (see chapter 3), this was the only type of case where Braid had a lower proportion of solemn cases than in other areas.

It is important to note that the research cannot judge the extent to which a case defined as solemn in one area would be similarly defined in another. However, it can be taken that a case defined as solemn in a particular area is, in that area, thought serious. In Doon and Tweed all undertaking accused were involved in summary cases but in Braid 16% of accused released on undertaking were involved in solemn cases (1 dishonesty case and 2 serious assault). These have been excluded from table 4.2.

Table 4.2 Sample Accused Detained in Custody: % Where Fiscal Opposed Bail at Marking

	Doon	*Tweed**	*Braid***
Summary	36%(36)	34%(47)	58%(67)
Solemn	56%(9)	57%(17)	91%(32)
All Accused	39%(45)	38%(64)	66%(99)

*Tweed excludes one case where attitude was unclear outstanding
**Braid one case excluded: PF expected a guilty plea as accused 'institutionalised' - a guilty plea was in fact given in court

Bail was opposed in around one-third of summary cases where the accused appeared from custody and just over a half of solemn cases at Doon and Tweed. In contrast, in Braid bail was opposed in just over a half of summary cases and nearly all of solemn cases where the accused appeared from custody. Prosecutors at Braid therefore opposed bail much more frequently in all cases than did prosecutors in either of the other areas. Indeed, the proportion of cases where bail was opposed in solemn cases at Doon and Tweed is similar to that for summary cases at Braid. Bail was opposed for just over half (53% or 10 cases) of accused who had been released on undertaking at Braid. Three of these were involved in solemn cases. In Doon bail was opposed in 6% (2) cases whereas in Tweed bail was agreed in all cases where the accused appeared from undertaking.

Figure 4.3 Accused Detained in Custody: % age of Case Types Where Procurator Fiscal Opposed Bail

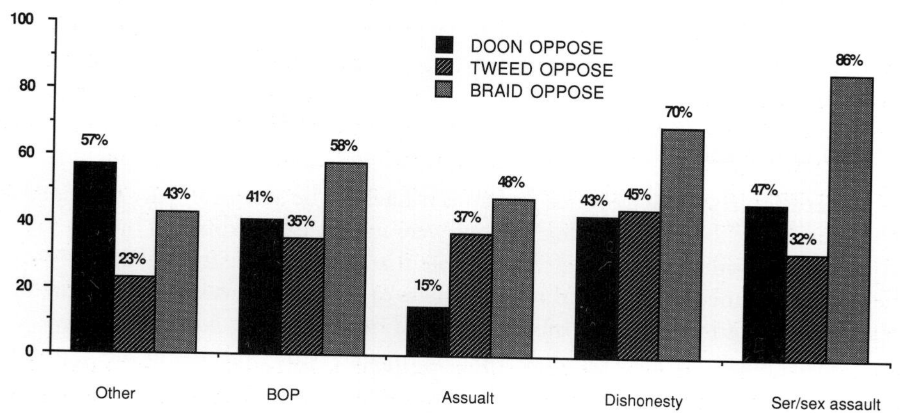

Figure 4.3 shows that for all categories of case where the accused was detained in custody, excepting 'other', bail was more likely to be opposed in Braid than in either of the other areas. For accused in serious assault cases at Tweed bail was less likely to be opposed than for those in dishonesty or assault cases, although serious assault was the case type for which fiscals were most likely to oppose bail in the other areas (excluding 'other' at Doon). For Tweed the highest proportion of accused for whom bail was opposed were involved in dishonesty cases. For all other case types Doon had the lowest percentage of cases where bail was opposed. Although the overall figures (table 4.2) for Doon and Tweed indicate that bail was opposed in a similar percentage of cases (39% in Doon and 38% in Tweed), this masks a considerable disparity in response to case types between the areas, particularly for those accused of assault.

Where accused appeared from undertaking, the fiscal in Braid opposed bail in half of those cases where the accused was charged with dishonesty and in two of the three accused charged with serious assault. In Doon, the fiscal opposed bail in two cases where the accused appeared from undertaking. One of these cases was the only accused in Doon released on undertaking charged with serious/sexual assault and the other was charged with a dishonesty offence.

CONSIDERING BAIL: REASONS FOR PROCURATOR FISCAL ATTITUDE

Some differences have been identified between the areas in case type and seriousness (more accused with previous custodial sentences at Braid and a higher proportion of more serious dishonesty there) and this could be seen as implying that only accused in more serious cases were kept in custody by police in Braid and that in Doon and Tweed more minor cases were being retained in the sample. Nevertheless it has been argued that this cannot totally account for differences between the areas in criminal justice response. In order to understand these differences it is necessary to consider the way in which the procurator fiscal's discretion to agree or oppose bail was being operated within these areas in relation to the configuration of elements which constituted individual cases.

The procurator fiscal guidance for opposing bail was discussed in chapter one. The increased qualifications which have been placed on the circumstances in which fiscals can oppose bail for administration of justice reasons and the increased number of principles described in terms of protection of the public, are likely to affect the types of reason given for decisions. As explained earlier in this chapter, marking takes place very quickly in most cases. When deputes are considering their attitude to bail during marking, they will consider both the police report and a print out of the accused's record. They are therefore not only considering the strength of the evidence of the accused's guilt but the extent to which the present case may be an aberration from that person's normal behaviour or part of a continuing pattern. This contributes to the view which they will form but, in addition, in considering their attitude to bail in individual cases, they must take into account not only the accused and what they may have done, but also what the police have done and what the court is likely to do in respect of that accused. In this section the general characteristics of decision making are described and, based on an analysis of individual cases with their reasons, more detailed discussion is focused on accused in illustrative cases.

For most deputes in all areas the prime consideration described in their accounts of how they consider cases was, once they had considered the sufficiency of the evidence, the record of the accused in close conjunction with the nature of the offence libelled.

"Record is important: whether there are any analogous offences; important if it is a bad crime, by that I mean a serious personal injury is involved and that then is the dominant factor". (depute at Tweed)

"I look at the age of the accused, the charges, police information, previous record, is it in the public interest that bail should be opposed? Danger to witnesses, evidence, further enquiries needed. When considering age I consider whether it's a young first offender or whether it's a mature first offender. Obviously if it's a first offender this is not a course of criminal conduct but I need to think about whether I am likely to have more trouble if the accused is let out". (depute at Braid)

Likelihood of further offences is generally seen as important in the prosecution assessment of record.

"Further offences I would say has greater priority for me rather than their likelihood of appearing, unless there is direct evidence on their record that they have failed to appear in the past". (depute at Braid)

Factors such as having a recent criminal record of analogous offences which might imply that the person was involved in a course of criminal conduct; having types of court order (probation, community service, deferred sentence, bail order) which imply that the commission of an offence would be a breach of the court's trust; a record of custodial sentences, or strong evidence of a serious or repetitive offence, are generally taken as contra-indications of bail i.e. they are factors which are likely to trigger prosecutors to consider opposing rather than agreeing bail. Where the evidence was considered weak, deputes were reluctant to oppose bail and this was the situation for accused in a number of cases, especially at Doon (classified as 'nature of evidence' in the 'facilitate justice' sections of tables 4.3 and 4.5).

PROSECUTION VIEWS ON USE OF BAIL ORDERS: UNDERTAKINGS

Information was collected about the reasons for prosecution attitudes to bail for the accused who had been released on undertaking. Though a presumption operates in favour of bail at court, and in Doon and Braid this also operated as such within the fiscal's office, in Tweed the presumption was, for those on undertaking, in favour of having the accused simply ordained for a subsequent court appearance: "the question of bail shouldn't arise unless there are exceptional circumstances" (depute at Tweed). Views about attitude to bail are therefore shaped by the police response, as well as contributing to the court response (the census recorded Tweed sheriff court as making more use of ordaining than the other areas). This was also clearly illustrated at Doon where a depute explained that, "If it's an undertaking then I would tend not to oppose bail....though there are exceptions". The depute continued that, if an accused had been released on undertaking by the police and then subsequently turned up for court, then the prosecution would have no strong view about that person being bailed or ordained. Nevertheless, the prosecution had a preference for the court to make bail orders in these cases although, if the defence requested that the accused be ordained, they would not feel sufficiently strongly about this to object. Given this view at Doon, the high level of police use of custody and the high level of police use of undertaking can also be understood as contributing to the low use of ordaining and the high use of bail by the court there (chapter two).

In 94%(30) of undertakings at Doon, 55%(11) at Tweed and 47%(9) at Braid, bail was agreed by the depute because they wanted bail conditions to be attached to the release of an accused rather than simply to have them ordained.

Deputes in all areas were asked to explain their view of the use of bail rather than simply having people ordained for subsequent court appearances. Most saw bail as placing constraints on people, although the extent to which they thought these constraints were necessary for all those granted bail was variable. In Braid deputes were almost all uniformly in favour of bail, although those who had come to work in the area more recently thought that bail orders were not always necessary.

> "This is a strange court here. In (previous court)... not many were admitted to bail, defence agents here do not ask for their clients to be ordained. I am surprised at that. I suppose there are cases where bail is required, the sheriffs here do not like to grant bail. It is not at all clear why defence agents do not ask for their clients to be ordained more often.....on occasion I would have been happy for an accused to have been ordained". (depute at Braid)

In Doon a similar, though more extreme, version of this view was held by a minority who also believed that bail was used too frequently by the court there. However those who were generally involved in marking maintained that if someone had come to court from police custody then it was important, if the accused was to be liberated after court, that this should be on bail conditions since a bail order would afford some protection to the public. Ordaining an accused, it was argued, would only ensure their appearance at court, it made no further injunction on them about their behaviour.

Most deputes in Tweed were similarly in favour of bail, since it would allow the court to be alerted to any offending in which the accused might become involved. One depute noted that:

> "I like bail orders. The accused is given a bit of paper on which the conditions are stated. You will have heard the accused being asked in court whether or not they understand the conditions and are willing to accept them.......The old system of money bail was not as effective as new style conditions. In my experience in the district court under the old system people used to treat money bail as a fine. If they had to pay £10 to be released on bail, then they wouldn't turn up for court. Whereas now people do have to turn up and that allows the court to deal with them". (depute at Tweed)

A bail order signifies that the court has formally placed an accused on trust to adhere to the conditions of their bail. Favourable views about the use of bail therefore expressed a recognition that bail is conditional liberation granted to people on the basis of undertakings about their behaviour. This was tempered by the recognition that, while placing people on bail might constrain the behaviour of many, for those for whom it was less effective, the existence of bail offences would act as a signal to the court that there had been a breach of trust and this would affect how that person would be dealt with if they should subsequently come into contact with the criminal justice system.

UNDERTAKINGS: THE NEED FOR CONDITIONAL RELEASE BY THE COURT?

When asked about their attitude to bail in individual cases deputes were asked about their reasons for agreeing as well as for opposing bail. Since there is a presumption that bail should not generally be opposed, in some cases deputes found it more difficult to explain their reasons for agreeing bail than for opposing it. This was particularly the case in Doon where in nine undertaking cases it was simply noted that the accused were not currently on bail and in Tweed, where in thirteen custodies it was stated that bail was agreed because there was no reason to oppose it.

Where bail was agreed for undertakings deputes often indicated that if the defence sought unconditional release (ordain) they would be prepared to accept this. However, this was not uniformly the case, and in some instances deputes were seeking conditions being attached to the release of accused who would otherwise have been candidates for unconditional release. In Tweed it was unusual for deputes to be looking for bail conditions to be attached to the release of an accused who had been given an undertaking. Though bail conditions were generally sought in Doon and Braid, in none of the cases was it sought as an alternative to remand.

In all areas deputes argued that the fact that accused had been released on undertaking by the police made it more difficult to oppose bail in court. For example, in an instance at Braid where a depute was concerned that a man accused of assaulting his wife had not been kept in custody, the depute argued that his potential for action in court was restricted by the man having been released,

> "This way my hands are tied as he's no previous convictions and he's 55....the accused's attitude shows no remorse; but he's been released back to the same address; I don't know whether the victim was forewarned of his return.....In the normal course I would have liked bail with a special condition. But I don't know if a special condition would be appropriate, and the fact that he has returned to live with the victim and witness means its difficult to make a request for a special condition"[2].

CIRCUMSTANCES OF UNDERTAKINGS: OVERVIEW

It could be expected that, being at a greater remove from the immediate incident than police, fiscals would give less prominence in their deliberations to the immediate circumstances of a case and this was borne out by observation. During the court observation in the areas where bail was opposed for undertakings, it was noted that defence agents would argue that the fact that an accused had been released by the police implied that there was no need for that person to be detained in custody by the court.

Tables 4.3 and 4.4 identify, respectively, the reasons which were given by deputes for their agreement and for their opposition to release on bail. The content of criminal records was more likely than any other factor to explain fiscal attitude to bail. Where bail was agreed for accused with problem records, the offences tended to be minor and, had their records also been thought minor, then these accused would have been released for summons or sent to the district court. In Tweed, because it was believed that the court would not remand undertakings, deputes did not oppose bail. Deputes at Braid, while acknowledging this as a difficulty, did not consider this to be insurmountable and were prepared to oppose bail for such accused. Having an outstanding bail order or a record containing Bail Act convictions was, of itself, considered by deputes in Braid to be sufficient reason for opposing bail.

2 The police report maintained that the accused had assaulted his wife because "the kitchen was untidy" and had ordered her and their sons to leave the home. Within twenty minutes of being apprehended he had been released on undertaking to the same address. Police had released him for medical reasons as they were concerned that he had a very bad heart condition, looked frail and was on medication "I don't think he posed a threat to her...the last thing I want is a cell death". (Braid police)

Table 4.3 Undertaking Cases: Factors in Fiscal Agreement to Bail (%age of Mentions)

Reason Type	*Doon*	*Tweed*	*Braid*
RECORD CHARACTERISTICS	**44%**	**44%**	**33%**
Few previous convictions	26%	26%	33%
Analogous prev. convictions	3%	7%	0
On probation/CSO/SD	1%	0	0
On bail	1%	0	0
Not on bail	13%	0	0
Prev breaches of Bail Act	0	7%	0
Prev breach CSO/probation	0	4%	0
RISK TO COMMUNITY	**19%**	**37%**	**8%**
Nature of crime (low risk)	15%	33%	8%
Nature harm/low risk to victim	4%	4%	0
FACILITATING JUSTICE	**16%**	**4%**	**16%**
Co-accused on bail	0	4%	0
Nature of evidence	13%	0	0
Has fixed address	3%	0	16%
PERSONAL CHARACTERISTICS	**0**	**0**	**24%**
Age (older)	0	0	16%
Drunk	0	0	8%
PROCESS FACTORS	**19%**	**15%**	**16%**
Released on U-T by Police	18%	15%	0
Expect to plead guilty	1%	0	8%
Unruly certificate	0	0	8%
N	**68**	**27**	**12**

Table 4.4 Undertaking Cases: Factors in Fiscal Opposition to Bail (%age of Mentions)

Reason Type	*Doon*	*Braid*
RECORD CHARACTERISTICS	**83%**	**78%**
Number previous convictions	17%	14%
Analogous previous convictions	33%	0
Analogous pending cases	0	7%
On probation/CSO/SD	33%	7%
On bail	0	29%
Previous breaches of Bail Act	0	21%
RISK TO COMMUNITY	**17%**	**0**
Nature harm/perceived risk to victim	17%	0
FACILITATING JUSTICE	**0**	**7%**
Nature of evidence	0	0
No fixed abode	0	7%
PROCESS FACTORS	**0**	**14%**
Released on U-T by police	0	7%
Unruly certificate	0	7%
N	**6**	**14**

BRAID- excludes one not stated

Numbers total higher than sample as more than one factor was mentioned in some decisions.

%ages in each table do not add to 100 because of rounding

AGREEING BAIL IN UNDERTAKINGS: RECORD

Bail, for accused on undertaking, was usually an alternative to unconditional release rather than to remand. Whereas record was not often mentioned by police in explaining their response of releasing on undertaking, it was more frequently mentioned than anything else in prosecution accounts of decisions. Where record was mentioned and bail was agreed it either meant that accused did not have records which implied that a remand would be appropriate (e.g. six accused each at Doon[3] and Tweed and three at Braid had no previous convictions at all), but that the incidents were sufficiently serious to imply that conditions ought to be attached to an accused's release; or that the incident was minor and bail conditions would not have been necessary had the accused's record not been thought problematic.

In those instances where there were aspects of individual criminal records which might have led the fiscal to interpret them as being serious but nevertheless bail was agreed, accused had been released on undertaking by police either because of a policy to use undertakings for certain sorts of incidents, or because of factors associated with co-accused. For example, in Doon bail was agreed for one person charged with challenging fans near a football ground (breach of the peace) despite that accused having analogous previous convictions[4] within the previous year, having had ten analogous convictions in the past two years; having two pending (non-analogous) cases; having had seven charges of offending on bail within the previous three years; and having a current community service order. The accused was on deferred sentence for non-analogous matters and the fiscal wished him to be granted bail rather than ordained because of this record.

Similarly in Tweed, for example, bail was agreed for one person whose record was described by the depute as "horrendous". He was charged with breach of the peace (involving an argument with bar staff in the city centre)[5] and had similar convictions in the previous year; two custodial sentences within the previous three years and had a non-analogous pending case. His record showed offences committed on bail during the previous three years, as well a history of failure to attend court; breach of community service order and convictions for attempting to pervert the course of justice. The fiscal agreed bail because the offence had been such that, if this accused's record had not been considered problematic, he would have simply been ordained for a subsequent court appearance.

In one example at Braid where the accused was just out of a young offenders institution, remand was not a consideration because of the minor nature of the crime (shoplifting, value £20)[6]. The fiscal saw this as a borderline district court case but, since the local district court rarely used custodial sentences and as the accused was just out of prison, it was put to the sheriff court because there was a greater possibility of the accused receiving a custodial sentence. Police had asked the fiscal to seek a special bail condition that the accused should not enter shopping areas of the town, but the fiscal thought this was unrealistic as it was hard to avoid the town centre. (Bail was ultimately granted with a condition not to approach the shop from which the goods had been stolen).

The impact of police action on fiscals was clearly illustrated at Tweed where, because

---

3 Though one of the Doon accused was on bail for a pending case.

4 Police had originally arrested this man because they had been concerned that the incident might escalate.

5 Police had made a policy decision to release him on undertaking.

6 Police had stated that if his co-accused had not had a warrant outstanding, then he would have been released for summons.

deputes believed that there was no point in opposing bail if police had released someone on undertaking, deputes would agree bail even if they believed that police ought not to have released particular accused. Thus, an accused released by police on undertaking for medical reasons, was charged with having caused a disturbance in a bar and threatening staff with a knife (breach of the peace and possession of an offensive weapon)[7]. The depute would rather have seen the case as a custody as he was described as having a bad record with a number of analogous previous convictions, although none of these had been within the last three years. The depute stated that, "given that he's been released on undertaking there's no point even trying to oppose bail".

AGREEING BAIL IN UNDERTAKINGS: RISK TO THE COMMUNITY

Where risk to the community was mentioned as minimal it was because incidents were minor (often breaches of the peace) and confined (and therefore unlikely to recur), either because they were associated with particular events which were finished (such as football matches) or because the problematic activity was contained to a small identifiable group.

For example, three accused at Doon had been released by police because it was felt that they presented no harm to the general public. They were charged with assault, as the result of a fight amongst themselves, and they were making counter allegations against each other[8]. The fiscal agreed bail as unreliable witnesses meant that the case was weak, there were no substantial injuries and the behaviour was not a problem for public safety as it was confined amongst the three accused.

OPPOSING BAIL IN UNDERTAKINGS: RECORD

Where deputes opposed bail for accused on undertaking, this was always a signal that they disagreed with the police release decision. Disagreement tended to arise as the result of police using undertaking for policy reasons or because they were prioritising the immediate circumstances of an incident or an accused, whereas the fiscal prioritised record in their response to a case.

For example police at Doon, had released one man accused of indecent exposure because there had been some time between the alleged incident and the arrest[9]. The fiscal thought that the accused's record was indicative of there being a risk to the community and therefore opposed bail. This accused had a record of analogous offences within the past year, he had a pending case of a similar type and was on deferred sentence for an analogous offence.

Similarly, bail was opposed at Braid for a man accused of driving while disqualified and without insurance and attempting to pervert the course of justice. Police had released him on undertaking because he had given a fixed address and the officer concerned believed it was local policy to use undertakings with disqualified drivers. However, the depute felt that the record was so bad that he should have been kept in custody (seven previous breaches of bail; four convictions for attempting to pervert the

---

7 Police would normally have kept someone involved in this type of incident in custody but he had been released on undertaking for the following day because he had a chronic heart complaint.

8 Police had felt that by arresting them they would reinforce to those involved that the matter was serious and that by not releasing them for summons the court would deal more quickly with the case.

9 This, together with the fact that his wife had attended the police station to speak on his behalf, had been the reason for the police release decision.

course of justice; and he had recently failed to answer an undertaking) and assumed that he would have no fixed address as he was a traveller.

At Doon and Tweed police practice of keeping those on bail as custodies rather than releasing them, meant that bail was not a prominent feature of decisions about undertakings in these areas. It was shown in chapter three that police at Braid did not give particular priority to current bail in their consideration of custody or release. Those accused at Braid and for whom record was mentioned by depute however, all had a history of bail offences or were currently on bail. However fiscal deputes in Braid considered bail history to be a priority and were prepared to oppose bail solely on the basis of the existence of a current bail order, even if an accused had no previous convictions, as in the case of one accused who nevertheless had two outstanding bail orders associated with housebreaking charges and two similar pending cases. The current charges were housebreaking, housebreaking with intent and four breaches of bail were being libelled(i.e. two breaches for each bail order). This sixteen year-old had been caught running away from a factory into which he was alleged to have broken.

Similarly bail was opposed because of the existence of a current bail order, for example, for an accused in Braid who was charged with being in possession of a flick knife and who was suspected of drunk driving. The marking depute believed that, in principle, bail should be opposed for anyone with a current bail order. This accused had convictions within the previous three years though they had no custodial sentences during that period and no similar convictions within the last year. They had four pending cases which were non-analogous and their most serious sentence had been a fine. They were on two bail orders associated with housebreaking charges, the last of which had been within one month of the present case. Police had said that if it had not been for the drunk driving charge this would have been a cited case as the bail orders were for non-analogous matters.

OPPOSING BAIL IN UNDERTAKINGS: PROCESS

The increased likelihood of bail being opposed at Braid was the case even for younger accused. This was the situation, for example, for one at Braid accused of theft of motor vehicles and driving while disqualified and with no insurance, and who, with his two co-accused, was resident at a children's home, having had involvement with the Children's Panel. Police had released the three to the care of the home. The accused in question was nearing 16 and the fiscal felt that he should come before the sheriff court because of the nature of the offence and because he must be absconding to commit these offences. Bail was agreed for the two co-accused but opposed for the other and an unruly certificate was sought. This accused had come to police attention at the age of 13 for dishonesty and had continued this, having recently taken to stealing cars. "He's involved with others in stealing cars, has driven recklessly and caused an accident...His address is [a children's home] where underage offenders are kept....Don't want him at liberty, he's been in trouble for a long time". The depute indicated that if it had been an adult facing similar charges with no previous convictions then bail would not be being opposed.

CIRCUMSTANCES OF CUSTODIES

The themes which were identified in decisions about accused on undertaking were also, as could be expected, a feature of fiscal responses to custodies. It was indicated earlier that prosecution reasons for wanting accused to remain in custody focused less frequently than police on immediate circumstances of an incident and were more frequently concerned with other aspects of cases. Table 4.5 shows that for accused in custody cases in all areas criminal record featured more frequently in prosecution explanations for bail attitude than any other factor.

Other factors associated with fiscal agreement to bail were assessment of risk to the community which was mentioned next often in all areas, and bail which ranked third in Doon, but was less prominent in decisions to agree bail in Tweed and Braid. There was no difference in the ranking of frequency of mentioning factors for opposition across the areas. Bail as a reason for opposition was mentioned more frequently than other reasons, apart from record. In respect of custodies, the prominence which bail had in decisions about undertaking cases at Braid was also characteristic of Doon and Tweed. However, prominence given to bail did not necessarily mean that bail would always be opposed if accused were already on bail. As illustrated in the discussion of undertakings, decisions are rarely made on the basis of a single factor in isolation, but rather on the basis of a particular configuration of elements which constitute the characteristics of a case. The focus for the discussion of prosecution responses to custodies will be record, bail and facilitating justice, all of which featured more prominently in decisions to oppose bail. Risk to the community concerns usually also accompanied these other concerns. Other factors will be illustrated in so far as they are linked with these three main categories of reason for attitude to bail.

ATTITUDE TO BAIL FOR CUSTODIES: RECORD

It was stated in chapter one, in the discussion of procurator fiscal guidance for opposition to bail, that evidence of a course of criminal conduct was important in considerations of bail and this notion was regularly referred to by deputes during the fieldwork. There are five elements to this: the number of previous convictions recorded, the type, their frequency, their seriousness - as defined by whether the conviction was from a district , sheriff or the high court and the type of sentence which was given for it, the existence of pending cases. Taken together, these produce what is defined as a more or less serious record. In many respects understandings of what counts as a serious record were shared across the three areas. For example, having previous custodial sentences was taken in all areas as being an indication of a serious record. However an important explanation for differences in fiscal attitude to bail between the three areas was in depute interpretation of criminal record and their views on bail history - defined as having current bail orders or previous convictions for bail abuse.

AGREEING BAIL FOR CUSTODIES: RECORD

Having no criminal record was likely to be a reason for bail being agreed, even in serious cases, such as serious assault. For 16% of those for whom bail was agreed at Doon, 18% at Tweed and 23% at Braid, the accused had no previous convictions and, with the exception of one accused at Braid who was also without an address, in all of these the fiscal agreed bail. In Doon and Tweed if previous convictions were non-analagous, bail also tended to be agreed. This happened less often in Braid, although it did occur on occasion there.

Even if an accused had analogous convictions bail might still be agreed if there were few convictions, they were thought to be for minor matters or if there was a significant time gap between them. For example, for two accused at Doon who had similar previous convictions, bail was agreed, as, in one instance, three years had elapsed since the last analogous conviction and, in the other, the accused had one analogous

Table 4.5 Police Custodies: Reasons For Procurator Fiscal Attitude to Bail (%age of Mentions)

	Doon Agree	Oppose	*Tweed* Agree	Oppose	*Braid* Agree	Oppose
RECORD	**39%**	**39%**	**32%**	**35%**	**51%**	**40%**
Number of previous convictions	21%	9%	25%	8%	40%	14%
Analogous previous convictions	5%	10%	3%	7%	1%	14%
Number of pending cases	0	0	0	1%	0	3%
Analogous pending cases	1%	2%	0	4%	0	<1%
Time since last conviction	4%	2%	4%	4%	7%	3%
On probation/CSO/SD	1%	13%	0	5%	1%	1%
Previous disposals	1%	1%	0	4%	0	4%
Prev. breach CSO/probation	0	0	0	2%	0	<1%
Likelihood custodial sentence	6%	2%	0	0	2%	1%
BAIL	**18%**	**27%**	**13%**	**26%**	**5%**	**23%**
On bail	4%	15%	2%	12%	4%	9%
Not on bail	10%	0	7%	1%	1%	0
Previous breaches of Bail Act	4%	11%	1%	6%	0	14%
Previous failure to appear	0	1%	0	4%	0	<1%
Co-accused on bail	0	0	0	1%	0	0
No prev. breach bail	0	0	3%	2%	0	0
FACILITATE JUSTICE	**9%**	**15%**	**11%**	**21%**	**5%**	**19%**
Nature of the evidence	8%	0	2%	0	2%	1%
Further enquiries	0	4%	0	5%	0	10%
Enquiries complete	0	0	0	0	2%	0
Co-accused untraced	0	0	0	0	0	1%
No fixed abode	0	11%	0	14%	0	7%
Fixed address	1%	0	9%	0	1%	0
Likely to abscond	0	0	0	2%	0	0
RISK TO COMMUNITY	**26%**	**13%**	**25%**	**9%**	**28%**	**8%**
Nature of offence	19%	4%	24%	4%	10%	5%
Nature of victim harm	4%	2%	1%	4%	10%	2%
Danger of recurrence	1%	2%	0	1%	8%	1%
Public safety/interest	2%	5%	0	0	0	0
PROCESS	**5%**	**4%**	**5%**	**6%**	**4%**	**1%**
Prev. released on undertaking	0	0	0	1%	0	0
In breach of interdict	0	2%	0	1%	0	<1%
On Children's Panel supervision	0	0	1%	0	1%	<1%
Expect to plead guilty	1%	0	1%	1%	1%	<1%
Encourage a guilty plea	1%	0	0	0	0	0
Time difficulties if remanded	2%	0	0	0	0	0
Inappropriate police custody	1%	0	1%	0	0	0
Warrant for another matter	0	2%	1%	3%	0	1%
Administrative reasons	0	0	0	0	2%	0
Time between offence & arrest	0	0	1%	0	0	0
PERSONAL FACTORS	**4%**	**5%**	**10%**	**6%**	**5%**	**2%**
Mental state/ Drunk/drugged	0	5%	3%	3%	1%	1%
"To secure better behaviour"	0	0	1%	0	0	0
Age of accused	3%	0	4%	1%	4%	<1%
Personal knowledge of accused	1%	0	0	1%	0	0
Job	0	0	2%	0	0	0
Offences against public justice	0	0	0	1%	0	1%
No reason to oppose	0	0	6%	0	0	0
N	**156**	**124**	**190**	**164**	**83**	**202**

Numbers total higher than sample as more than 1 factor was mentioned in some decisions.
%ages do not add to 100 because of rounding.
Excludes 1 accused each at Tweed and Braid where no prosecutor reasons stated.

conviction for which the disposal indicated that it was a minor breach of the peace. In Tweed one accused had only three convictions in total and in another case the fiscal noted that although the accused had analogous previous convictions, they were not thought to be serious.

OPPOSING BAIL FOR CUSTODIES: RECORD

Of those for whom bail was opposed, for 24% at Doon, 20% at Tweed and 29% accused at Braid the large number of previous convictions was a factor. Important in assessing previous convictions was their similarity to the offence currently alleged. Bail was generally opposed for accused with analogous convictions in all areas, with those in dishonesty cases being more likely to have this given as a reason for opposing bail (45% of such mentions at Doon, 53% at Tweed and 69% at Braid). Analogous previous convictions was, however rarely the sole reason for opposition to bail - in only one accused was this the case (where the accused had ten previous convictions for assault and robbery).

ATTITUDE TO BAIL FOR CUSTODIES: 'RECENT' CONVICTIONS

Most deputes in all areas had similar views about the significance of the timing of previous convictions and if the last previous conviction was not recent then it was not usually considered as a contra-indicator for bail. Nevertheless, definitions of what should count as 'recent' were variable. In all areas there were accused who had gaps of two or more years since their last previous conviction as well as those who were alleged to have offended within a few days, or hours, of having been released on bail by the court. In these extreme cases, the pattern of agreeing or opposing bail was generally consistent across the areas. However, within the range of a few weeks and three years, there was variation in working definitions of 'recent' with deputes at Braid being more likely to consider older convictions as contra-indicators for bail.

> "If there is no recent criminal record say, for example, somebody had a really bad record 5 years ago but had nothing since then I would not count those, unless of course they had been in prison all that time. I do not know if I would not consider anything much younger than that. It would only be that if there had been no record for a period and there was a significant gap". (depute at Braid)

Deputes at Doon and Tweed tended to define a gap of a year or more between present charge and last conviction as 'significant' and occasionally minor offences which were less than a year would also be considered as 'not recent'.

For example, in the case of an accused at Tweed alleged to have been involved in breach of the peace, the depute described it as "a long time" since his last offences as he had no similar convictions within the last year. Although he had 3 custodial sentences on his record, he had no history of breaching bail. Similarly bail was agreed for another accused at Tweed who had a history of petty theft. It was alleged that as a known thief he had been caught in circumstances where he was likely to commit crime. The depute described him as "just on the right side of the line", as he had no history of having breached bail, although he had similar convictions within the past year and four analogous pending cases; he was currently on bail, having been granted bail four weeks previously.

In Braid especially in cases where accused had records with custodial sentences, deputes were more likely to consider older convictions as contra-indicators for bail, although those who had come to work in the area more recently had different views.

This is illustrated in the case of one accused (attempted theft of motor vehicles and various road traffic offences (petition)) who was detained by the police because of "numerous and analogous previous convictions". The depute who initially marked the case opposed bail because of a "horrendous" record which had lots of breaches of bail. The record showed that the accused had no convictions in the previous three years. The depute dealing with the case at full committal stated prior to court that they would not oppose bail as they didn't consider the record to be "so bad...it wouldn't survive an appeal to the high court because the last previous conviction was in 1988 and though he got six months imprisonment for that, this would finish in 1989 - so there's been nothing for two years".

ATTITUDE TO BAIL FOR CUSTODIES: CURRENT BAIL

Though most who were on bail had bail opposed, deputes in Doon and Tweed were more willing to agree bail for those who were currently on bail than were deputes in Braid. The existence of a current court order is both an indication of court views of the seriousness of an accused's behaviour and an indication of the extent to which the accused can be seen to be responding seriously to the court. There are a number of types of court order to which accused might be subject. The significance of community service, probation and deferred sentence was examined in addition to bail orders. Deputes in all areas attached varying significance to different types of court order. Some thought that breach of any court order was of equal weight since it was a breach of the court's trust, whereas others thought that other court orders were more important than bail. More marked than any distinction between areas in interpretation of other aspects of record however, were variations in the weight attached to bail history, that is, having current bail orders or bail convictions.

Prosecutors at Doon and Tweed argued that, although at one stage in the 1980's a current bail order was a ground automatically for opposition to bail, this was no longer the case as they thought that this was too rigid a practice and therefore did not want to oppose bail simply on the grounds of the existence of a current bail order.

> "I don't want to clog up the system with too many custody trials. I would oppose, but it is a mixture of looking at the present offence, how serious it is and how many trials there are likely to be. It might be that you have to oppose bail in a more serious matter and you need to be free to do that. I suppose its not really wanting to cry wolf because we might really need to oppose bail next time". (depute at Tweed)

> "If they breach their bail by failing to appear then they would definitely be prosecuted. Other breaches I don't know." (depute at Tweed)

Deputes were asked about reasons for not opposing bail if accused are on bail already. In all areas a more recent bail order would have more weight attached to it than an older bail. However, as with interpretation of record, understandings of what should count as "recent" were variable, with those in Doon and Tweed being less likely to consider older bail orders as recent than Braid. For example, in Doon, "recent" was within one month of present charge.

Deputes at Braid were more likely to argue both that bail should be opposed in principle and that, if more than one bail order is outstanding, then multiple bail charges should be libelled.

> "This indicates a past record of offending and I am more likely to oppose bail in these cases. If there were, for example, three separate bail orders then I would libel

one breach of bail per bail order. I would not libel a breach of bail for each substantive charge". (depute at Braid)

"Importance of breach of bail because it creates a separate offence it adds an extra dimension to it. ... In cases where an accused has a bail order outstanding I would not expect that accused to have their case cited, neither would I expect to see them as an undertaking, I would expect to see them as a custody because of the bail. Exceptions would be for social reasons or if the offence was trivial where you might not want them to be brought in at all". (depute at Braid)

CURRENT BAIL ORDERS

The variation between the areas in deputes' approach to formulating attitudes to new bail applications was closely linked to the weight which was generally attached to bail in depute decision making. Deputes at Doon and Tweed in practice interpreted bail as a factor which was weighed no differently to others; whereas those at Braid often held firm principles about the need to oppose bail if a record showed a bail order or bail conviction. In Doon and Tweed, if the present charge was less serious than the charge for which bail had been granted, there was a likelihood that bail would be agreed. In Braid it was likely to be opposed because of the seriousness of the earlier charge.

For example, in Tweed bail was agreed for two accused because their offences were more minor (breach of peace; possession of cannabis) than the offences for which they had been placed on bail six weeks previously (assault; attempted housebreaking). In contrast, in Braid bail was opposed in a case where there was a current bail order for a petition matter (assault to serious injury) which was 8 months old and the present charge was for a breach of the peace and assault. This accused had no analogous convictions within the past year, although the depute was aware that he had intimated a guilty plea for the petition matter which was to call in court within a few days. The depute stated that they would not have opposed bail if the accused had not been on bail.

In many of the cases where other aspects of record were important, bail history could distinguish those accused for whom bail was to be opposed, especially at Braid, and those for whom it was to be agreed. For 75% of accused at Doon for whom bail was mentioned, 83% of such accused at Tweed and 86% at Braid the fiscal opposed bail because they were on bail. Two of the six accused at Doon for whom bail was agreed had one current bail order, the rest had multiple bails, most of which had been granted only a few weeks before. Generally where bail was agreed in these instances it was because the bail order was considered not to be recent, the present charge was considered to be minor, or because it was non-analogous.

For example an accused at Doon with a single bail order was charged with shoplifting valued under £100 and fully recovered. The charge was seen as minor, and bail was agreed because although there was an outstanding warrant it was a means warrant and the bail order, though for a similar offence, was considered old (7 months previously).

In the case of an accused in Tweed who had been placed on bail for a non-analogous matter just over one month previously; who had analogous convictions within the last year; a record of theft and petty offences; a recent community service order; and four analogous pending cases, the fiscal thought that there was a "reasonable gap" and agreed bail. Another accused had bail agreed as the offence (shouting and swearing at other residents in a hostel for people with mental handicap) was thought minor in itself. The depute thought that anyone else would have been given a warning but the accused had been placed on bail for similar matters the previous week and the behaviour caused upset to other residents in the hostel.

At Doon these considerations could lead to bail being agreed even for those who had more than one bail order current. For example, an accused at Doon who had two bail orders for analogous offences, both within the previous month, one previous conviction which was non-analogous; and had three analogous pending cases. Bail was agreed because the dishonesty was considered minor as the loss was valued at under £50 and it was recovered.

Three accused each had three current bail orders. One had eight pending cases for similar offences, three outstanding bail orders for similar offences and was at that time on deferred sentence. He was accused of dishonesty, but bail was agreed because he was sixteen years of age and the charge was thought minor (under £50 loss).

Another (one of five co-accused)was charged with assault, and in their report the police had asked for "an example to be made" stating that this accused hadn't been dealt with seriously enough in the past by the court. This accused had similar convictions within the past year, six analogous pending cases, two outstanding bail orders, both within the previous month and six bail convictions within the past three years. The offence was described as relatively serious but 'bailable' by the depute who agreed bail because they judged that the accused did not have "such a bad record" . Similarly another accused had convictions within the last three years but no analogous conviction within the last year. They had three outstanding bail orders (two for non-analogous offences, one of which had been granted within the last month), three non-analogous pending cases, two bail convictions in the previous three years. Police noted in their report that on three previous occasions within the past six months the accused had been sent to court for breach of the peace and had been released on bail. The prosecutor viewed the record as being non-analogous and the offence as relatively minor (breach of peace, resist arrest) and therefore agreed bail.

In contrast, deputes in Braid were rarely prepared to agree bail for those already on bail unless this was necessary to facilitate the administration of justice. For example, bail was agreed in the case of one accused who had a six month old bail order, no analogous convictions in the past year and no record for breach of bail. The fiscal stated that he would have opposed bail because of the existing bail order but he had to agree as a trial diet had been set for this accused on another matter the previous day and it was too far away for the cases to be brought together if the accused should be in custody. If the accused were to be remanded then two trial diets would have to be fixed and this would cause "inordinate complications".

ATTITUDE TO BAIL FOR CUSTODIES: BAIL CONVICTIONS

Fiscal response to current bail orders was mirrored in their response to previous bail convictions. In all the cases in Braid where the fiscal noted previous contraventions of the Bail Act on the accused's record, bail was opposed. In 91% of such cases bail was opposed in Tweed and in 70% in Doon.

For most of those at Doon and Tweed who had bail convictions and for whom bail was agreed, this was because the offence itself was minor or because of ameliorating factors associated with the accused's record. For example, for an accused who had 3 contraventions of the Bail Act in the past year and was on bail, the fiscal agreed bail as the offence was a "minor" housebreaking and also because the accused was only 16. The fiscal described this as a "borderline case" between agreeing and opposing bail because the accused was on bail already and had broken into the home of someone whom he had known was disabled. Another accused at Doon had 4 Bail Act convictions in the past 3 years and an extensive record including 10 custodial sentences in the past 3 years. The fiscal agreed bail as the offence was trivial (theft) and the accused had not had analogous convictions for two and a half years.

For a further accused in Doon, bail was agreed for an accused charged with an assault on his wife. The fiscal decided to agree bail but to seek a special condition for the accused not to approach the complainer. Bail was agreed because the accused only had one Bail Act contravention and it had been more than 3 years previously.

In Tweed bail was agreed where the fiscal noted that an accused had Bail Act charges, but that his record was for non-analogous offences and there were only 2 Bail Act charges over a 10 year period. In this case the fiscal noted "if we let him out this time and then he misbehaves, then we would oppose it".

One fiscal in Tweed stated that they attached no weight to contraventions of the Bail Act unless the current offence was serious enough to oppose bail. Despite this statement, bail was opposed in 10 of 11 cases although in none was the fact that the accused had a Bail Act conviction the sole reason for opposition and in these cases the other factors were mainly connected to the accused's record.

In 95% of all the cases at Doon and 91% in Tweed where the fact that the accused had previous Bail Act convictions played a part in the fiscal's decision, the Bail Act charges were within the last 3 years. However in Braid for almost a third of accused in this group the Bail Act convictions dated from more than 3 years previously. In one instance in Braid the fiscal opposed bail on the grounds that the accused had a history of Bail Act convictions. All of the contraventions were more than 3 years previously but the fiscal stated that the length of time since the convictions was not important saying that "that would be a defence argument" . In another example the Bail Act charges dated from 3 and a half years ago. The fiscal said that their existence at all showed a tendency not to comply with bail. In a further example in Braid, for an accused with a history of breaching bail this was the sole reason for the fiscal opposing bail. This accused was not currently on bail and had no pending cases. Currently charged with breach of the peace and possession of an offensive weapon, he had six convictions of breach of bail, all of which occurred four years previously. Since that time his record showed that he had two convictions for assault on which he had been admonished and one conviction for misuse of drugs for which he had been fined £150.

ATTITUDE TO BAIL FOR CUSTODIES: FACILITATE JUSTICE - ADDRESS

The two main types of reason in this category were associated with the accused's address and the question of further enquiries. The concern about having a fixed address is a concern that accused can have papers served on them or that they should be able to be contacted if they should fail to appear for court. Bail cannot be granted to an accused unless they have an acceptable address; however, not having an acceptable address was interpreted differently in different areas.

In Doon addresses were generally accepted by the police and deputes did not insist that the accused be resident but would, unless there were special reasons, accept an address of citation. In Tweed checking of addresses was not regularly insisted upon by the depute and addresses of citation were acceptable. In Braid addresses had to be checked and deputes, although aware that an address of citation was technically sufficient, were more reluctant to accept this and more likely to insist on residence than the other areas. There were 14 accused at Doon, 23 at Tweed and 14 at Braid who, at this stage, were defined as having no acceptable fixed address. However, in 9 of those at Doon, 12 at Tweed and 3 at Braid the depute indicated that any opposition to bail was a "formality", and noted that any fixed address offered at court would be acceptable. "He's down as no fixed abode but that's hardly ever true. Usually they'll come up with an address at court" (depute at Tweed). In all of these cases the fiscal opposed bail (31% of all custodies where bail was opposed at Doon, 33% at Tweed and 14% at Braid).

REASONS FOR GIVING NO FIXED ADDRESS

In a third of this group at both Doon and Braid, and 65% at Tweed the reason for accused not having an address was unknown. For a further third of this group at both Doon and Braid, and around 20% at Tweed, accused were deemed as having no fixed address because the incident had occurred in their home and they were unable to return. Another third in Braid were defined as having no fixed address as they had provided addresses which did not check out when police made enquiries. In Doon one had been expelled from social work department accommodation, another had absconded from a social work centre and one had been evicted from a local authority house. One accused from each area lacked an address because they were just out of prison; one at Tweed refused to return to a children's home and one, also at Tweed, had refused to give any details.

In the cases of about two thirds of accused overall who had no fixed address, the fiscal opposed bail for additional reasons and the existence of an acceptable address would not have removed opposition.

IMPLICATIONS OF HAVING NO FIXED ADDRESS

The implications of not having an address were wider than influencing deputes' attitudes to bail and in Braid a depute considered that the fact that the co-accused was NFA was the reason for not proceeding with a charge of theft by opening lockfast place in the district court. The prosecutor noted that the district court would not remand accused or give prison sentences and therefore the sheriff court was more appropriate for this case. The prosecutor stated specifically that they would require any address offered to be residential rather than simply an address of citation, noting of one of the accused, "she's been living rough and that lifestyle lends itself to repeated offending".

Concerns about the provision of an acceptable address are concerns about being able to contact an accused and about the likelihood of that person turning up for court. However lacking an address was not the only reason for people being seen as likely to abscond from Tweed where bail was opposed for 6 NFA accused whose record indicated that they had previously failed to attend court. Bail was usually opposed for foreign nationals on the grounds that it would be more difficult to apprehend them if they failed to appear for court.

OPPOSING BAIL FOR CUSTODIES: FACILITATING JUSTICE - FURTHER ENQUIRIES

The need for further enquiries relates solely to the need to obtain additional information which will enable a case to be fully prepared. In some instances it is expected that additional charges may result from the enquiries if, for example the case involves dishonesties and recovered property can be linked to earlier thefts. Often it can mean that an identity parade is required or that further witnesses need to be interviewed. It is a reason for opposition to bail for which , at first court appearance of solemn cases, bail will always be refused. The impact of fiscal attitude to bail on defence agents was acknowledged by deputes who, if they needed to make further enquiries would often tell defence agents prior to court "I'll tell solicitors that I'm making further enquiries so that they won't ask for bail". (depute at Braid)

In Braid opposition to bail was regularly marked for this reason at this stage and some deputes described this as routine. Where this was the prime reason most accused were released at their next court appearance a week later. All accused, where further enquiries was a reason for opposition, except for one at Doon, were involved in solemn cases. The only summary case with this reason at Doon was primarily detained because of three outstanding bail orders. However, in none of the accused at Doon was further enquiries a primary reason for opposing bail: seriousness of record and nature of an offence were important factors. Both cases involved sexual offence charges (one of which was ultimately a high court case). In one, where incest was alleged, further charges were also expected, however the fiscal indicated that they would agree bail with a special condition if an address outwith the area were offered at court; and this was in fact the outcome of the first appearance. In the final case bail was opposed not only because of the need for further enquiries but because of the seriousness of the charge, the harm to the victim, (a child, who had needed to be taken into care); the continuing threats being made against the victim and their family; and the witnesses were considered by the fiscal to be problematic.

All those in Tweed where this reason was mentioned were solemn cases, and in half of these this was the only reason for bail being opposed. For example, in a case of attempted extortion where the charges involved sending packages of shotgun pellets to local business men and threatening violence to their families unless large sums of money were paid, further enquiries were needed about an unauthorised shotgun found at the accused's home, police having stated that they thought the accused might interfere with these enquiries. The fiscal did not expect to need a remand at second appearance as they would have completed the case by then.

In the other cases additional factors were involved, for example, in an attempted murder where the charge was that the accused had fire-bombed the family home while his wife and children were inside, the need for further enquiries was a secondary reason and a remand was sought primarily because of the danger to the family.

In two instances where the fiscal believed that accuseds' records indicated a course of criminal conduct, it was indicated that if bail was granted at first appearance then the prosecution would appeal but that they would not appeal if it were granted at a later stage as by then the necessary police enquiries would be complete(both were remanded).

Unlike in Doon and Tweed where most further enquiries were linked with dishonesty cases, in Braid serious/sexual assaults were more likely to have further enquiries mentioned and accounted for seventeen of the twenty-one accused where this was mentioned. Ten of these were accused of involvement in robbery or assault and robbery. Most of these needed identity parades and where this was the prime reason for bail being opposed it was often only opposed at first appearance.

Those accused who had serious and analogous records tended also to have bail opposed at full committal (eight were remanded at full committal). Three co-accused in a case of armed bank robbery, two of whose records were marked as "Risk: Violent Behaviour Likely to Escape Custody" were remanded at first appearance. Although two of these were remanded at the subsequent appearance, their co-accused who had no record, had admitted the charge and had given further information to the police, had bail agreed at full committal. A further four co-accused of armed robbery (value £12,000) had bail initially opposed primarily for further enquiry and because of the nature of the crime, although two were subsequently released on bail at second appearance.

Other types of serious/sexual assault involved rape, incest and attempted murder. In some instances the immediate circumstances were coupled with the need for further enquiries. This is illustrated in a case where the accused was charged with attempted rape of his daughters over a period of time. The accused had a non-analogous record with the last conviction fourteen years previously. The depute indicated that though they were not likely to oppose bail at full committal if the accused could offer an address in another area, even if an address were available that day they would oppose bail, "There's an element of outrage and a need to defuse matters. I can't put that into acceptable legal terminology. The legal reason is that I want further statements from the girls before deciding on the charge and to see the strength of the case".

CRIMINAL JUSTICE CULTURE : IMPLICATIONS OF FISCAL ATTITUDE TO BAIL

Record in general and bail history in particular were important in prosecution attitude to bail. Those for whom the fiscal agreed release on bail would not necessarily have been potential candidates for remand. Many accused were found for whom prosecutors sought release on bail conditions because their alleged offence was so minor that, had the fiscal not considered their record to be problematic, would either have been sent to the district court or the prosecution would have accepted them being ordained for the next appearance. Police responses to the accused were important in prosecution views of the need for bail conditions, with deputes at Doon seeking bail for police custody and undertaking cases and those at Tweed preferring not to have bail conditions attached to the release of those appearing from undertaking. In Braid, where police released most accused for summons, fiscals were more likely to disagree with this decision and to believe that accused should have been kept in custody. In both Doon and Braid deputes stated that they would have been prepared for more accused to be ordained rather than bailed by the court. (In both areas the court census showed that around 20% of accused are ordained as compared with 40% of accused at Tweed.)

Prosecutors tended to see bail as a means whereby any problem behaviour of accused could be linked to a breach of the court's trust and, to the extent that bail was not an effective constraint, would signal to the criminal justice system that the particular person could not be relied on not to breach that trust. Some argued that this meant that the 1980 Act was more effective than previous bail legislation since prior to this Act there was no record of people having breached bail. Accused paid money to gain release and this was simply forfeited if they failed to appear at court. There was no mechanism for recording the level of offending during release. Now, a breach of bail is a permanent indication on a criminal record that the accused is not reliable. As such, in the future it would be a contra-indicator for release. Depute views of the significance of bail history were a major factor in accounting for differences in depute responses to bail.

When marking cases, deputes not only consider how police have responded to a case, they take into account the likely court response and in particular they are instructed to consider the likelihood of a custodial sentence. Often, in addition, they consider the likelihood of the high court granting an appeal against the refusal of bail. The response of the court to offences is therefore important in their attitude to bail. This was displayed in individual cases by the attention which was given to previous court disposals recorded as part of the criminal history for individual accused and the assessment of likelihood of custodial sentence. Prosecutors at Doon explained that sometimes it may be in the public interest to prosecute a case even if the evidence, while sufficient, is not as strong as would be desirable. If it was felt that a case was likely to end up in acquittal then the prosecution would not consider opposing bail. Similarly if they did not think a custodial sentence likely then they would not oppose bail. Some deputes stated that an increased use of non-custodial sentences had increased the likelihood that they would agree bail and gave as an example the impact of community service orders which they believed to be significant since, by reducing the number of accused likely to end with custodial sentences, they had increased prosecution willingness to agree bail. Sheriffs at Doon made little use of custody and this was identified by deputes as a strong factor in how prosecutors approached bail.

This assessment of likely court outcome is an important way in which court practices influence decision-making prior to court. In Braid, where the court made greatest use of remand, deputes were more likely to oppose bail, and, as will be shown, were more likely to be criticised in court if they did not oppose bail. This pressure toward remand was absent in the other areas where the pressure for bail was such that in cases where police had not kept accused in custody the fiscal would not consider opposing bail. The implications of this pressure to remand or bail may have been that fiscals were more likely to agree/oppose bail, however it did not necessarily produce acquiescence. Whereas deputes in Braid were more likely to consider the court as being too willing to remand, prosecutors at Tweed were more likely to wish to see an increased use of remand and those at Doon to see a reduction in the use of bail and an increase in the use of ordaining.

CHAPTER 5

COURT BAIL DECISIONS

INTRODUCTION

When they were considering cases prior to court, procurator fiscal deputes often commented on likely court response. In this chapter we shall consider how the elements of cases and of police and prosecutor action impacted on court decisions and we shall illustrate the ways in which shrieval response to prosecutors could publicly indicate acceptance or questioning of prosecution response to cases.

Once the procurator fiscal depute has marked a case, a complaint (statement of charges) is typed and is then served on the accused by the police on behalf of the procurator fiscal. Accompanying the complaint will be a list of those previous convictions which the prosecution intends to present to the court (it excludes pending cases, disposals from children's hearings and may, if a record is very lengthy, exclude very old convictions). At that point, if they wish to be represented, the accused will see a defence agent to discuss the complaint. Typically defence agents may have ten or twenty minutes prior to court to see all their clients. This means that they are sometimes unable to verify information offered to them by clients. The defence agent will then attend the custody court and, if there is an opportunity, they may have a brief discussion with the court procurator fiscal depute in order to ascertain the prosecution attitude to bail, including whether the depute is seeking bail conditions at all. It was identified in chapters three and four that disagreements between police and prosecutors over release decisions were primarily explained by these agencies giving different prominence to different aspects of cases. Record tended to be given greater prominence by fiscals, whereas police tended to give more prominence to immediate risk to the community and the facilitation of justice. All accused in the sample had the opportunity to be legally represented under the duty solicitor scheme and in each area 99% had legal representation[1,2].

MAIN FINDINGS

Analysis of courtroom encounters showed the way in which pressure to remand or to release on bail was manifest. In Doon and Tweed sheriffs rarely commented on fiscal

---

1 A small number in each area chose not to be legally represented - in two cases (one at Doon and one at Tweed) accused initially entered a guilty plea and refused representation. When told by the sheriff that they should reconsider obtaining legal advice, they named solicitors who were at that time working in another court. Pleas of not guilty were recorded for these accused and they were admitted to bail. In Braid an accused with a large number of previous custodial sentences told the court that he did not want a solicitor.

2 **Court Bail Decisions: Some Methodological Limits**
All of the summary cases were observed at their first appearance and researchers were present at some of the later appearances. It was not possible to observe all appearances and it was found that later diets revealed little extra information. Researchers were not able to observe initial proceedings in solemn cases. Information about bail applications in solemn cases is therefore taken primarily from the details recorded on the case papers. Wherever possible the researchers observed the second court appearances for those in summary cases who were initially remanded. In addition bail reviews were observed whenever feasible. The discussion in this chapter focuses on police custodies, information about undertaking cases is provided in annex 5.

attitude to bail and the only occasion on which it occurred at Doon, a fiscal who was working temporarily in the court was criticised for opposing bail. In Braid deputes were regularly reproached in court for not opposing bail. Offenders at Braid were more likely to be remanded during a deferred sentence than were offenders in other areas. Most accused in all areas applied for bail. However, accused at Braid who did not apply for bail were more likely to be remanded than were such accused in the other areas. A not guilty plea makes it possible for the fiscal to present the grounds of opposition to bail to the court. For those accused pleading not guilty the focus of court discussion was usually the prosecution's interpretation of their criminal record. Only where the fiscal interpretation of record was successfully challenged or where the court accepted the defence's interpretation of additional social information presented in court, were accused granted bail. Social information was generally marginal to courtroom decisions. A plea of guilty precludes the prosecutor from agreeing or opposing bail in court. For those who were pleading guilty, there was no discussion of their criminal record in court and this had usually been the reason for fiscal opposition to bail having been marked.

Court responses to bail charges were tempered by their response to the substantive charges. Whereas courts did not always remand those with bail charges, in no area did release on bail preclude the court using custodial sentences. The implications of different court use of bail and remand were identified. Those accused in Braid who were ultimately not convicted, were more likely to have spent time on remand than such accused in other areas. Further when accused in similar cases from the different areas were compared, those in Doon and Tweed were more likely to have been repeatedly released and to have received non-custodial sentences than accused in Braid who were more quickly brought into custody.

DESCRIPTION OF THE INITIAL COURT PROCESS

Until an accused's case is called at court, the individual decisions taken are not subject to discussion in public. For accused in summary cases the first court appearance and, for those in solemn cases, the second court appearance is the forum in which their liberation or their remand in custody are first publicly discussed. The prosecution decides which cases are to be called in court and a list of these will already have been provided for the clerk of court who will be advised by the fiscal depute in court of any alteration to the content of the list or the order in which the cases are to be called. When the clerk of court has called a case and the accused have appeared, they are asked to confirm their identity. The defence agent will then indicate that they are appearing on behalf of the accused and will state the plea to each charge. In solemn cases it is usual for there to be no plea and no further comment by the suspect on the charges for which they are appearing, the standard response at this stage is 'no plea and no declaration' at this first appearance, which is in private.

If there are any not guilty pleas the prosecution will say whether or not they are accepted. Pleas which are not accepted will go to trial and an appropriate date for this will be set before the end of this appearance. Sometimes, when indicating the prosecution response to a plea, the court depute will also state their response to bail should an application be made. At this point an application for bail can be made to the court by the defence who may, if the prosecution have indicated that they have no objection to bail, request that their client be ordained (i.e. simply ordered to appear at court on the next appointed date). The prosecution may have no objection or may state that they wish bail conditions to be attached to the release of that accused. If the prosecution objects to bail they state the grounds of their objection; the defence will then present their argument for bail, sometimes stating special conditions which their client would accept in order to secure release.

If the accused pleads guilty, they are no longer the prisoner of the fiscal, but become the prisoner of the court. As such, if sentence is not passed immediately but is being deferred, a bail application may be made by the defence and the fiscal's attitude to bail is no longer relevant, although occasionally the sheriff may seek information from the fiscal to assist the court with its decision.

Courtroom discussions of bail tend to be very brief, usually taking no more than two or three minutes. The volume of cases and the short time available for processing them together promote the routinisation of practice and help to foster the development of shared assumptions necessary for practitioners to get through court business. It is on the basis of these shared assumptions that norms are established through which practitioners work to interpret the law and they serve to reduce the number of cases over which the appropriate course of action is disputed. It should be stressed that the existence of shared assumptions did not mean that prosecutors always agreed with court outcomes, or that sheriffs necessarily refused bail when it was opposed. Nor did it mean an absence of defence or prosecution argument on bail applications. Rather it meant that most courtroom exchanges focused on the details of individual cases rather than on how the cases should be approached or on the position on bail adopted by prosecutors or defence agents.

These norms are not only a product of past criminal justice decisions, but also of present practice. For the most part practitioners' awareness of norms tends to take the form of the anticipation of likely court responses to cases and a recognition that the way things are done in one court differ from the way in which they are done in another. This difference is often understood as being about the preferences and idiosyncrasies of particular sheriffs, however, we have argued that the understandings and practices of others within the criminal justice system make an important contribution to this. Nevertheless, given their position within the criminal justice system, and their role in granting or refusing bail, sheriffs are of particular importance.

SHRIEVAL VIEWS: USEFULNESS OF BAIL

In all areas most sheriffs argued that bail was both valuable and effective, placing more constraint on accused to remain beyond further suspicion that they are involved in offending and to ensure their appearance at court. In this, their views paralleled those of most prosecutors.

> "It means that the accused is subject to a degree of control, it ensures their future presence and it is a deterrent to further offending; it affords a degree of protection to members of the public. If an accused fails to appear and they are subject to a bail order then that goes on record therefore on another occasion this gives a clue as to their reliability..." (sheriff at Braid)

Sheriffs in all areas indicated that the fact that accused are generally asked to read bail conditions or have them read to them in court is taken as further reinforcement of the court's requirements and it is believed that this makes accused more likely to take them seriously. This is felt to be particularly important if the police have detained accused in custody or released them on undertaking rather than released them for summons.

> "If they're kept in custody there must be a reason. But if they're not on bail and they don't turn up there is little sanction...by bailing accused have sanction. If you ordain them and they've got the story right - its very difficult to exercise court powers if the accused has got the date muddled up.."(sheriff at Doon)

Some sheriffs argued that, apart from at the stage of deferring sentence, they were only able to exercise their discretion in granting bail if the prosecution opposed bail since unless this happened bail must be granted. While for some this was an acceptable high court ruling, others felt that this was more problematic.

> "In summary crimes there are few reasons for not giving bail.....you appreciate that the high court decision has reduced our discretion, if the procurator fiscal does not oppose bail then I cannot keep him....." (sheriff at Braid)

Nevertheless, the assumptions upon which courtroom practices operated differed between the areas and this is illustrated by considering the implications of not making bail applications in each area.

FIRST COURT APPEARANCE: BAIL APPLICATIONS IN SUMMARY CASES

A bail application may not be made for a number of reasons: for example, if an accused is not eligible for release on bail because they are in custody on other matters; or because they could not provide an address. Occasionally an accused may instruct their defence agent not to make a bail application. All these situations were observed during the course of the study. In Doon and Braid an application for bail was almost routinely made (for respectively 90% and 92% of accused) and there were more accused in Tweed where there was no formal bail application (79% of accused there applied for bail)[3].

The outcomes for those in the sample who failed to make an application for bail (table 5.1) mirrored those of the census, showing that in the courts in Doon and Tweed no explicit application was more likely to result in release on bail or being ordained whereas in Braid such accused were more likely to end up being remanded.

Table 5.1 Summary Cases From Police Custody:Outcome of Court For Accused Who Did Not Apply For Bail

	Doon	*Tweed*	*Braid*
Ordain to appear	*57%*	*41%*	*18%*
Bail	*29%*	*41%*	*0*
Remand	*14%*	*18%*	*82%*
Total	*100%*	*100%*	*100%*
N =	7	22	11

Discussion in court was generally very brief and the reason for no application was not always clear[4]. Some accused were already in custody on other matters and the practice at Tweed and Doon was for these accused to be ordained, whereas in Braid the practice was for them to be remanded. In some instances the defence had requested that the accused be ordained to appear (three at Doon, five at Tweed and two at Braid). In one instance at Doon there was no application for bail made as the accused was initially

3 Braid one case information was not available as court hearing could not be observed and no information was recorded on the court sheet. These figures exclude cases which reached final disposal at first appearance or where a warrant was issued. Doon n=114; Tweed=106; Braid=103
In 12% (3) of cases appearing from undertaking in Doon and 72% (8) in Tweed no bail application was made. All these accused were ordained to appear. In 7% (one) in Braid no bail application was made. The accused was remanded in custody.

4 This was the case for one in Doon - who was ordained, thirteen in Tweed - four of whom were ordained and nine granted bail and one in Braid who was remanded.

not represented and then asked for a solicitor who was working in another court. He was admitted to bail. In three accused at Tweed there was no explicit application as the sheriff initiated the discussion without the defence making a formal request for bail. One accused at Tweed who appeared from undertaking was ordained as the sheriff believed that they were unable to understand the terms of a bail order.

CRIMINAL JUSTICE CULTURE: COURT RESPONSES TO THOSE NOT MAKING A BAIL APPLICATION

It was argued earlier that a culture sets the assumptions in terms of which formal procedures are operated. Localised cultures and practices can be illustrated by data collected from court room observation. At Doon there was a clear assumption that release would be the norm and in only one case where there was no application for bail was the accused remanded. In this instance the accused stated that he did not wish to instruct his solicitor to apply for bail and there was evident disbelief at this in court from the sheriff and the defence agent who both tried to persuade him to make an application for bail. This accused was sixteen, charged with theft by opening a lockfast place and breach of two bail orders (both for dishonesty, from the same court in the previous month)[5]. He was kept in custody by the police because he was a "known active housebreaker" who had admitted more offences when interviewed. The fiscal did not intend to oppose bail because he had little record, no breaches of bail and the offence was thought trivial. In court this accused pled guilty and the defence stated that they had been instructed not to apply for bail. The sheriff asked the agent to confirm this with the accused, they did so and then the agent asked the sheriff to seek further confirmation. Before remanding the accused the sheriff asked him directly to confirm that he did not wish bail and the accused agreed.[6]

In Tweed an assumption that release was the norm was also illustrated by court response and encouragement to defence agents that they should not prevent the release of a client by an ill-timed bail application. In three of the four accused at Tweed where no application was made and accused were remanded, the accused lacked a suitable address. All were granted bail after an address was found. In one instance where an accused was unable to provide an address and there were no available hostel places, the sheriff advised the defence solicitor not to make a bail application stating that "if you do not apply for bail and I remand, you can ask for a review any time you can come up with an address. If you make an application and I refuse it, then you can not make another for 5 days". Several days later a bail review was held and the accused was bailed to an address obtained by the court social worker.

In contrast at Braid when accused were not making a bail application there was little discussion of this in court.

In all of the solemn cases at Tweed and Braid where a bail application was not made, the accused were remanded in custody. In Braid this represented 76% of all accused in solemn cases (including those appearing from undertaking). In all the cases at Braid the fiscal opposed bail at marking. In 26 of these cases a bail application was made at

5 The theft was from commercial premises, value of theft £11-£50, (fully recovered) he had a temporary address in a local hostel. His record showed one non-analogous previous conviction for which he had been admonished, he had three analogous pending cases.

6 The social enquiry report subsequently revealed that this accused had spent most of his life in care. He was unwelcome at home; he had previously had a job which he had lost during the period when he had no address; he had been unsuccessful in claiming benefit because he had difficulty completing the necessary forms (though he had completed three applications for benefit they had on each occasion been returned to him). He spent 31 days on remand, sentence was deferred for 6 months and he was eventually admonished.

FIRST COURT APPEARANCE: BAIL APPLICATIONS IN SOLEMN CASES

Table 5.2 Accused in Solemn Cases From Police Custody: Whether an Application for Bail was Made*

	Doon	*Tweed*	*Braid*
Bail application	*100%*	*96%*	*21%*
No application	*0*	*4%*	*79%*
Total	*100%*	*100%*	*100%*
N=	14	28	33

*In 2 accused in Doon, 2 in Tweed and 2 in Braid it was not known whether an application for bail was made. This was because the information was not recorded on the case papers. Three accused in Braid appeared from undertaking. In all of these no bail application was made.

the second appearance (full committal). Table 5.3 shows that there were differences between the courts in the proportion of accused with solemn charges who were kept in custody after full committal. In Doon all were released whereas in Tweed and Braid approximately a third were remanded in custody. For solemn cases the increased likelihood of being remanded at Braid was associated with the tendency there to seek a remand for the initial seven days rather than for there to be a much higher proportion of custody trials as the proportion of accused remanded after full committal is similar in Braid to that in Tweed .

Table 5.3 Court Action for Accused Appearing from Police Custody in Solemn Cases

	Doon	*Tweed*	*Braid**
Bail at first diet	56%	50%	14%
Bail at full committal (2 diet)	44%	20%	57%
Remand at full committal (2 diet)	0	30%	29%
Total	100%	100%	100%
N=	16	30	35

*In Braid 3 additional solemn cases appeared from undertaking. These were all remanded in custody after full committal (second diet).

FIRST COURT APPEARANCE: IMPACT ON PLEA OF FISCAL ATTITUDE TO BAIL

The importance of plea in understanding bail is that plea dictates who has the authority to speak about bail in court as well as what can be said. Any response other than a plea of guilty to the charges on a complaint, enables the fiscal to continue their authority over a case and to state their view as to whether or not that accused can be released prior to trial. At the first court the customary reply to charges in solemn cases is 'no plea and no declaration', but for summary cases it is usual for a plea of guilt or innocence to be entered. Procurator fiscal deputes commonly believed that the knowledge that the prosecution was going to oppose bail could increase the likelihood of a guilty plea being offered in court by the defence and occasionally some deputes would refer to this in individual cases.

A guilty plea forecloses on prosecution opposition, precluding the fiscal from laying before the court the grounds of opposition, removing the authority of the fiscal over what subsequently happens with a case and transforming the discussion about bail into a dialogue between the defence and the court. A guilty plea, of course, removes any presumption of innocence, to the extent that that is relevant. Although many sheriffs and prosecutors argued that the presumption of innocence was important, others maintained that it was irrelevant to the question of bail. Those who held this view argued that the presumption of innocence related solely to questions of proof which means -

"....when a person faces trial....it is a presumption that he is innocent and that...will remain until that presumption has been displaced by proof beyond reasonable doubt to the contrary....that so called presumption of innocence has got no place until the trial starts so it is entirely irrelevant". (high court judge)

A guilty plea opens up the possibility of a final disposal being given at that appearance and, in removing any concern about the need to protect witnesses or secure evidence from interference, it strengthens the significance of likely sentence if sentence is to be deferred and a bail application is made, since considerations about matters such as interfering with the administration of justice are no longer relevant.

Defence agents often had a brief discussion about bail with the fiscal depute prior to the start of court so that they were usually aware of the fiscal attitude to bail prior to entering a plea on behalf of a client. It is possible therefore that fiscal attitude to bail could affect plea and some deputes believe this to be the case. Table 5.4 shows the attitude of the prosecution to bail at marking for those who entered a guilty plea at their first court appearance.

Table 5.4 Summary Cases from Police Custody: Percentage of Accused Pleading Guity by Marking Depute's Attitude to Bail*

	Doon	*Tweed*	*Braid*
Agree	13%(8)	39%(35)	6%(3)
Oppose	42%(15)	53%(25)	37%(24)
Total	*24%*(23)	*44%*(60)	*23%*(27)

*Excludes one at Tweed where the fiscal attitude to bail was unclear. Information for accused appearing from undertaking is included in annex 5

Accused at Tweed were much more likely to plead guilty than accused in either of the other areas. With the exception of those at Tweed whose bail was being opposed, most accused pled not guilty at their first court appearance. In Doon accused for whom the fiscal was going to oppose bail, were three times as likely to plead guilty and in Braid six times as likely to plead guilty as those for whom bail was to be agreed.

There was limited evidence during observation to suggest that such manipulation of pleas operated in practice. The procurator fiscal has the discretion to accept pleas entered by the defence and there were occasions where it was stated to the researcher by a depute that they had not accepted a plea in order to give themselves the opportunity to oppose bail. In one instance the depute had opposed bail at marking on the grounds that one accused had a bad record of analogous offences and for the co-accused because they had numerous pending charges, were subject to a current bail order and had been hostile towards the police at the time of their arrest[7]. In court the depute accepted pleas of guilty from each accused on all charges but one and opposed bail arguing that each of the accused was repeatedly offending. Both accused were remanded (later one appealed to the high court but the appeal was refused).

However any claims about the relationship between fiscal attitude to bail and plea in a large number of cases needs to be carefully qualified. While it is likely that there is a relationship, it is likely that this is usually mediated by other factors, not least the strength of the prosecution case, the innocence of the accused, the court's propensity to defer sentence and its propensity to remand.

FIRST COURT APPEARANCE: BAIL APPLICATIONS AFTER NOT GUILTY PLEAS

The greater likelihood of fiscal opposition to bail at Braid was associated with an increased chance that the court there would refuse bail once it had been opposed. In around half of the cases in Doon and Tweed where the fiscal opposed bail the accused were remanded in custody by the court whereas 62% of the cases in which the fiscal opposed bail in Braid were subsequently remanded.

Figure 5.3 Accused in SUmmary Cases Appearing from Police Custody: Not Guilty Plea: Procurator Fiscal Attitude to Bail by Outcome of First Court (%ages)

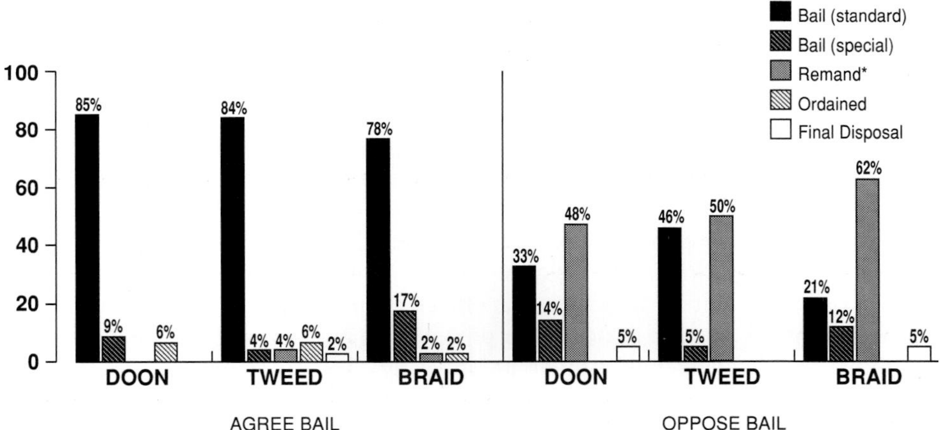

AGREE Doon n=55; Tweed n=55; Braid n=46; OPPOSE Doon n=21; Tweed n=23; Braid n=42

Agree Doon n=55; Tweed n=55; Braid n=46; Oppose Doon n=21; Tweed n=23; Braid n=42

Tweed includes 2 accused where the fiscal agreed to them being ordained. These have been categorised as 'agree'. Tweed excludes one case where fiscal attitude to bail unclear; Braid excludes one accused where the fiscal expected a guilty plea and one case where the accused failed to appear at court and a warrant was issued. Figures for undertakings are given in annex 5.

* The fiscal attitude to bail was recorded at marking. In 2 cases in Tweed where the fiscal agreed bail, the accused was unable to apply for bail as NFA, in one case in Braid where the fiscal agreed bail, the accused was in custody on another matter.

---

7 Police had been concerned that these accused might abscond as the elder had a conviction for prison breaking, had been released from a young offender's institution the previous week and had been hostile to police on arrest. The hostility was shown in court by a lack of co-operation and the sheriff commented, "You've been in court often enough to know how to behave." After being remanded this accused was led away swearing and banging on the dock.

BAIL APPLICATIONS AFTER NOT GUILTY PLEAS - ACCUSED UNDER 21

Court responses to those under 21 are particularly important since this group has less experience of the criminal justice system than older offenders, they are also more likely to come into contact with the system and once this has happened to have further contact within a short period. As such, they are more likely to be alleged to be in breach of bail. This is particularly the case for those who have been involved in dishonesties. A comparison was made of accused aged under 21 and involved in housebreaking cases in order to examine the circumstances under which the court would agree bail for those in this group for whom it was opposed. All were either on bail, had previous bail convictions or both. Bail history was rarely an explanation of court outcome for this group. Rather, it was either referred to in underlining the importance of other factors or its significance was overshadowed by other factors in an accused's circumstances.

When the fiscal was opposing bail on the basis of record the provision of social information rarely impacted sufficiently on the court for bail to be granted. Social information provided by the defence resulted in the release of two of the three accused in this category being bailed at Doon. For three from Doon who were remanded and all at Tweed who were remanded, either no additional information was offered or that which was offered was not sufficient to sway the court in favour of bail. In Braid social information influenced the court to release one accused on condition that he lodged money, and in the other case where bail was agreed the grounds of opposition were ruled as inadmissible.

IMPACT OF SOCIAL INFORMATION - SUCCESSFUL BAIL APPLICATIONS

Two in this group at Doon and two at Braid were allowed bail by the court because of additional information provided by the defence about changes in their personal circumstances. Each at Doon was already on one bail order and each had a number of bail convictions in the previous three years (between three and eight), all had analogous pending cases. In one instance bail was primarily opposed because the accused lacked an address, an address was offered at court, bail was granted and the case was eventually marked as no further proceedings. For another at Doon, whose bail record was described by the sheriff as "appalling" and for whom bail was nevertheless allowed, the defence argued that the accused had recently been out of trouble, that part of the explanation was that his four month old daughter had recently been in hospital with pneumonia and gastro-enteritis and that he was therefore required at home. The sheriff stated that "normally you're not entitled to bail with this record" but allowed bail because of the family circumstances. (This offender was eventually given six months probation).

An accused at Braid for whom bail had been opposed had bail granted on condition that he lodge £50 with the clerk of court. He had a record of convictions in England but not in Scotland. Police had kept him because they thought he was likely to abscond and because he was on bail on a petition matter (assault and robbery). He had no bail convictions. The fiscal opposed bail because of the recent petition bail. The defence stated that this accused was a student at a local college who would be sitting highers in two months time. The sheriff granted bail if he lodged £50 with the court, "if he's trying to study then I don't want to stand in the way of that".

Defence agents, if they judged that a bail application was unlikely to be successful, would occasionally not make an application for bail at the first appearance, but seek a review of bail when they felt an application would have a greater chance of success. For example, in one instance at Tweed an accused with two bail orders for analogous, though petition matters, and who had no convictions for breaching bail would have had bail opposed by the fiscal on the grounds of him having a bad record for his age (he had ten pending cases) and because he was officially recorded as having no address[8]. At court the defence did not apply for bail and this foreclosed on any discussion of record. In interview the defence agent explained to the researcher that their client had an address but that there had been no application for bail as they thought that the sheriff would not grant it. Under these circumstances they would not have been able to reapply for five days and even then there would be no point unless circumstances had changed as a different sheriff would only "interfere" with a previous sheriff's decision if there had been a material change in the accused's circumstances. The agent said that they would have applied if it had been a different sheriff as they believed that some would have granted the application. They planned to ask for the case to be called again in a few days either to lodge a change of plea or to seek a bail review. Nine days later the accused pled guilty. The dialogue at this appearance was brief, with the sheriff simply noting that this offender had been in custody for nine days and indicated that he was considering deferring sentence for reports. The agent indicated that the offender had a fixed address, bail was granted and the sheriff told the offender, "If you get into trouble between now and then it will be much worse."[9]

IMPACT OF SOCIAL INFORMATION: UNSUCCESSFUL BAIL APPLICATIONS

In Tweed although defence agents all offered social information about the accused (need for treatment for drug misuse, forthcoming job interview, ailing mother requiring care) none of it was acceptable to the court as a reason for granting bail. In these instances bail was being opposed on the basis of record. For example, in one instance the fiscal opposed bail because of the length and seriousness of an accused's record[10]. In court, passing the record of previous convictions to the sheriff, the fiscal opposed bail stating that in addition to its length it included four contraventions of bail, a conviction for failing to turn up for court, that the accused had five convictions already that year alone and that he was on deferred sentence for similar matters. The defence agent responded,

> " I am conscious of my client's previous convictions and contraventions of bail; but the section 338 matter (i.e. the failure to appear at court) was dealt with by way of discharge. He has a permanent address and the contraventions of bail are now quite old and date from a period when he lived a nomadic lifestyle. Though he is only 18 my client has a severe drug habit and attends counselling three days a week. He is on daily methadone maintenance from his GP. If he is remanded then

8 This sixteen year old male had broken into commercial premises and escaped from police before reaching the police office. Police re-arrested him one week later and detained him because of his initial escape, he had since made a further attempt to escape. Though police described him as having "no real fixed abode" they were sceptical about this as they had tried to trace him at his previous known address though those staying there maintained they hadn't seen him. Police expected an address to be offered in court.

9 At his next appearance this offender was ordained as he was in custody on other matters for which he had failed to appear at court and as a result of which he had been remanded. Eventually he was sentenced to 30 days detention on each of the housebreaking and bail charges.

10 This accused faced housebreaking charges and police asked the fiscal to seek a remand because several thousand pounds worth of property had been stolen and the co-accused in this case was still at large. Though the fiscal marked bail to be opposed they indicated that they would not appeal if the sheriff did not remand. "The practice of the high court in summary matters is to follow the decision of the sheriff - you rarely succeed in these appeals - only if the first decision is ludicrous....If there's any room for doubt then the high court would back the sheriff...."

> the methadone will be stopped as the local prison doesn't allow this type of treatment for inmates. This matter will proceed to trial and there may be a complaint to the Chief Constable about police behaviour and if my client is on remand there will be difficulty in this being lodged within the necessary 40 days."

However, the sheriff refused bail,

> "There's no getting away from this appalling record - there is no doubt that when he gets bail he doesn't pay attention to it."[11]

Where bail was being opposed both because of record and because of other reasons, such as the lack of an address, even if the defence were able to meet the non-record objections by, perhaps offering an address, this would not usually be sufficient to sway the court in favour of bail. For example, this was the situation for an accused in Braid alleged to have been found in circumstances where he was likely to commit crime. Described by police as NFA and as regularly coming to their attention, he had convictions within the previous three years, including six bail convictions, but no analogous convictions within the previous year. His most serious sentence had been a fine. The fiscal opposed bail "most strongly" because of there being no address and because of the bail convictions. An address was offered by the defence, the fiscal repeated opposition on the basis of the number of previous bail convictions and the sheriff refused bail[12].

IMPACT OF RECORD - SUCCESSFUL BAIL APPLICATIONS

In general, for the fiscal's opposition to bail to be successfully challenged, it was necessary for the court to be convinced that the prosecution interpretation of criminal record was inappropriate. For example, there was a dispute over the significance of the record of an accused in Doon who had six bail convictions and was currently on bail. Bail was opposed because of this bail history. However, the defence agent argued that the bail order was for a matter alleged to have occurred over a year previously and that this could not therefore be considered as recent. Bail was allowed and eventually this accused's not guilty plea was accepted.

An accused in this group who was released on bail at Braid and who had an outstanding bail order, was released on bail by the court because the grounds on which the fiscal opposed bail were inadmissible. Though this accused had no convictions he had analogous pending cases. Kept by the police because of the outstanding matters and the bail order, bail was opposed by the fiscal for the same reasons. The defence disputed the number of pending cases. However, the sheriff rejected the pending cases stating that those which had not come to court should be disregarded and bail was granted.[13]

IMPACT OF RECORD - UNSUCCESSFUL BAIL APPLICATIONS

For those where bail was refused in all areas the discussion in court revolved around their record and in Doon and Braid no new information came to light. Those at Doon were all currently on bail (three, two and one current bail order). In all cases the fiscal opposed bail because of their records and they were on recent bail. In one instance the

---

11 After 33 days on remand the offender pled guilty and was bailed for reports; he was ultimately sentenced to 120 hours community service.

12 This accused was ultimately found to have no case to answer.

13 Ultimately given one month prison on a housebreaking charge and two months (consecutive) for breach of bail.

depute thought a custodial sentence was likely. This involved charges of housebreaking[14] and the fiscal opposed bail stating,

> "he has a record of breaches of bail and analogous convictions. His most recent deferred sentence and probation order were made two days ago."

The defence argued that,

> "For this charge he has an alibi defence. The other charges (which dated from earlier but had been added into this complaint) are previous to the bail order and the probation order and so my client is not in breach of them....The probation order was made in the knowledge that there were other charges and therefore bail is being sought to allow him to comply with the probation order and to give him the opportunity to deal with his persisting offending and alcohol problem. This cannot be done if he is remanded."

In remanding this and one other accused, the sheriff stated that he was giving priority to the protection of the public.[15]

In one instance in Braid the fiscal argued that the record showed a course of criminal conduct and opposed bail. The defence argued that despite a bad record, most of it had occurred two years previously. The sheriff remanded the accused mentioning the recent bail order which had been granted from that court. The accused was eventually given 3 months detention and 30 days concurrent for the bail act charge.

In those cases where bail was granted either new information had been given to the court or the interpretation of the accused's record which had been given by the fiscal, was rejected by the court. However, granting bail did not necessarily mean that a custodial sentence would not be given at the final disposal of the case if this was thought appropriate by the court.

CRIMINAL JUSTICE CULTURE: COURT DISCUSSION OF BAIL APPLICATIONS

Record was usually the focus of courtroom discussions of bail and usually fiscal opposition to bail consisted of the prosecution interpretation of an accused's record being presented verbally to the court. Where bail is being opposed by the fiscal, the court will generally only grant bail if the prosecution interpretation of record is rejected by the sheriff (for example, because the defence's interpretation has been accepted) or, less usually, if it is overshadowed by social information provided by the defence. There is pressure from the court for prosecutors to conform to shrieval definitions of appropriate use of bail and remand and this was most clearly evident at Braid. In Doon and Tweed, while deputes did not always agree with court outcomes and sheriffs did not necessarily refuse bail when it was opposed, disagreement was rarely expressed in court and courtroom exchanges focused on individual cases rather than on the position adopted by prosecutors. The reason for this is that usually most participants in court operate within the same localised criminal justice culture and therefore most court interaction occurs within a shared understanding of appropriate

---

14 Police detained this accused because of his record, describing him as a 'habitual housebreaker' who was usually drunk when he offended. The fiscal marked bail to be opposed as he was in breach of two bail orders and had a record of six bail convictions and of analogous offences. It was anticipated that this case might lead to a custodial sentence.

15 One accused had their case recalled later the same day, changed their plea and were given 90 days detention each on a housebreaking and a bail charge. Of the other two accused, one was ultimately given 150 hours community service and the other had their plea of not guilty accepted.

behavioural ground rules. It is only necessary for these ground rules to be referred to, to the extent that any understanding is not shared by all participants, for example, because they normally work elsewhere or because there is conflict over the ground rules. This occurred, for example, in Doon when a depute who normally worked elsewhere violated local norms by opposing bail in a case where the sheriff indicated that there should have been no question of a remand. The sheriff, on granting bail turned to the fiscal and said that it would be "draconian" to remand in a case which would not receive a custodial sentence.

In Braid there was little shared understanding of the relative role of the fiscal and the sheriff in relation to bail and the interaction which occurred around this area of conflict threw localised norms into relief. In contrast with the incidents in other areas which took the form of sheriffs questioning the appropriateness of opposition to bail, defence agents being questioned about their failure to make a bail application, or being advised about the timing of an application, in Braid they were always about the prosecution's failure to oppose bail and therefore the court's inability to remand an accused. Deputes in Braid would often be reproached in court for not opposing bail. Sheriff (sarcastically and incredulously):

> "Bail is not opposed, Mr Procurator Fiscal. Well, well - there's something - disqualified driving and drunk driving and bail is not opposed.."

The reason for this type of reproach was stated during a bail review when the sheriff interrupted the defence agent who was starting to make an application for bail.

> Sheriff: "What is the Crown's position?"

The fiscal started to respond and was interrupted by the sheriff,

> "I don't want to know your thought processes I just want to know what your attitude is. The High Court has made it clear that if the Crown does not oppose bail then bail must be granted. I just want everyone to know that its not me that's granting bail but it's the Crown that's granting bail. So that if he goes out and commits further offences it's not my fault....Bail will be granted solely on the grounds that it is not opposed."

In Braid this last statement, that bail was being granted because it was not being opposed, was regularly made to express shrieval disapproval when the fiscal did not oppose bail for those who the court would have preferred to remand. Such comments were not restricted to particular cases and would sometimes be made between cases. For example, as one accused left the dock and another was brought in, the sheriff addressed the depute directly,

> "I thought that the public interest was a consideration in deciding on bail."

This type of courtroom incident was referred to directly in interview,

> "I really do resent in some cases having to grant bail on the directions of the high court because the Crown does not oppose it in a case where I think it should be refused....I have adopted a formula in a case such as that, of saying that bail is granted solely on the ground that the prosecutor does not object and I insist that that appears in the bail interlocutor, because the newspapers, who are the people who are always bleating about this that and the other, don't consider the niceties of things and always blame the court,...the position I don't like...is being made to look as though I am making decisions when I am not...." (sheriff at Braid)

In the context of this pressure by the court for remand, it is unsurprising that a higher proportion of those accused for whom the fiscal opposed bail were remanded in that area. Sheriffs in the other study areas expressed a reluctance to remand people pre-trial, especially if they were young, and argued that in summary cases there should rarely be any question of a pre-trial remand,

> "..I remain to be convinced that the public will be any better protected by such containment for a limited period before conviction rather than after it....." (sheriff at Tweed)

> "..If its a young person, by that I mean someone under 25, I'd be very, very reluctant. If it is someone with a bit of a criminal record brought to my attention by the procurator fiscal I might have to think about it... I prefer on summary criminal matters to allow them bail. Especially young people..." (sheriff at Tweed)

Though in general comments sheriffs at Braid were likely to share this view ("In summary crimes there are few reasons for not giving bail....." (sheriff at Braid)); prior to trial they thought that remand was useful for some younger accused,

> "...there are lots of problems caused by young people. If they are left out then they will simply commit more offences... Regular housebreakers are a worry to the public and they should be remanded." (sheriff at Braid)

FIRST COURT APPEARANCE: BAIL APPLICATIONS AFTER GUILTY PLEAS

A small number of accused in summary cases pled guilty at their first court appearance. For these accused any discussion would take the form of a dialogue between the defence agent and the sheriff.

Table 5.5 Accused in Summary Cases Appearing from Police Custody: Guilty Pleas - Outcome of First Court

	Doon	*Tweed*	*Braid*
Bail (standard)	62%	59%	29%
Bail (special)	8%	3%	0
Remand	15%	10%	65%
Ordained	15%	28%	6%
Total	100%	100%	100%
N =	13	29	17

Doon excludes 10 cases final disposal, Tweed excludes 31 final disposal; Braid excludes 11 cases final disposal. The majority of accused in Doon and Tweed appearing from undertaking reached final disposal - 86%(6) in Doon, 78%(7) in Tweed. In Braid 33% (1) final disposal, 33%(1) ordain and 33%(1) remand.

The likelihood of a custodial sentence is considered not only by the fiscal when marking, but by the sheriff when considering bail. A guilty plea at Braid was four times as likely to result in remand as a similar plea in Doon and six times as likely as at Tweed to result in remand. While the numbers here may be small, these results are consistent with the findings of the census.

FIRST COURT APPEARANCE: BAIL APPLICATIONS AFTER GUILTY PLEAS - ACCUSED UNDER 21

In order to compare the circumstances under which the court would agree bail or would remand those for whom bail would have been opposed by prosecutors, a comparison was made of accused aged under 21 and involved in housebreaking cases.

For all those for whom bail was granted after a guilty plea there was no discussion of record in court and this had been the main ground for which the fiscal would have opposed bail. In these cases there was no opportunity for the pattern of behaviour which was provoking police and prosecution response to be displayed to the court. Although the sheriff does see an offender's record, they do not hear the prosecution interpretation of the record, which is normally presented verbally when a not guilty plea has been entered by an accused and the fiscal is opposing bail. In the example of one case at Doon, fiscal attitude was linked to awareness of forthcoming charges and as such would not have been admissible in court. In an example at Tweed there was one offender for whom bail would have been opposed had he not pled guilty and he was also given bail by the court. This offender was on two current bail orders for analogous offences, one of which was five months old, the other more recent, he was also on deferred sentence. He had seven convictions for breaching bail in the previous three years. Detained in custody by police because of his two bail orders and described as a "prolific housebreaker", the fiscal would have opposed bail for this reason and because his record was considered "major" - "If we don't block him he would just commit more crime". Sentence was deferred for a social enquiry report and bail was granted with little discussion at court, though, when granting bail the sheriff reiterated the condition not to offend on bail and warned this offender that he was near to custod.[16].

Only at Braid were any of this category of accused remanded (this included the only offender in this group for whom the fiscal would have opposed bail because he was already on bail). Social information given by the defence in these cases did not lead to their release and in one instance the presentation of information to the court was taken as a signal for remand by the sheriff who refused bail stating, "The fact that the defence agent has to go over these matters underlines to me that I should refuse bail."

The greater use of custodial sentences by sheriffs at Braid is an important explanation for the high use of remand after a plea of guilty. The likelihood of a custodial sentence was not viewed by Braid sheriffs simply as one potential contra-indication for the granting of bail at this stage, rather it was seen as shifting the presumption to one in favour of remand. As one sheriff there stated, they thought it was inappropriate **not** to remand an accused in these circumstances when sentence was being deferred.

> " I believe in backdating....I sometimes say to agents if they talk of bail and want to raise the matter, 'is this a good idea?' I will keep people for reports as I can take into account (a period of remand when I) sentence. If there is a gap, that is if I release them on bail during the case, I cannot backdate a sentence and it is better to backdate as the high court says that an accused is entitled to this." (sheriff at Braid)

> "One's powers of sentence are now hedged around with all sorts of safeguards for people under the age of 21 and first offenders and people who haven't been to gaol before that one has got to get reports in dozens of cases where, I must confess but for the statutory constraint, one wouldn't bother to get a report. And there are some cases where it is perfectly clear that whatever the report says the only sentence is gaol. And so one I suppose is prejudging the case slightly but I feel they might as

16 Ultimately the offender received 4 months custody in a young offenders institution - the bail charge being concurrent with this.

> well go to gaol now and the sentence is backdated to the date of the plea of guilty, or the finding of guilt." (sheriff at Braid)

Nevertheless, custodial sentences were not only given in cases where people had been remanded. There were occasions when accused granted bail at Braid, as well as accused bailed at Tweed custodial sentences were also imposed.

USE OF SPECIAL CONDITIONS

Most bail orders did not have special conditions attached (in total, 12% of bail orders in Doon, 8% in Tweed and 20% in Braid had special conditions attached). The court can attach special conditions to a bail order at the request of a fiscal, the defence (usually offered if the agent thinks they will increase a client's chances of release on bail), or simply if the sheriff considers them appropriate. In interviews many sheriffs and prosecutors had given little thought to the use of special conditions beyond that of not approaching a named person or place, which was the most commonly used special condition, especially where alleged incidents had involved relatives or ex-partners. Other special conditions which people had either asked for or granted (though not necessarily during the research) were exclusions from certain parts of a town (such as a shopping area), curfews, reporting to a police station, surrender of passport; attendance at identification parade, attendance for medical examination to enable forensic samples to be taken, not to drive (given to a drunk driver), money. Police discourage the use of reporting conditions and they were not used at all in the study areas during the research.

There was more use of special conditions at Braid, where sheriffs were in favour of money bail.

> "I make more use of special conditions as its better to make conditions than to keep somebody in custody .....I do think you have a duty to consider them.....I have returned to money bail. I regret the end of money bail....It is not set at a sum which people could not meet .... It is not as great a burden as people pretend - it brings other sanctions....If an accused has not appeared and then they are willing to offer money then I would be willing to consider release again on bail." (sheriff at Braid)

Although some sheriffs objected in principle to any further use of special conditions, for most the objection reflected a concern with their practicality and enforceability. Often it was the fiscal who would ask for a special condition in court although occasionally discussion would be instigated by the defence or by the sheriff. In Tweed some were instigated by fiscal at the suggestion of police. Some deputes said they would like to make more use of curfews and exclusions but had reservations about their enforcement in practice. Others had reservations in principle about asking for special conditions,

> "I am not keen, its attacking democratic rights too far....I don't like curfews but I would be more willing to use them if the process in getting cases to trial were shorter as this would be more of an inconvenience than a prolonged infringement of liberty." (depute at Tweed)

> "My understanding is that bail should not be custody in a different guise, you should not be restricting a person's liberty." (depute at Braid)

Most special conditions involved telling an accused to keep away from a complainer or a certain area (usually the location of the incident or the complainer's address). This accounted for seven instances at Doon, seven at Tweed and ten at Braid. On most occasions the discussion of special conditions was instigated by the fiscal. In one instance at Tweed, at marking the depute had said of the accused, "if he'd been older then I would have wanted to lock him up" (the accused was fifteen years old). The accused was alleged to have abducted a young girl to make her withdraw a complaint she had previously made against him for assault with intent to ravish. Police suggested the special condition in their report to the fiscal. The fiscal agreed bail on condition that he did not approach or communicate with the complainer.

In the two cases at Doon where other special conditions were used, one was a condition to attend an identity parade which was set in a solemn case where the fiscal had marked the case as bail to be opposed for further enquiries. In the other, the condition was suggested by the defence agent whose client was charged with breach of the peace because they had attempted suicide. The fiscal opposed bail explaining that it was the opinion of the accused's GP that he needed urgent psychiatric help and that the court should remand the accused for a psychiatric report. The defence agent suggested a special condition saying their client was anxious to seek help. Bail was granted with a special condition - that this accused attend their GP and accept psychiatric treatment as instructed.

MONEY BAIL

The 1980 Bail Act removed the need to lodge money as a requirement for release on bail. Many within the criminal justice system believe that the use of money bail has virtually been abolished. Nevertheless in our sample accused were required to lodge money with the court in two instances at Tweed and in four instances at Braid. The one of two occasions in Tweed where money bail was used the fiscal opposed bail in court on the basis that the accused was a foreign national with a permanent address abroad and it was felt unlikely that he would attend trial. There was some discussion of an appropriate condition to secure his attendance and the sheriff initially suggested surrender of passport but the accused needed this to attend work, as he worked on a boat, and reporting conditions would have been impractical, as he was at sea for several days at a time. The sheriff eventually suggested lodging money and the accused agreed to lodge £200 pre-release.

In the other case involving money bail in Tweed the fiscal opposed bail on the basis of the accused's analogous previous convictions and because he was in breach of a recent bail order. In court, the defence agent argued that the other charges were not yet proved and said that he would lose his job if remanded. Bail was granted with a special condition to lodge £50. The accused did not lodge the money and the next day appeared at an accelerated diet where he received a custodial sentence.

In Braid other special conditions all involved the requirement to lodge money with the court and in all of these money was the only special condition which was mentioned in court. Unlike the other areas where special conditions tended to be used in cases which had involved violence or the threat of violence (breach of the peace, assault) money bail at Braid was used for dishonesty cases or driving offences. Money bail is always at the suggestion of the sheriff. These were all cases where the fiscal opposed or intended to oppose bail in court and it was highly likely that without this special condition the accused would have been remanded. For one being dealt with for housebreaking under solemn proceedings, the fiscal opposed bail on the basis of record and bail was granted subject to a £100 being lodged with the court. In another (summary) case the accused was about to sit exams, a remand would have interfered with this and bail was granted subject to £50 being lodged with the court. In the case of one accused of failing to give a breath test, unlawful use of vehicle and for whom bail was also being opposed because of his record, the defence agent pointed out that he had no convictions for three years and bail was granted subject to a £100 being lodged with the court because of the gap in the record.

SECOND APPEARANCE

Wherever possible, information about subsequent appearances was collected about accused who were remanded in custody at their first court. Solemn cases were discussed at table 5.3. Only eleven accused in summary cases in the total sample remained in custody throughout the process of their case. Nine of these were in Braid and one each in Doon and Tweed. For accused in summary cases in Doon the average (mean) length of time in custody was 23 days, in Tweed 19 days and in Braid 26 days.

Table 5.6 Summary Cases from Police Custody: Outcomes for Accused Remanded at First Court*

	Doon	*Tweed*	*Braid*
PRISON	*25%*	*38%*	*50%*
CSO/PROBATION	*25%*	*26%*	*10%*
MONETARY PEN.	*8%*	*19%*	*24%*
ADMONITION	*25%*	*0*	*3%*
NG/NO FURTHER PRO	*17%*	*6%*	*8%*
OTHER	*0*	*13%*	*6%*
TOTAL	*100%*	*100%*	*100%*
N =	*12*	*16*	*38*

*One accused in each of Doon and Braid and who appeared from undertaking, was remanded and was given probation and in a further case in Braid sentence was deferred.
All not guilty accused, with the exception of one at Braid, were not convicted of any offences. The accused at Braid was found not guilty of housebreaking but was convicted of attempting to pervert the course of justice (he had given a false name to the police) and was fined £200.

Table 5.6 shows that most people were not given a custodial sentence on conviction. In Braid half of the accused in summary cases who were remanded subsequently received a custodial sentence and in Doon only a quarter of those remanded in custody received a sentence of imprisonment. It is important to note the small numbers discussed in this section. Nevertheless, in the context of the processes and pressures identified by the research we would maintain that the findings in table 5.6 and figure 5.4 have substantive, if not statistical, significance.

As would be expected, all areas made a higher use of imprisonment for solemn cases with Braid also having a higher use for summary cases. Both Doon and Braid had a high proportion of accused whose cases were marked as no further proceedings or who were found not guilty, especially in solemn cases. This high level is particularly important if it is considered in the context of local propensities to remand or release on bail. At Doon 80% (24) of those who were not convicted had either been bailed or ordained during the case. In Tweed the proportion was 82% (14). However, in Braid 48% (14) were remanded. The impact of a propensity to remand is that more people who will not be convicted of the crimes of which they have been accused will spend

FINAL DISPOSALS

Disposal

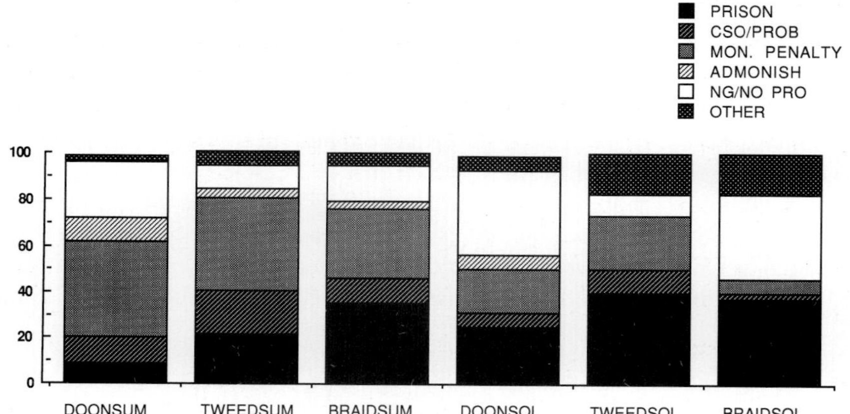

Summary Doon n =99; Tweed n =138; Braid n =117; Solemn Doon n =16; Tweed n=30; Braid n =35
*Includes compensation orders - 1 at Tweed, 3 at Braid.
** 'Other' = sentence deferred, hospital order, warrant, case incomplete.
The number of cases categorised as 'other' is higher at Tweed and Braid. A cut-off point for data collection had to be set which was September 1992 for Doon and Tweed and March 1993 for Braid. These dates were 15 months after the end of fieldwork in Doon, 9 months in Tweed and 11 months in Braid. Cases remaining incomplete after this date were recorded as 'other'. Information for cases appearing from undertaking is contained in annex 5.

time in prison. The two summary cases remanded at Doon spent an average of fourteen days on remand, the one accused at Tweed spent 29 days and the three at Braid spent an average of 26 days in prison. Those in solemn cases who were remanded, the four at Doon spent an average of eight days, the two at Tweed spent an average of 20 days and the eleven at Braid spent an average of 28 days in custody. Though most in Braid were released after seven days, two spent over one hundred days on remand. (One accused at Braid has been excluded from these calculations as they received a long custodial sentence for a separate matter shortly after being remanded.) It is important to note the small numbers on which this and the previous section are based. Nevertheless, in the context of other processes and pressures identified in the research, we would argue that these findings have substantive (though not statistical) significance.

COURT RESPONSES TO OFFENDING ON BAIL

Most (though not all) sheriffs in all areas argued that likelihood of failing to appear at court was a more of a consideration than further offending when they were thinking about granting or refusing bail.

> "..But the most important one of all, the most important breach of bail conditions is the time, ...where a person has failed to appear for a diet of trial. Whereas there is the other kind, where the person simply commits another offence while on bail......."(sheriff at Doon)

"The main purpose of remand has to be if it is in the interest of the public...and it is the interest of the public that people do not fail to appear - and that is the main reason for remanding someone...regular housebreakers are a worry to the public and they are people who should be remanded." (sheriff at Braid)

Court responses to the existence of a current bail order were variable since factors such as recency of bail; whether it is for an analogous offence; whether it is for a pending matter or associated with a deferred sentence; whether it is for a summary or a solemn case; and whether the present case is summary or solemn, as well as likelihood of custodial sentence, all affect the court response.

The Wheatley guidelines state that if an accused is already on bail and has therefore abused the court's trust, there is a presumption for the refusal of bail unless there is a reason for the decision to be otherwise. In Doon 29%, Tweed 24% and Braid 19% of the total sample were on bail when they were arrested. Although in all areas accused with a Bail Act charge libelled were more likely to be remanded in custody than accused who were not on bail, it was not possible to identify a presumption in favour of refusing bail operating. In Braid just over half of accused with a Bail Act charge were remanded in custody but in Doon 70% and Tweed around half were released on bail either with standard or special conditions. In all of these instances other factors overruled any presumption of the refusal of bail. This is explored further in chapter seven.

Table 5.7 Accused appearing from Police Custody: Where a Bail Act Charge Libelled by Outcome of First Court*

	Doon		*Tweed*		*Braid*	
	Bail charge	No Bail charge	Bail charge	No Bail charge	Bail charge	No Bail charge
Bail (standard)	62%	58%	46%	55%	32%	36%
Bail (special)	7%	12%	2%	5%	4%	11%
Remand	21%	14%	35%	13%	57%	42%
Ordained	2%	5%	4%	8%	0	2%
Final disposal	7%	11%	13%	20%	4%	10%
Warrant	0	0	0	0	4%	0
Total	100%	100%	100%	100%	100%	100%
N =	42	73	46	120	28	123

* In Doon one accused released on undertaking had a Bail Act charge libelled - released on bail; In Braid 5 had Bail Act charge libelled - 1 ordained, 2 remand, 2 warrants after failure to appear in court.
Braid 1 case missing.

In interview sheriffs were asked about the circumstances under which they would consider for release an accused who already had an outstanding bail order.

"... if the bail order is old and it is obvious that nothing much has been done about it. I am interested in those who have been bailed from my court recently and are in again. For example if an accused was bailed (6 months ago)..in (other sheriff court)... then I do not bother about it as this prejudices an accused simply because of the slowness of court procedures...but usually I take a bail order well into account." (sheriff at Braid)

SENTENCING OF BAIL ACT CHARGES

Table 5.8 Accused Appearing from Police Custody: Sentencing of Bail Act Charges*

	Doon	*Tweed*	*Braid*
Concurrent with main charge	*33%*	*39%*	*29%*
Custody	*2%*	*11%*	*25%*
Fine	*7%*	*15%*	*18%*
Admonition	*17%*	*0*	*4%*
Not guilty	*31%*	*11%*	*7%*
Case incomplete	*0*	*9%*	*18%*
Unclear if sentence concurrent	*10%*	*15%*	*0*
Total	*100%*	*100%*	*100%*
N=	42	46	28

*Outcomes for accused from undertaking with bail charges libelled - in Doon 1 admonition; In Braid 2 were admonished, 2 received custodial sentences concurrent to the main charge, in one it was unclear if the sentence was concurrent to that of the main charge.

Once someone had been convicted of breaching bail, the sentences given by courts generally reflected their pattern of sentencing on other charges. With those convicted at Braid being more likely to receive custodial sentences than those convicted in other areas. Most of "concurrent with main charge" are probation orders, community service orders, although a few received custodial sentences which were concurrent to the sentence for the main charge. However, court sentencing of bail charges was not the only way in which sheriffs said that they took breach of bail into account when sentencing. Sheriffs maintained that sometimes a more serious or a consecutive sentence may be imposed on a number of convictions for which, had there been no bail charge, the sentences might have been concurrent. It is notable that in Doon, where the sample had the highest percentage on bail, nearly a third of those accused were ultimately not convicted.

IMPACT OF CULTURES ON RESPONSES TO INDIVIDUAL ACCUSED: ILLUSTRATIVE CASE HISTORIES

A clear pattern has been identified of high police custody at Doon, high fiscal agreement to bail and high court use of bail; lower police custody at Tweed, increased fiscal acceptance of ordain and increased court use of ordain; and at Braid low police use of custody, high fiscal opposition to bail and high use of remand by court. These patterns are not simply outcomes of pressures from one part of the system, such as the police or the court, to liberate or remand. They are also outcomes of experience of the criminal justice system in different localities. Each part of the system is in constant interaction with the rest. These patterns described are the results of these inter-relationships and are indicators of the local cultures which are produced. The way in which local criminal justice culture was manifest both in criminal justice responses to accused prior to court as well as in courtroom exchanges have been illustrated. The risks of a culture of remand are that those that are not ultimately convicted are more likely to have spent time on remand than accused in an area with a culture of bail. The impact of local criminal justice cultures on individual cases will be demonstrated by contrasting responses to similar cases in the study areas.

The first examples were older accused both of whom had long records for drunkenness and breach of the peace. Both were the type of case which was going to recur. In Braid, the offender was immediately given custody and it was clear from his record that this had been the response of courts to him for many years and that he was now so institutionalised that he was actively seeking custody. The impression was of a system which had washed its hands of this accused and was resigned to locking him up. For the accused in Doon, although all criminal justice personnel showed dismay at having to deal with him, the fiscal and court actively sought ways of avoiding the use of custody (the police usually kept this accused because he was generally drunk on arrest) despite the fact that he reappeared regularly.

In the case of the accused in the example in Braid (breach of the peace and vandalism) who was just out of prison that day, he had broken a window in the town centre saying to a witness that he wanted a bed for the night. When police apprehended him he swore and shouted at them. The duty officer described him to the researcher as having told police that if they did not arrest him then he would break more windows. His record, which went back to 1955 and until three years ago was primarily for dishonesty, in the last three years had been for vandalism, breach of the peace and police assault. Most of his sentences were 3 months custody. Since 1971 every time he had been released he had committed an offence and had ended up in custody. He had spent most of the last 21 years in custody. The only time during this period when he had received another sentence was apparently from a temporary sheriff who had admonished him in September 1991. His record showed that 3 days later he was in court again for vandalism.

The fiscal at marking said that this was only going to the sheriff court because of the length of the accused's record. They did not have a formal opinion on bail as they expected the accused to plead guilty "he's a product of the system - he's institutionalised". In court he refused legal representation, pled guilty and was given a three month custodial sentence; the sheriff when passing sentence stated that he was unable to do anything else other than impose custody.

This contrasts with an accused at Doon with a similar record who was arrested ten times for various breach of the peace and drunkenness offences during the 12 weeks of the study. He was generally described by police as being of no fixed address. On six occasions the case went to the district court; in one the fiscal didn't prosecute as they thought that it was not in the public interest. On one of the occasions the fiscal opposed bail because of the recurrent offending of the accused during that week (he had been arrested three times). On later occasions the depute did not oppose bail as the offence would not have attracted a custodial sentence (accused offered an address before court). On another occasion the fiscal agreed bail and expected an address to be provided at court "to be honest I don't have the heart to oppose bail." The sheriff in court expressed the view that this sort of case should not be appearing in court, fined the offender £20 with an alternative of seven days custody. In the other two cases, the offender was fined.

The two previous cases referred to accused with long experience of contact with the criminal justice system. Both had records which initially involved dishonesties but which had primarily become drink related breaches of the peace. Although the accused at Doon had spent some time in custody, he was not institutionalised and deputes attributed the spate of appearances to a recent bereavement. The offender at Braid had spent so little time out of prison that he was unable to cope with liberation and the criminal justice system was unable to respond by doing anything other than returning him to custody.

Cases of younger accused in each area who had similar characteristics were also examined. All were sixteen, each had appeared more than once in the sample and each was involved in a mixture of dishonesty, breach of the peace and minor assault. In Doon and Tweed these accused were released on bail and ultimately given non-custodial sentences, in Braid the accused was remanded at his second court appearance and then given a custodial sentence.

One accused in Doon came into the sample five times during the twelve week period of the study, mainly in connection with dishonesty offences[17]. On his first appearance the fiscal agreed bail as, though he had a record of having appeared before the children's panel, he had no previous convictions. During the study this accused was released on bail three times by the court. However, at the fourth case the fiscal opposed bail because of the three bail orders for analogous charges and the fact that thirteen other charges were expected. On this occasion the accused pled guilty and was granted bail. On the fifth appearance the fiscal agreed bail because of his 'relatively short record' and also they believed that the evidence in this case was not strong. Bail was granted by the court. For none of these cases did the offender receive a custodial sentence.

An accused in Tweed who came into the sample three times also in connection with dishonesty, breach of the peace and minor assault[18]. In the first case, the fiscal agreed bail - knowing that the accused had substantial previous involvement with the children's panel and a pending case. However the fiscal stated that this accused would look to the court as if he had no previous convictions. At court the accused entered a guilty plea and sentence was deferred for a social enquiry report. At the second case, the fiscal opposed bail as it was only one week since the accused had been released on bail for analogous offences. However the fiscal said that it was unlikely that the accused would be remanded as he had only one previous conviction on which sentence was deferred, " but it's my duty to try and get him locked up if these [charges] are true". In court the depute opposed bail on the grounds that the accused had already been put on bail the previous week and that the present charges related to two incidents, saying "offences of this nature and escalating in this way indicate that there is no evidence that this young man is prepared to behave himself." The defence agent emphasised the age of the accused saying that he was very young to be remanded and reminding the court of the presumption of innocence. The defence agent also stated that the accused lived with his mother and required medical treatment regularly. The sheriff granted bail saying that they were "reluctant to lock someone up at such a young age and with such a short record." In the third case the fiscal agreed bail saying that they were reluctant to have someone of that age kept in custody. There was no discussion of bail in court. The offender received a community service order for all the charges.

For both these individuals, their youth and their short record, prompted prosecutors and courts to try to avoid remand.

The example from Braid, an accused who did not have any adult convictions although he was currently on a children's panel supervision order. He came into the sample

---

17 There was no loss and no victim in the first case which was a breach of the peace and the loss to the victims in the other cases was, respectively, £10-£50 recovered; £101-£250 not recovered; £51-£100 (damage), £10-£50 (damage). The offender was sentenced to probation, two fines of £40 each, and two periods of community service.

18 There was slight injury to the victim in one case and the loss to the victims in the other cases was, respectively, £51-£100 recovered; no loss or damage).

twice[19]. During the period of the study the supervision order ceased as the panel felt it was having no effect. In the first case the fiscal agreed bail saying that the accused had been under supervision since 1988 but had repeatedly offended and this was increasing. The depute said that this incident would under other circumstances have gone to the district court but said that "I'm not being vindictive, it's not in the public interest for him to think that he can go on behaving in this way. He has to understand what's involved if he is going to embark on an adult life of crime." In court the depute agreed bail, asked for a special condition and this was granted. In the second case the fiscal opposed bail, saying that the accused had 'numerous outstanding charges' with a history of dishonesty dating back to 1988 (when he had been on supervision). The other reason given was that he was on a recent bail order and had since been arrested again and released for summons. The depute said he would oppose bail "to let him see what would happen to him". In court the fiscal opposed bail saying that although this accused had no previous convictions, he had numerous appearances before the panel, and was currently on a supervision order which was about to be terminated. They stated that he was on bail and yet was again attracting the attention of the police three days later, "it is obvious that he intends to continue offending". The defence agent emphasised the age of the accused "very young and impressionable if remanded". Bail was refused. An appeal on the grounds of age was also refused. When he appeared again, he plead guilty and was remanded for social enquiry reports. However bail was granted on this complaint at a bail review where the fiscal did not oppose bail. After release from his initial remand this accused did subsequently fail to appear for the sentence deferred and the trial diet for the earlier charge, and was later remanded when he appeared from police custody having been arrested on warrant. He eventually received a 3 month custodial sentence concurrent on both charges with 1 month imprisonment to run consecutively on the Bail Act charge.

In this case, although the prosecutor was initially not prepared to oppose bail, at the second case bail was opposed on the grounds of pending cases and the accused's history of dishonesty which had been dealt with by the children's hearing. This offender did appear at court after his initial release on bail but he failed to appear after he had experienced remand. 'Letting him see what could happen to him in the criminal justice system' did not secure this accused's compliance with the wishes of the court. Whereas the accused at Doon was repeatedly being detained in custody by the police and this resulted in repeated use of court bail for offences which ultimately attracted non-custodial sentences; the response of the criminal justice system at Braid was to bring the offender quickly into custody.

CONCLUSION

In this chapter we have described court responses to accused and offenders in the cases which were examined in the study. Criminal justice decisions in particular cases not only have immediate impact on what happens to people in their present case but also have a long term impact on how criminal justice practitioners will respond to that person in the future. The research has found that experience of imprisonment and bail convictions contributes to the production of criminal records which in the future will make these people more likely to be candidates for custody than for release. Those coming into contact with criminal justice agencies in an area with a high use of bail, especially those under 21 who are likely to come into more frequent contact, will in the longer term develop records which make them appear poor bail risks. Those

19 The loss to the victims in each case was respectively, £20 unrecovered; and £101-£250 unrecovered.

coming into contact with the system in an area with a high use of remand are also more likely to experience imprisonment earlier and ultimately to have custodial sentences on their record.

The impact of different use of bail and remand is not, of course only at the level of individual cases. In chapter seven its more general impact recorded bail abuse will be assessed.

CHAPTER 6
BAIL APPEALS

INTRODUCTION

This chapter discusses the appeals which occurred in main sample cases as well as providing a high court perspective on the operation of bail. The appeals discussed illustrate some of the features of bail decisions and show how they may be contested. However, because they are simply those appeals which happen to have been lodged from a sample of cases, which was drawn on the basis of criteria set for other purposes, they cannot be taken as being representative of bail appeals generally or even as being representative of those which result from decisions in the study courts. Wherever possible, a short interview was conducted with those defence agents who were appealing refusal of bail in these cases. A high court perspective on bail appeals generally has been sought by interviewing crown counsel and high court judges who hear bail appeals.

It has been argued that case type and seriousness provide a partial explanation of differences in decision making and that attention needs also to be given to the operation of localised criminal justice cultures. These cultures are produced by local criminal justice experience but also by the way in which that experience is impacted upon by the authority relationships of the high court to the rest of the criminal justice system. The high court has the authority to define sheriff court bail decisions as having been either correct or incorrect. It therefore operates to constrain localised decisions to within currently authoritative interpretations of legislation. This is illustrated at the stage of appeals to the high court against bail decisions made locally. If either the defence or prosecution do not want to accept a sheriff's decision to remand or to grant bail, then they may appeal to the high court. The exception to this is at the first appearance of accused in solemn cases where there is no right of appeal for the defence (see figure 1.2). If bail is granted by the court despite opposition by the prosecution and the prosecution wishes to appeal, then the accused is remanded until the outcome of the appeal is known.'Appeal if granted' or a similar marking will usually have been noted on the case papers at the time of initial marking if bail is to be appealed against by the prosecution. An appeal against a sheriff's decision to bail or remand is an appeal to the high court that, in the case in question, the sheriff has exercised their discretion wrongly.

MAIN FINDINGS

Prosecution bail appeals are infrequent and did not occur in any cases in the main sample. There were few defence appeals identified. About 30% of remands in Doon and Braid were appealed, most appeals were unsuccessful, though a higher proportion from Braid than from Doon were successful. Though Tweed had only two appeals there was a greater tendency there to seek reviews of bail and these are held in the sheriff court. An advocate depute will not support a prosecution bail appeal unless they believe that the sheriff has exercised their discretion wrongly. High court judges interviewed confirmed that this was the only basis on which an appeal would be successful. Although bail appeal judges maintained the continuing importance of the Wheatley guidelines for bail decisions in the lower courts, they pointed out that the guidelines were not binding on the high court. In contrast, most sheriffs thought that the Wheatley guidelines were irrelevant to present bail decisions and many prosecutors showed only a vague knowledge of the guidelines. More prominent in their view were current high court decisions about bail appeals and most maintained that there was little evidence that the high court continued to adhere to the principles set out by Wheatley.

THE BAIL APPEAL PROCESS

A bail appeal will usually be lodged with the sheriff clerk immediately after court and written intimation will be given to the other party of the intention to appeal. A letter will then be sent from the local procurator fiscal's office to the high court unit at Crown Office and the defence agent will instruct an advocate on the grounds for appealing the sheriff's decision.

On receiving papers for a bail appeal, staff at Crown Office will highlight the relevant sections, such as, for example, highlighting Bail Act convictions on a record, and attach a brief summary of the key points in the papers which are then passed to the advocate depute who will appear before the high court judge on behalf of the Crown. The papers consist of a report from the fiscal, attached to which will be a copy of the complaint, copy of the record, if there is one, and a copy of the police report. The advocate depute receives these papers either the day before a hearing or on the morning of a hearing when there can be up to 25 appeals against the refusal of bail pre-trial. They read through the report in which the fiscal narrates the points made in favour of the bail application that have been made on behalf of the accused by their solicitor. The report also narrates the arguments that the fiscal depute put forward against the granting of bail and the reasons, if any, which the sheriff gave for refusing bail.

The advocate depute takes a view on whether bail should still be opposed at this stage and then proceeds to court where bail appeals are called before a single judge in chambers.

> "What happens is that there are a queue ...of defence agents there and they might have two or three bail applications each; and they come in in turn with most of their instructing solicitors and they mention the case....then they explain the reasons why (an accused) should be getting bail...quite often repeating the argument that was put to the lower court. If....I, as an advocate depute, feel that there's some merit in what they are saying, or I don't feel the person should be kept in custody, then I would simply indicate to the court that the Crown were not opposing the application and if the Crown don't oppose the applications the judge would let them out." (advocate depute)

If the fiscal takes the view that the sheriff had exercised their discretion wrongly by not keeping someone in custody, then the process is the same.

> "..the defence agent would mention the case...and then it's up to us to assess whether we are going ahead with the bail appeal or not. If we are then it's for us to argue why the man should be kept in custody. If we don't agree and we are not arguing that the sheriff exercised his discretion wrongly then we just say, 'we are not supporting that bail appeal' and again the effective result would be the man would be released, but the decision there would be the Crown appeal failed." (advocate depute)

Just as the prosecution might decide not to argue in an appeal which they do not feel should be supported, interviewees indicated that defence agents might also not present an argument to the bail judge if they feel there is little point to an appeal but have nevertheless been instructed by their clients to appeal,

> "in that case responsible counsel come in and say they are instructed to move the bail appeal but that is as far as they go....." (advocate depute)

SAMPLE BAIL APPEALS

There were few bail appeals identified in the sample and none of these were prosecution appeals against the granting of bail. All interviewees indicated that Crown bail appeals were unusual, with advocates depute indicating that they might each see perhaps one or two over a ten week period. Around thirty per cent of remands were appealed in Doon and Braid, with appeals from Braid being more successful than appeals from Doon.

In Doon there were twenty remands and six bail appeals of which one was successful. Four accused were already on bail and in none of these was the appeal successful. All appeals were in summary cases. Five out of the six had been police custodies and one had been released by police on undertaking.

In Tweed there were thirty-one remands and two bail appeals (one summary case, one solemn case) one of which was refused. Both were already on bail at the time of their arrest and both were police custodies.

In Braid there were seventy-four remands and twenty bail appeals. Six (30%) were successful. Six were on bail at the time of their arrest and in four of these cases the appeal was successful. Thirteen were in summary cases, seven in solemn cases. Nineteen had been police custodies and one had been released by police on an undertaking.

Some defence agents at Doon indicated that they would always appeal a remand decision, arguing that there was little work involved in this for them and that they might be "lucky and get a sympathetic judge" (most of the study appeals in this area originated with one firm of solicitors). This view was not widely held though and in Braid, the belief amongst defence agents was that while clients should routinely be advised of their right to appeal, a bail appeal should not be routine.

PROSECUTION VIEWS ON BAIL APPEALS

Procurator fiscal deputes who dealt with the sample cases had either never appealed a bail decision or had not recently done so. Some stated clearly that they would not appeal summary matters though others indicated that they would be willing to consider appeals in some summary cases.

> "An appeal of a sheriff's bail decision would have to be a solemn case. Either that or an extreme case of summary - for example a serious driving offence and you thought the accused was likely to drive again or perhaps there was a psychiatric element to a case (where the public interest really means public safety). You would have to get Crown Counsel's co-operation....If the granting of bail seemed contrary to what the court ought to have done, for example, if it is a very serious offence and the accused has a history of breaching bail. Our view though is that generally we would not appeal. I have not appealed a case within memory; though I have appealed a case it is just that it is so long ago." (depute at Braid)

The anticipated attitude of Crown Counsel was stated by fiscal deputes as being an important consideration in whether or not to mark a case for an appeal if bail is not refused by the sheriff, as an appeal would only be taken forward in the high court with their support. Fiscal deputes recognised that Crown Counsel did not always support an earlier decision to oppose bail by opposing bail at the appeal. However they stated that the reasons for this were not always clear to them. Advocates depute were asked in interview about such apparent differences in view. They confirmed that often there were differences in opinion as to whether bail should initially have been opposed; however, they maintained that bail appeals needed to be considered in the context of whether or not the sheriff's decision could be said to be a wrong use of discretion.

> "..it's the sheriff's discretion which counts; and, given a series of factors, whether you agree with them or not is neither here nor there quite often....Sometimes it's fairly thin, somebody's been done for a breach of the peace and maybe was on bail for something else at that time, technically speaking......that would certainly be grounds for supporting it....But quite often you would say, oh well given the nature of the offence, given his age, sometimes given his personal circumstances, sometimes then you would come to the conclusion that perhaps it would be as well if he wasn't kept in custody." (advocate depute)

More often than not, appeals are by the defence against the refusal of bail and this means that the Crown generally are arguing that shrieval decisions are correct in law. However, in a Crown appeal against the granting of bail the situation is reversed.

> "....... we argue in the main that the sheriff at first instance is exercising his discretion properly, that's basically 99% of bail applications, that is our position. When you come to put the boot on the other foot and we are arguing he has exercised it wrongly, then...it has got to be a fairly extreme example of that. Extreme examples would be if he...was intending to release somebody who the Crown thought, and had information, that he was a severe danger to society then...we would support the bail appeals - but its got to be fairly extreme before any depute would support a Crown bail appeal generally." (advocate depute)

> "in other words if his (the sheriff's) decision is perverse, either that he has not taken into account relevant factors that he should have taken into account or he has taken into account irrelevant factors. You do actually get cases where it's quite clear on the face of it that it is a perverse decision and you have no hesitation in those circumstances in going ahead with the Crown bail appeal....On the other hand...if you think the sheriff should not have granted bail but you cannot say that he has exercised his discretion wrongly then you're in the position when you cannot argue with it. So in the borderline case you may not be able to proceed ....." (advocate depute)

Whereas earlier decisions can be understood as being about particular cases in the context of the law, at the stage of appeal, decisions are about the application of law in the context of the individual case. Crown Counsel said that there was generally less difference between their views of whether bail should have been opposed and those of procurators fiscal. However, the difference in focus at the stage of appealing bail is particularly important in understanding why, in the case of Crown bail appeals they stated that, more often than not, they do not support the appeals that are lodged by local fiscal offices.

> "...quite often I think...that person probably should be kept in custody. That's not quite the point though, because you're arguing..... in the main that ...the sheriff didn't fail to exercise his discretion properly...Now if...we are...then saying that the

sheriff didn't exercise his discretion properly...you can see that that makes your credibility.....a little silly...." (advocate depute)

COMMUNICATION OF BAIL APPEAL RESULTS

Those advocates depute who were interviewed confirmed the comments by fiscals that there is little feedback about appeals to local fiscal offices. Such as there is tends to be simply the result of the appeal; there is not usually any information about either the reason for the decision or the reason for the view which advocates depute took of a case if it has been decided not to continue with the Crown's opposition to bail.

> "The outcome of a bail appeal is always reported by a letter from Crown office....which is in a standard form with the name of the accused as a heading saying, 'The above named accused appeal against the refusal of bail was heard today by Lord X who refused the appeal.' New Paragraph. 'Bail is therefore refused.' And the procurator fiscal knows that the sheriff's decision has been upheld, or it will of course indicate if bail has been granted on appeal and has been refused in the Sheriff Court....or will also indicate if Crown Counsel have decided not to proceed with a Crown bail appeal or indeed if Crown Counsel have decided not to oppose a defence bail appeal.....If nothing is said in the letter then it means that the appeal has proceeded but it may be that the letter will say 'when this appeal called Crown Counsel decided not to support the appeal and the appeal was therefore refused'....so they know if Crown Counsel have taken a view on the matter that has resulted in there being no argument before the bail judge" (advocate depute)

Explanations for not supporting a Crown bail appeal or for not opposing a defence bail appeal may occasionally be given to local fiscals but this does not happen routinely. Nevertheless if a fiscal decides to enquire, then interviewees thought that they would probably be given an explanation. An exception might be made if a succession of appeals were received from a particular office and which Crown Counsel thought were similarly inappropriate then it may be decided to give reasons in order to discourage further such appeals being lodged.

> "..one office, a while ago,....was taking a very strong line in opposing bail for shoplifters and these were people perhaps charged with stealing goods of very little value who may have had 2 or 3 convictions resulting in fines. We made it clear in that particular case that they were taking too strong a line on opposition to bail." (advocate depute)

CROWN COUNSEL ATTITUDE TO BAIL

Though it was indicated in chapters three and four that 'nature of the crime' was a reason regularly given by police and fiscals for their bail decisions in both summary and solemn sheriff court cases, (although record tended to be the deciding factor at sheriff court), advocates depute argued that 'nature of the crime' would not, at the appeal stage, be likely to be applicable for sheriff court cases and that only in high court cases was it likely to be a strong reason for not granting bail on appeal.

> "..there are many serious crimes in which bail is granted. It is almost invariably granted in cases of rape, because of the difficulty of proving the crime at the end of the day...it is usually only in cases where an accused is already on bail for a similar type of offence....that bail is opposed in the case of rape....On the other hand if you had someone who was a first offender and was charged with a post office robbery

with a sawn-off shotgun it would be unlikely that he would be granted bail, simply by reason of the nature of the crime." (advocate depute)

When asked to explain what features of a criminal record might lead them to oppose the granting of bail on appeal responses indicated similar considerations to prosecutors in the sheriff courts: number, type and penalties which previous courts had imposed for these.

Views on the significance of breaches of current bail orders and of convictions for bail offences were similar to prosecutors in Doon and Tweed. Though a range of views had also been expressed by prosecutors at Braid, those involved in marking cases in the study were more likely in practice to consider that the existence a current bail order or of any breach of bail charge on a criminal record should be ground for opposing bail. However such views were not shared at the level of the high court.

> "I would say that it depends on the offence charged, I mean if someone is charged with assault with a knife in the course of a fracas outside a discotheque and he has a lot of convictions for dishonesty and maybe two or three convictions for breach of bail, in that situation it may be obvious that he has got no record of violence, for example, and there wouldn't be any reason on the face of it for refusing bail for the type of offence with which he's charged. On the other hand, if he was being charged with his seventh or eighth theft by housebreaking, the breaches of the Bail Act would be highly relevant..."(advocate depute)

JUDICIAL VIEWS ON BAIL APPEALS

High court judges interviewed stressed their role as assessors of the original sheriff's decision,

> "It is not for us to decide on a bail appeal whether we would have given bail...it is sometimes difficult to explain to people that we are not there to grant or refuse bail in the proper sense of the word, we are there simply to make sure that we think that the Sheriff has exercised his discretion properly." (J1)

The judge who considers a bail appeal is provided with information both by the prosecution and the defence and their assessment is that of whether a reasonable sheriff, given the same information, was entitled to have come to a particular decision. Occasionally new information which was not available to the sheriff will be put to the bail appeal judge. Just as prosecutors are not routinely told the reason for a prosecution appeal not being taken forward, neither are sheriffs given a reason if the bail appeal judge decides that they have exercised their discretion wrongly. Those in the high court maintain that the work involved and the present volume of appeals would make it excessive if reasons for individual decisions were to be given in all bail appeals. This is because bail appeals need to be dealt with swiftly in order to expedite the release from custody of those who are to be given bail and to enable those who hear bail appeals not to delay their other high court business which cannot be conducted till the bail judge is free.

> "There is no point in it. Unless the sheriff has gone off beam.....then we would take steps to ensure that he was told and one way would be to write an opinion.." (J2)

The whole process of bail appeals is very swift, "You get through them at the rate of about one every two minutes." (J2)

Judges indicated that analogous previous convictions and any history of failing to appear, or defeat the ends of justice as well as a history of Bail Act convictions were central considerations in assessing records. In addition interviewees said that they would be reluctant to interfere with a sheriff's remanding of anyone with an outstanding bail order (though in five of the eight successful appeals in this study the accused were already on bail on arrest). However, it was also said that if the Crown were to appeal against the granting of bail on the basis that an accused was already on bail in relation to another matter, this was equally likely not to be successful.

> "..the Crown might make that point but again...I take the view that the sheriff has exercised his discretion properly. I won't interfere and if in the unusual situation of a bail order being outstanding and the sheriff allowing bail, I would expect that there would have to be very good reason indeed for me to interfere with the sheriff's decision...." (J1)

> "...there are very few Crown appeals, that's not because the Crown is delighted with every result it gets, it's just because it doesn't on the whole bring appeals unless there are very substantial grounds, and with those circumstances the Crown wouldn't have a hope." (J2)

It was stated that Crown appeals tended to be based on more substantial reasons than some defence appeals, nevertheless the criteria for allowing or refusing a bail appeal were the same,

> "....it comes to asking whether or not the sheriff...has taken a decision which is defensible....and if the answer is, yes....then you don't allow that appeal either." (J2)

Judges thought that recent bail convictions would be important contra-indicators of bail (although one said 'recent' would be within two or three years, the other was unwilling to specify what he generally considered to be recent) and, whereas there was a tendency for sheriffs to accord a higher priority to failure to appear, both advocates depute and high court judges thought that further offending was the more serious of types of bail abuse. The prevention of further offending was seen as a central purpose of remand prior to trial. Interviewees stressed that Bail Act convictions could not of themselves be considered as reasons for granting or refusing bail on appeal and emphasised the importance of assessing them in the context of other information about an accused.

Remand pending reports is generally frowned upon.

> "...one of the things that is important....if one is asking for background reports, these should be obtained when the person is living in his normal circumstances, not in prison, because you don't get anywhere if you try and take a social report for instance from somebody who is confined to Barlinnie. It is far better that you should see him in his family background and social background..."(J1)

THE WHEATLEY GUIDELINES

Those prosecutors who maintained that the existence of a current bail order was, of itself, a ground for opposing bail, reflected views which were formulated by Lord Wheatley in the appeal in the case of Smith V McCallum 1982 and in which he set out his views on the granting and refusal of bail (see chapter one). These guidelines continue to have formal importance both in terms of police and prosecution regulations for custody/liberation decisions. Procurator fiscal deputes, sheriffs, crown counsel and high court interviewees were asked to give their views on the continuing relevance of the guidelines to their current bail decision making.

Both high court judges argued that the case of Smith V McCallum was currently important in high court consideration of bail appeals.

"Lets distinguish between the case as an authority and the case which has the authority of its own reason as it were. So far as I am concerned its got no authority in relation to me at all. It's just one other judge has expressed certain views. There is no binding force. I am not obliged to follow his opinion. I don't think that is true in the courts below, they should be following the opinion of a high court judge......the other feature of it is that it actually contains reasons which I think most judges would agree were sound....so it has the authority of its own actual worth....it's a very useful guide...and ought to be followed unless there is some very good reason for not following it." (J2)

However, in the rest of the criminal justice system there is more ambivalence about these guidelines. Many deputes were vague about the continuing relevance of the guidelines and this is perhaps unsurprising given that, since they were not generally considering Crown bail appeals, the guidelines would primarily impact on their approach indirectly, through the procurator fiscal guidance on agreeing/opposing bail which is issued from Crown Office (see chapter one). Deputes were more aware of Crown Office guidance and of recent high court decisions and some were of the firm view that these guidelines were in the past and not relevant to current court practice. This was the general view in Doon, where the Wheatley guidelines were not viewed positively, as well as in Tweed and Braid.

The range of views about the guidelines was reflected at other levels in the criminal justice system and one depute who had spent a period working on bail appeals in Crown Office in 1985 said that they felt there had been 'a distinct backlash' against the Wheatley guidelines at that time. Counsel at that time reported that any mention of the guidelines was likely to provoke a response from the bail judge to the effect that they didn't use guidelines. The result was that counsel gradually stopped referring directly to the guidelines although it was believed that their arguments continued to follow them.

Sheriffs at Doon and Tweed had clear views on the continuing relevance of the Wheatley guidelines although those at Braid had divergent opinions. Of the nine sheriffs interviewed in all areas only one (in Braid) stated unequivocally that the guidelines had continuing relevance. Sheriffs in Doon and one in Tweed thought that they were enforced less rigidly by the high court and argued that this set the tone for sheriff court practice, implying that it was beneficial.

"The Wheatley guidelines died with Wheatley though their inherent common sense still has force." (sheriff at Doon)

However, most sheriffs in Tweed expressed strongly critical views of the guidelines and indicated that they saw them as irrelevant.

"Let me put it this way, my experience of how the high court has dealt with bail appeals has led me to believe that these are not very relevant to modern times." (sheriff at Tweed)

"I can unreservedly tell you that I have disregarded the Wheatley guidelines . . . I don't think that they are regarded as being serious by serious men now. I have no respect for them whatsoever." (sheriff at Tweed)

Although sheriffs in neither of the other areas saw the guidelines as desirable, this was not uniformly the case in Braid.

"I think Wheatley set out proper consideration for granting of bail. Unfortunately the procurator fiscal has been given a particular role and often I see him release on

> bail people who violate these guidelines....the procurator fiscal has to apply Wheatley now. He protects the public interest and has to determine whether someone can be released and often the Wheatley guidelines have little relevance to that decision.......I would like to see us (sheriffs) given the proper discretion to apply them. It would mean the court granting bail not the procurator fiscal. The difficulty we are placed in now is that of consistency as our role is now limited." (sheriff at Braid)

These differences of view were reflected by the advocates depute who were interviewed one of whom thought the guidelines were relevant. The other, however, only thought that they were partially relevant, indicating that they thought that judges were less strict about applying the view that if someone is on bail then they should not get bail again.

> "In the time of Lord Wheatley that was applied quite rigorously, that if someone was on bail he did not get bail. If he looked at the complaint and he'd say there was a Bail Act charge....then he would simply refuse the defence application against refusal of bail." (advocate depute)

> " ..someone said 'they're guidelines not tramlines'. You know you don't just look at them as rules cast in iron and say, 'you're in breach of this particular guideline therefore bail is not granted.'...if someone already has bail once or even twice, or more than twice and he is applying for bail again, it may still be relevant and proper to grant bail if the substance of the offences with which he is charged right through are all offences which are unlikely to carry a period of imprisonment or detention on conviction." (advocate depute)

Whereas the interviewee who thought that they were relevant said that they found the bail appeal process to be consistent and that little had changed since the inception of the Bail Act, their colleague had a different view, stating that they were unable to identify a pattern to high court decisions on bail appeals which would guide them in their consideration of bail matters.

> "For a start you now have several judges hearing bail appeals...the variation you get is exactly, in my view, in parallel with the kind of variation you get in sentencing in the high court and, to put it bluntly, there is no rhyme nor reason to it.." (advocate depute)

Nevertheless this interviewee did not want a return to closer adherence to guidelines,

> "No....on the other hand, not to have any guidelines at all just leads to chaos...and I think that's the position at the moment....It's the uncertain and crooked cord of discretion, as it was once described....." (advocate depute)

CONCLUSION

Prosecutors and sheriffs look to current high court decisions to guide their practice. This is particularly the case with prosecutors when assessing whether a case should be marked for appeal if bail should be granted by the sheriff. While prosecutors and sheriffs clearly recognised the general principles on which bail decisions are assessed, there was widespread uncertainty of the rationale for applying those principles in practice. The lack of information from high court prosecutors and judges about those cases where they believe that the decision of the fiscal or the sheriff has been inappropriate or wrong, contributes to a view, frequently expressed by respondents in the research that high court decisions in bail appeals are inconsistent or unfathomable.

CHAPTER 7

BAIL ABUSE

INTRODUCTION

The level of offending while on bail recorded by the police is often taken as an indicator of the effectiveness of the Bail etc (Scotland) Act 1980. In chapter one we pointed out that recent rises in levels of bail abuse charges recorded have been taken by some to indicate that bail is presently ineffective and that its current use limits the extent to which the public are presently being protected from persistent offenders. In this chapter we assess this interpretation both in relation to the study areas and as an accurate account of the significance of bail statistics generally. Bail abuse is a generic term for breach of any condition of a bail order. In Scotland breaches of bail conditions can involve: failing to appear at court at an appointed date and time (section (3)(1)(a)); breach of any other bail condition by committing an offence while on bail, interfering with witnesses or evidence, or failing to adhere to a special condition imposed by the court(section (3)(1)(b)). Prosecutors and courts regard any offence under the Bail Act as a breach of the court's trust. In this respect most prosecutors and sheriffs saw it no differently to breaches of other court orders such as probation and community service. The most commonly recorded of these breaches is committing an offence while on bail. This is the breach which is often being referred to in discussions of bail abuse and on which the discussion in this chapter will focus.

MAIN FINDINGS

Most people released, whether or not released on bail conditions, were not alleged to have committed further offences, even though the sample consisted primarily of accused whose release was considered by police to be problematic. A high level of recorded bail abuse was associated with a high use of bail by the court. However, when the proportion of accused who were not convicted was taken into account, there was no evidence that the higher use of remand at Braid was providing greater protection for the public there. No evidence was found that in the areas with a propensity to grant bail the public were being placed at increased risk from large scale serious further offending.

In all areas most who breached their bail did so within the first twelve weeks of their bail order. It was notable that in Doon over half of those who were recorded as having breached their bail had done so within its first four weeks. However, the tendency of police at Doon to detain accused in custody and therefore report them to the fiscal more quickly, the fiscal tendency to seek bail conditions and the court to grant these, meant that those at Doon who are going to be charged with committing further offences are also going to contribute to the production of high levels of recorded bail abuse. Most of this group were under 21. Many such accused at Braid are likely not to be detained by police there but to be released for summons. The reports take several weeks to reach the fiscal from the police and, as these accused would not have been to court, they could not be on bail for the original matter. They would not therefore be in breach of the court's trust if they became involved in any offending during that period and would not be identified in official statistics in a way which would indicate that such accused had recently had contact with the criminal justice system.

Prior to the 1980 Act there was no information collected about the extent of offending on bail. The Bail Act has allowed the criminal justice system to make recidivism of bailees statistically visible in a way which was not previously possible and therefore, in areas with a culture of bail there is likely to be increased awareness of this type of problem. However current concern about the level of bail abuse recorded is based on a misconception about the meaning of the statistics. Levels of recorded bail abuse are often discussed as if they signified the level of repeat offending. The statistics record alleged breaches of the court's trust, with a high level of recorded bail abuse being associated with a high use of bail by the court. Offending on bail statistics are recorded by the police at the point of arrest and at that stage no account can be taken of whether accused will ultimately be convicted. The present study has found that guilt was not established for around ten per cent of those in the sample at Tweed and Braid who had bail charges, but that in Doon, where more people were on bail, thirty per cent of bail offences in the sample there were not proved. Bail statistics give no indication of the significance of the breaches. The study has found however, that the type and seriousness of either initial or subsequent offences as well as recency of bail orders were central to criminal justice responses to those breaches.

FAILURE TO APPEAR

Failing to appear at court is the breach which many sheriffs consider to be the most serious. Failing to appear at court without a reasonable excuse can be dealt with as a contempt of court, as a charge under section 338 of the Criminal Procedure (Scotland) Act 1975, or, if the accused is on bail, by a charge under section 3(1)(a) of the Bail etc. (Scotland) Act. The advantages of dealing with failure to appear by other than contempt of court is that a conviction which is recognisable as being for non-appearance is recorded against the offender whereas convictions for contempt of court give no indication as to the nature of the incident which led to the conviction. In most cases where accused failed to appear a further charge was libelled unless there was a specific reason for not doing so.

In Doon 6% (9), Tweed12% (22) and Braid 9% (16) of the sample failed to appear at court. In six out of seven accused in Doon and all accused in Tweed where a bail charge was not libelled, there was a reason for the failure to appear which was accepted by the fiscal. At Doon one defence agent had instructed the accused that it was not necessary to appear for the hearing although the court took a different view, in another at Doon and one at Braid, the accused was in custody on other charges and was not brought to court.

OFFENDING ON BAIL

Because it consists primarily of accused whose release was considered by police to be problematic, the sample could be expected to contain a higher proportion of accused likely to abuse their release. For the purposes of this research, further offences alleged were identified by the police checking an accused's record with the Scottish Criminal Records Office in order to identify charges libelled between the date of liberation by the court and the date of final disposal of their initial case. The discussion of bail abuse in this chapter focuses on accused involved in summary cases. This is because at Braid there was a shorter period of time than there was for the other areas, between the end of fieldwork and the end of the study. This means that fewer summary cases at Braid had reached final disposal at that stage and no solemn cases where the accused had been at liberty. (Full details at annex 1)

For all accused in the sample who were released during the process of their case, information was collected on the number of charges [1] libelled as having occurred during their release. Most accused were not alleged to have abused their release. The highest group were those released on bail at Doon and Braid around forty per cent of whom had subsequent charges. Around thirty per cent of those released on bail at Tweed had subsequent charges alleged. In all areas those released on bail with either standard or special conditions at the end of their first court appearance were more likely to have further offences libelled than those remanded and later released and those ordained to appear. These accounted for 93% of those with further charges alleged at Doon, 84% at Tweed and 87% at Braid. Few accused were ordained to appear for their next court date and only a small proportion of those had further offences libelled. This shows that those accused for whom the fiscal was prepared to agree that they could be ordained (see chapter four) were less likely to have further charges alleged. Most of those with further charges had one or two new charges, however a few in each area had a larger number of offences subsequently alleged. Accused at Tweed had the highest average (mean) number of further offences libelled (5 compared with an average of 2 in Doon and 3 in Braid).

OFFENDING ON BAIL: TIME BETWEEN RELEASE ON BAIL AND FURTHER INCIDENTS BEING ALLEGED

Most of those with further charges at Doon, where the level of bail was highest compared with Tweed and Braid, were alleged to have offended within 4 weeks of their release on bail. For most accused (over 90%) who had further charges, the offences were alleged to have occurred in the local area and they would therefore be likely to appear to answer any complaint in the same court as they had appeared previously.

Figure 7.1 Summary Cases: Time Between Court Release on Bail and Alleged Incident Resulting in Further Charges

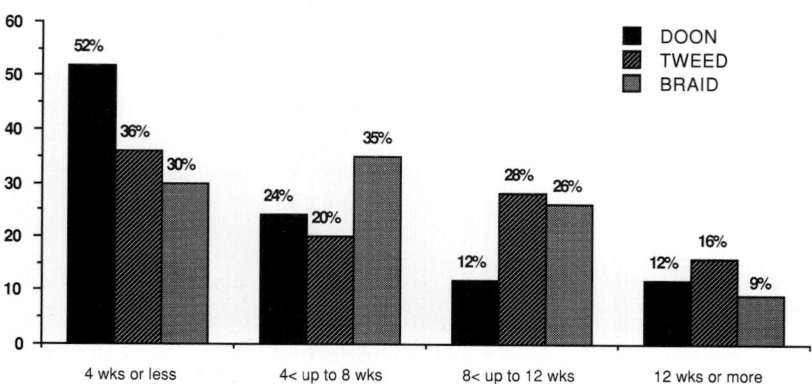

Doon n =42; Tweed n =25; Braid n=23

1 Later in this chapter we examine different measures of bail abuse. Because of recent concerns about offending on bail we have tried to consider the most serious picture of this problem which could be generated by our sample. It should be emphasised that we recorded **charges** rather than **cases**, ie. a case often consists of more than one charge. This inflates the levels of bail abuse in the discussion.

PROTECTION OF THE PUBLIC: LIKELIHOOD OF CUSTODIAL SENTENCE

In view of the concerns referred to in the introduction to this chapter, it is important to look at whether this group of people were found, at the end of their initial case, to have been people from whom the court considered that the public needed to be protected by giving them a custodial sentence. The likelihood of a custodial sentence has been identified in this study as a factor which both prosecutors and courts take into account at the time of considering whether bail should be granted for an accused. If a custodial sentence is unlikely, then the only alternative justification for remanding someone is to enable the case to be properly processed (i.e. to prevent interference with witnesses or evidence, to enable further enquiries to be made, to ensure appearance at court).

Figure 7.2 shows the outcome of the initial case for sample accused. Most of those at Tweed and Braid with further charges were ultimately to receive either a custodial sentence or a community service order (which is considered to be an alternative to custody). However, few of those at Doon who were alleged to have committed further offences ultimately received either of these types of disposal. Whatever kinds of problems may have been posed by the pre-trial or pre-sentence release of those who received a non-custodial disposal, a remand to protect the public would not have been consistent with the final outcome of their case.

Figure 7.2 Final Disposal by Whether Accused had Further Charges (%ages)*

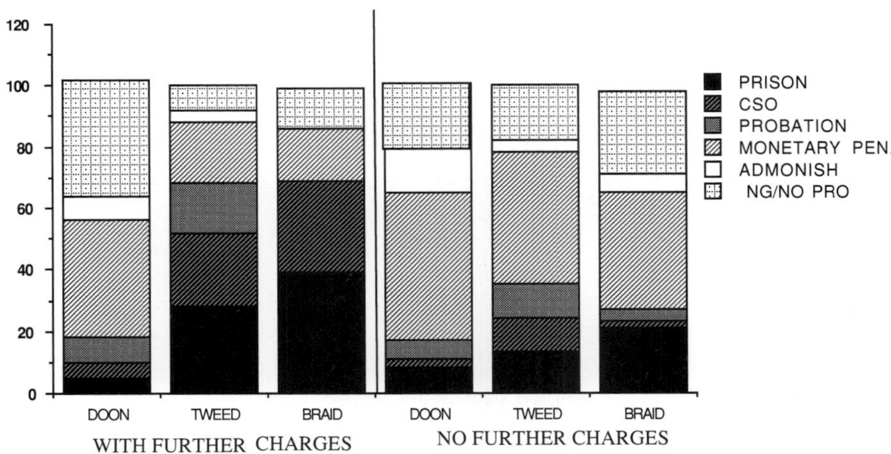

With charges Doon n= 40;Tweed n =25; Braid n =23; No charges Doon n=65; Tweed n =72; Braid n =47.
*Excludes 2 accused with further offences alleged at Doon for whom warrants had been granted.
Doon Chi-square = 4.86 (DF = 6) significance = 0.561; Tweed Chi-square = 9.17 (DF = 6) significance = 0.164; Braid Chi-square = 19.267 (DF = 6) significance = 0.0037. Only in Braid was the relationship between whether an accused had further charges and the disposal of the original case statistically significant. (In Doon and Tweed figures not significant at 5% level).

PROTECTION OF THE PUBLIC: REPEAT OFFENDING

Anxieties about bail abuse are anxieties about repeat offending. The official police category of *'re-offending while on bail'* presupposes that people are guilty of both the initial offence for which bail was granted and the subsequent offence on the basis of which it is alleged that bail has been breached. But for a high proportion of accused at Doon (38%) and for 8% at Tweed and 13% at Braid who were either not guilty or whose case was not proceeded, even if they had been guilty of the subsequent charges, although they would have committed an offence while on bail, they could not accurately be described as having *re*-offended. Proportions of alleged *further* offences were calculated by removing those accused found not guilty or whose case was ultimately not proceeded with. Tweed and Braid were found to have a similar percentage of alleged further offending (30% at Tweed, 29% at Braid), Doon had a much lower percentage (24%). This implies that the higher use of remand at Braid was not necessarily providing greater protection for the public from repeat offending there, and neither was there evidence that the higher use of bail at Doon and Tweed was placing the public at greater risk of a high volume of crime.

BAIL ABUSE: TYPES OF OFFENCES

It is important, nevertheless, to look beyond the volume of offences and to consider in more detail the types of offences both for the original charges and for the subsequent charges, in order to assess further the risk at which the public was being placed[2].

Previous research has found that those charged with crimes of dishonesty were more likely to breach their bail (Morgan 1992:iii). Figure 7.3 shows that, with the exception of the small number of accused at Tweed and Braid whose alleged offences were classed as 'other', the findings of this study confirm this for Doon and Tweed, though for Braid those charged with breach of the peace were more likely to have further offences alleged.

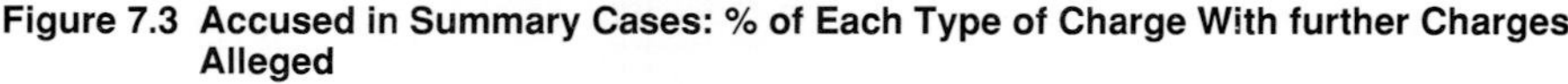

Figure 7.3 Accused in Summary Cases: % of Each Type of Charge With further Charges Alleged

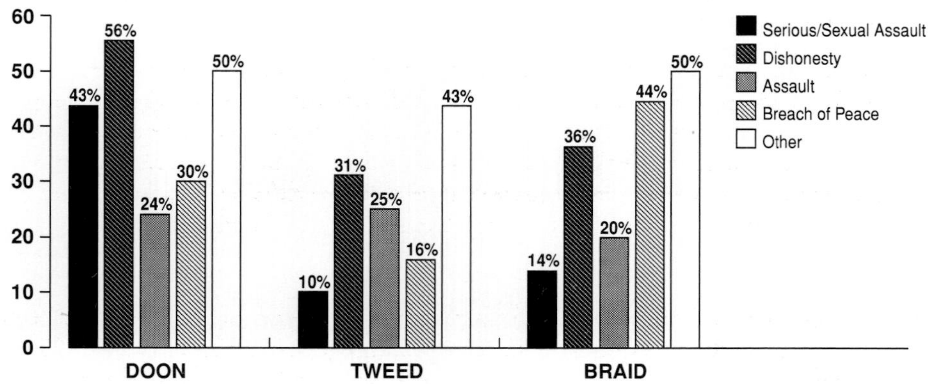

Doon n =42; Tweed n =25; Braid n=23

2 The following figures have not excluded those found not guilty or whose cases were not proceeded. Arguably these accused ought to be removed from this section, however, since responses to the generalised 'problem of bail abuse' are based on statistics which assume guilt and neither take into account guilt and innocence nor whether the offences are indeed *further* offences, the statistics here have not been adjusted and will therefore *over-state* levels of bail abuse.

Figure 7.4 shows that in all areas crimes of dishonesty were the most frequently libelled for people at liberty. In addition, those with further offences alleged and who were originally charged with dishonesty were the most likely to have offences alleged which were analogous to the original offence (58% of such accused in Doon, 83% in Tweed and in Braid 90%).

Figure 7.4 Accused in Summary Cases: Type of Further Offence Alleged During Release

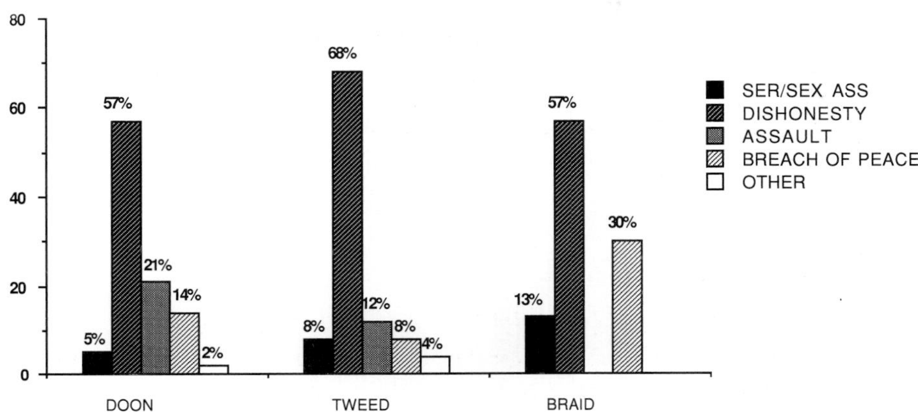

Doon n=42; Tweed n=25; Braid n=23

In Doon and Tweed half of those with further charges alleged were on bail when initially arrested whereas around a third of those in those areas and who had no further charges had been on bail at initial arrest. In Braid those with further charges alleged were almost as likely to have been on bail as those with no further charges (around 20%).

CHARACTERISTICS OF ACCUSED WITH FURTHER OFFENCES ALLEGED

Record has been found to be a key indicator to criminal justice personnel as to whether it is appropriate to release someone on bail. However during our observation we noted that an accused with pending cases was sometimes regarded as being currently involved in a course of criminal conduct. It was found that there was a significant relationship between whether the accused had further offences libelled and whether they had cases pending at the time of being charged as well as with their age.

In Doon and Tweed, those with alleged further offences were more likely to have been on bail when they were arrested than those without alleged offences. In Doon, 50% and in Tweed 44% of accused with alleged offences were on bail when they were arrested compared with 23% of accused with no further offence alleged in Doon and 17% in Tweed. In Braid accused with further alleged offences were as likely as those without alleged offences to have been on bail when they were arrested. 17% of both groups were on bail when they were arrested.

In each area around half of accused under 21 had further alleged offences. These accounted for around three-quarters of those with further alleged offences at Doon and Braid, and around half in Tweed. This is similar to findings of previous research that young offenders are more likely to be involved in allegations of offending on bail. The lower level of alleged further offending at Tweed is associated with the lower representation of this age group in the sample[3] since those under 21 at Tweed were just as likely to have further charges as those in this age group at Doon.

Figure 7.5 Summary Cases: %age of Accused With and Without Further Offences Alleged by Whether Any Charges Pending When Originally Charged

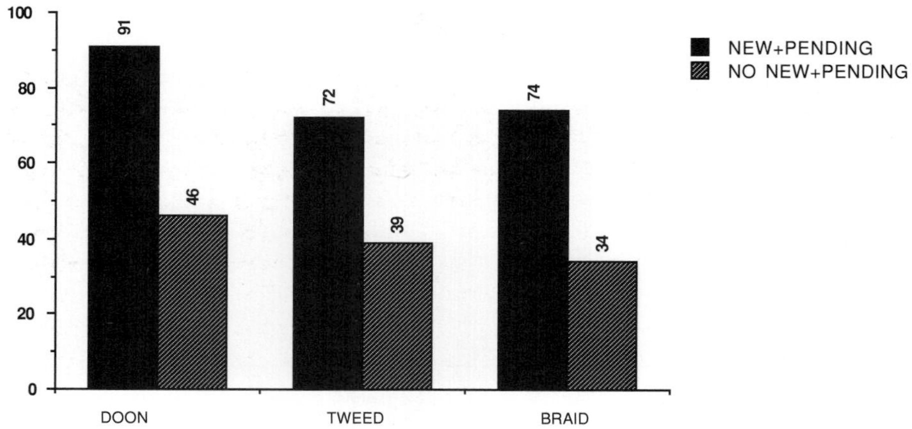

With new charges Doon n=42; Tweed n =25; Braid n=23; No new charges Doon n=65; Tweed n=72; Braid n=47 Doon chi-square = 21.64 (DF = 1) significance = 0.000, r = -0.45; Tweed chi-square = 8.16 (DF = 1) significance = 0.004, r = -0.29; Braid chi-square = 9.9 (DF = 1) significance = 0.001, r = -0.38.
The relationship between whether accused had cases pending at the time of arrest and whether they had further charges was significant at the 5% level in each area.

Figure 7.6 Accused in Summary Cases: Age by Whether Further Offence Alleged (%age)

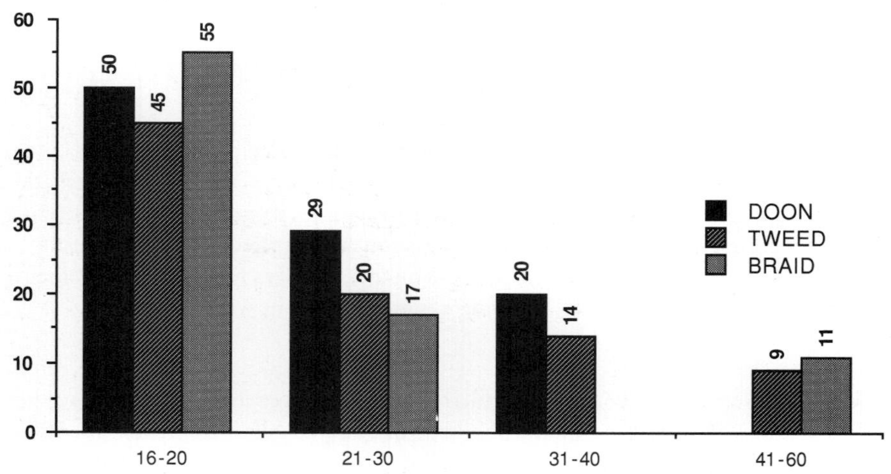

Doon n=42; Tweed n=25; Braid n=23
Doon chi-square = 8.5 (DF = 3), significance = 0.037, r = 0.28; Tweed chi-square = 9.24 (DF = 3) significance = 0.026, r = 0.23; Braid chi-square = 11.23 (DF = 3), significance = 0.010, r = 0.34. The relationship between the age of accused and whether they had further charges was significant at the 5% level in each area.

3 Under 30% of accused in the main sample in Tweed were aged 16-20 compared with over 40% in Doon and Braid.

YOUNG PEOPLE AND BAIL ABUSE

Figure 7.7 shows that most young people who had further charges had these alleged during the first twelve weeks of their release. Doon had a particularly high proportion within the first 4 weeks and many of these were within two weeks of release by the court (31%). In Tweed and Braid few aged 16-20 appeared in the sample more than once. However, in Doon there were 3 accused who appeared twice, three who appeared 3 times, one who featured 4 and another, 5 times during the 12 week period.

Figure 7.7 Accused Under 21 Years Summary Cases: Time Between Court Release on Bail and Alleged Incident Resulting in Further Charges (%ages)

	DOON	TWEED	BRAID
4 wks or less	58%	31%	28%
4<up to 8 wks	13%	31%	33%
8<up to 12 wks	16%	31%	33%
12 wks or more	13%	8%	6%

Doon n=31; Tweed n=13; Braid n=18

Doon n=31; Tweed n=13; Braid n=18

The findings in figure 7.7 are particularly important if we take into account the findings in chapter three (table 3.1) which showed that there was little difference between the areas in likelihood of people in the sample having cases pending, that in general police at Doon detained people in custody at twice the rate of police at Braid and that police at Tweed detained people in custody at one and a half times the rate of police at Braid. The release of more accused at Braid for summons (77% of all accused compared with 56% of all accused at Tweed and 43% at Doon) means that accused who are likely to be dealt with as custodies or undertakings in other areas may be being released by the police at Braid. At the time of the research police said that it was taking about five weeks for them to send a report to the fiscal on summons cases in that area. This means that, unlike their counterparts in Doon, many accused at Braid who may be involved in further incidents at that stage would not yet have been to court in connection with the initial incident and could not therefore have bail orders. This suggests that the higher level of recorded offending on bail at Doon may in part be a result of police practices of detention, fiscal practices in seeking bail for police custodies and the greater court use of bail. This allows the behaviour of those initially detained in that locality to be monitored in a way which is not possible in localities with different criminal justice practices which release more people for summons to court and which make less use of release on bail.

ILLUSTRATIVE CASE HISTORIES

Examples of details for individual accused are presented at annex 6 in order to illustrate the features of the decisions which were made about initial cases and the types of difficulties which are associated with those alleged to be involved in repeated offending. Criteria for selecting the examples were that the first further incident should have occurred in the middle of each time range and that, where more than one accused met this criterion, the accused with the highest number of further offences recorded has been selected. The examples therefore focus on those accused with an increased incidence of further offending.

The examples illustrate that accused at Doon had much less experience of the criminal justice system than accused in the other areas. This is consistent with earlier findings (chapter three) that accused in this area had less serious records than those at Tweed or Braid. They show that none of those at Doon had analogous offences in the previous year, although the accused in the examples of X79 and X90 (these codes identify cases described in annex 6) had had involvement with the children's panel, whereas those with further charges within the first twelve weeks of their bail at Tweed and Braid had similar convictions. Three at Doon with charges within the first 12 weeks had been on bail at the time of their original arrest and, though the accused charged within four weeks at Tweed was not on bail, the other three Tweed accused were. None of those at Braid had been on bail at the time of their original arrest. Only one of the accused at Doon had a bail conviction within the last three years, and he had one conviction. In contrast, accused at Tweed and Braid were more likely to have bail convictions - one in each area had no bail convictions, two in each area had one conviction and one in each area had three convictions.

The complexity of features associated with court decisions for individual accused especially if the accused currently has other involvement with the criminal justice system is illustrated in particular by the example of Y247 who was released on bail because he was just about to be given probation for another matter. This, together with the wide range of sentences given for breach of bail during this study (Table 5.8) underlines the importance of the criminal justice context of a breach of bail in the court's assessment of the significance of this breach of trust.

ASSESSING MEASURES OF BAIL ABUSE: OVERVIEW

In England and Wales offending on bail is not a separate offence and therefore is not routinely monitored there. Recent studies of offending on bail in England and Wales have been reviewed by Morgan (1992) who has commented on the different methodologies used in the police surveys and has highlighted the need for a common methodology to allow reliable estimates of the rate of offending while on bail. Morgan argues that the rate of bail abuse (measured by offending on bail) found by these studies is largely dependent upon the methodology adopted. The most frequently used method of estimating offending on bail in these studies has been to sample accused who were granted bail and then to search records to find if they had been convicted of an offence committed while on bail (Used in Home Office 1978, Metropolitan Police, RPU, Northumbria). The second method has been to sample accused either at the point of arrest or charge and to check the proportion who were on bail (Greater Manchester and Avon and Somerset). The third method has been to examine all crimes cleared-up and link these to the accused's bail record in order to estimate the proportion of cleared-up crime committed by accused on bail. (Northumbria) (Morgan 1992:2)

The various studies in England and Wales have estimated that the proportions of people found guilty of offences committed while they were on bail were 10% in three areas outside of London in 1986 and 1988, 12% in London in 1988 and 17% in Northumbria in 1989. (Henderson and Nichols 1992, Northumbria Police 1991) However, Morgan comments that the Northumbria figure also counts offences which were taken into consideration by the courts and those who were formally cautioned. When this was allowed for, the studies showed that the rate of offending on bail was 12% in London and 9% outside of London. The highest rate of conviction for offences committed on bail was in theft of or from a vehicle (23% in London) and burglary (housebreaking) (20% in London and 16% outside of London). The lowest rates were for those charged with violence offences (6% to 8%) (Morgan 1992:iii). There are no comparable figures for Scotland.

The present study compared three sources of data for offending on bail and compared the results of adopting different sampling strategies. Information on these was collected from a number of sources - police detention sheets, the bail census and the sample . Table 7.1 summarises these and illustrates that the proportion of those alleged to have committed offences on bail is dependent on the stage of the criminal justice system at which a measurement is taken, as well as the population against which the proportion is being calculated.

Table 7.1 Measure of Offending on Bail

	Doon	*Tweed*	*Braid*
Sample			
On bail when charged	*27%*	*24%*	*19%*
Alleged to breach study bail order	*43%*	*29%*	*35%*
Police Detention Sheet Data			
On bail when arrested	*12%*	*3%*	*8%*
Court Census Data*			
With offending on bail charges	*18%*	*14%*	*11%*

*Details of court census results on bail abuse are given at annex 7

The study has found that a person on bail was more likely to be detained in custody by police than they were to be released on undertaking or for summons. For this reason the sample could be expected to have an over-representation of accused with outstanding bail orders and this is confirmed in Table 7.1. The most accurate measure of the extent to which the court's trust is being breached is provided by looking at the proportion of those granted bail who were subsequently found to have offended while on bail. The study has not measured the extent to which those in the sample were found guilty of these subsequent offences therefore these percentages are likely to overstate the level of bail abuse in the sample. It may also be affected if the police record is not correct e.g. if pending charges have not been recorded on the computer at the date of checking.

If we consider the court data and the sample data for those found to be on bail on arrest, then Doon would be taken to have the highest and Braid the lowest level of offending on bail. However earlier in this chapter we indicated that, of those in the sample whose case had reached final disposal and who had been granted bail at first appearance, accused at Braid were almost as likely as those at Doon to have further charges recorded during their release. The court at Braid had the same level of use of bail as the court at Tweed and a lower level than the court at Doon. However, the figures discussed earlier in this chapter would imply that those on bail at Braid were no less likely to have further charges than those at Tweed and therefore that a higher use of remand there was not clearly associated with increased protection of the public from those suspected of further offending.

ASSESSING MEASURES OF BAIL ABUSE: SIGNIFICANCE

Initially when the Bail Act came into force, there was some uncertainty as to the propriety of libelling both the substantive charge and a charge of offending while on bail and procurators fiscal had to choose which they would libel (amendment to Crown Office Circular No.1671 in May 1980). The belief at this time was that libelling both charges would constitute double jeopardy. However, after a High Court ruling in the case of Aitchison V Tudhope (1981, SLT231) it was decided that it was competent to libel both the substantive and the breach of bail charges (amendment to Crown Office Circular No.1671 in May 1982). The explanation being that if someone has committed an offence while on bail then they have breached the trust of the court and a sentence for this type of offence is a sentence for the breach of trust rather than an additional sentence for a substantive offence.

Most criminal justice practitioners maintained that a major advantage of having breaches of the Bail Act separately recorded was that it provided them with fuller information as a basis on which to assess an accused as likely to breach the trust of the court.

> 'If they don't have a bail order then the sheriff won't find out how often an accused has committed further offences prior to trial. Apart from this though it doesn't stop the persistent offender from offending.' (depute at Tweed)

> "...... it allows an extra charge for those who commit further offences and an accurate record of their reliability by the recording of bail offences." (depute at Braid)

There was variation in practices for libelling charges of committing an offence while on bail, especially for accused who had more than one bail order outstanding (51% at Doon, 31% at Tweed and 13% at Braid). In areas Doon and Tweed the practice was for deputes to libel one charge of offending on bail on a complaint and for the narrative of the charge to contain information about the number of bail orders outstanding. For example, instead of simply stating that the accused 'having been granted bail in ... Sheriff Court on ....(date)' had committed a further offence while on bail, the convention in these areas was for the complaint to state that the accused 'having been granted bail in ... Sheriff Court on ....(date) and .... Sheriff Court on ....(date)....'. Occasionally police in these areas would report more than one offending on bail charge, but the practice was for the deputes to combine these charges into the narrative of a single charge.

Deputes in Tweed said that they would libel a separate charge for each bail order from each court on separate dates, but if the bail orders were from the same court then they would libel the breach of bail as one charge. In practice though some accused were from different courts, only one bail charge would be libelled. This was also generally, though not uniformly, the practice at Braid.

> "Normally I libel a separate bail charge for each bail outstanding. I cannot imagine rolling all the charges together in one Bail Act charge.... it is likely that the sheriff

would only sentence the accused on one charge and admonish him on the others and I think that that is right." (depute at Braid)

Though sheriffs had mixed views on the practice of libelling multiple bail charges, all held the view that they would either sentence on the first charge and admonish on the rest or give concurrent sentences on all charges.

"I don't think it matters very much (how bail act charges are libelled) because the maximum sentence which you can impose for breach of bail order by commission of another offence is not very great...." (sheriff at Braid)

CONCLUSION

The sample selected for this study was selected on the basis that the cases would be those where a bail decision would be relevant. This is likely to explain the fact that the proportion of this sample who were alleged to have offended on bail was higher than in previous studies. The proportion of the accused involved in summary cases alleged to have offended while at liberty ranged between 26% and 39%. However, it should be emphasised that the sample consisted of those who were judged by the police in their custody/undertaking decision as being problematic for release and that in Doon a high proportion of charges both in the census and for the initial charges for those in the sample , were not ultimately resulting in convictions. Those most likely to have further offences libelled were those with charges pending at the time of the original charge and accused aged between 16 and 20 years.

Current concern about the level of bail abuse recorded is a concern about increased risk to the public by those who repeatedly offend. However bail statistics record alleged breaches of the court's trust; they are not an indicator of large scale recidivism, nor of criminal justice failure to treat breach of bail seriously. The range of disposals used by courts in response to breach of bail is indicative of the significance accorded to particular breaches in the context of the other criminal matters for which an offender is being sentenced. Recorded crime statistics of re-offending while on bail assume that accused will be convicted of the original offence and, in addition, take no account of those who are not convicted of the further offence. A high level of recorded bail abuse was associated with a high use of bail by the court. However, although the court census recorded a lower level of bail abuse in Braid, the area with high level of remand, those released on bail there were only slightly less likely to those in the high bail area, to be alleged to have breached their bail orders.

ANNEX 1

METHODOLOGY

CENSUS

The purpose of the court census was to enable us to describe the pattern of use of bail by the study courts. It took place in Doon and Braid sheriff courts for 52 weeks from March 1991 to March 1992. In Tweed it was curtailed after 36 weeks because of pressures of work on court staff as it coincided with computerisation of the court office and relocation to another building. For the purpose of this report information is compared for the 36 week period in the three areas. Information was recorded by court staff on cases where the accused appeared in person at the first calling of their case (pleading diet) and was collected by a researcher. Information was also collected on accused who failed to appear in person and a warrant was granted for their arrest. Accused who appeared on warrant were included although checks were made to ensure that they had not previously appeared in relation to this case.

The information collected from the census was: age, sex and race of the accused; charges; how the accused appeared before the court (ie whether from police custody etc); whether solemn or summary procedure; whether a Bail Act charge was libelled; plea entered and the outcome of the appearance; whether a verbal application for bail was made and whether the procurator fiscal opposed bail in court.

Quality of data. To ensure quality and consistency of data recording, pilot tests of the census took place in Doon and Tweed and a researcher sat in court with those who were to complete the census in order to assess the ease with which information could be recorded. Accuracy checks were also carried out in Braid, although consistency was less of an issue there since only one member of staff was involved in recording the census there. In all areas court staff recording the information were issued with guidance notes. The data was collected by a researcher initially on a weekly basis and then every 4-6 weeks. Wherever possible, random checks on the accuracy of data recorded were carried out by a researcher.

Limitations. It was difficult for those recording the data to identify accused who were appearing from prison or remand (custody) on other charges. This was because in court they appear from the police cells as do those appearing from police custody and there is not necessarily any indication on the court papers that an accused has not recently been at liberty. Those collecting the information relied upon their local knowledge of the accused and the police officer in court to inform them if the accused was in custody. The census may therefore underestimate this group.

Missing Information. There was some information missing in all courts. Where the level was low this was accepted as unavoidable given the constraints upon the amount of time those collecting the data could devote to it. However in Doon the level of missing information tended to be higher than the other areas and data from this court was monitored more closely. The higher level of incomplete data primarily affects the information on verbal bail applications and opposition to bail in Doon. As such, the data on this in Doon has to be treated with caution.

Classification of cases. The charge was selected at the beginning of the process. For those accused of serious/sexual assault this was always classed as the main charge. Dishonesty was taken when most of the charges were dishonesty (for example, if someone had 5 charges of theft of motor vehicles plus one charge of police assault then this was classified as dishonesty). Charges of assault were taken in preference to charges of breach of the peace and charges were classified as 'other' only if there were no other charge types.This is different to the way in which criminal statistics are collected. Here the most serious charge is selected at the end of the process when the most serious charge is indicated as that receiving the most severe sentence.

The information on solemn cases is taken from the case papers and consists of the plea entered in court, whether a formal application for bail was made, and the result of the court appearance. The discussion in court was observed for summary cases and the details of the courtroom interaction about bail/remand was noted. In cases where information was unclear or the researcher was unsure of the argument presented in court, it was possible to clarify this later with the fiscal and defence agents who were also approached after court. It was not possible to observe the second and subsequent appearances of all cases.

Final disposal of census cases. The cases of all accused recorded in the first twelve weeks of the census in each area were followed through to final disposal. Data was recorded for the main charge and there is the possibility that an accused may have been found guilty and sentenced on a lesser charge. (See above for how the main charge was selected). The number of not guilty final disposals in the census may therefore be an over-representation. (For discussion of over-representation of not guilty outcomes for sample cases see below). It was also noted if the accused had failed to appear at a diet. Information was recorded on whether a Bail Act charge (Bail Scotland Act 1980 S(3)(1)(a)) was libelled and the final disposal of the Bail Act charge. In many cases there was no separate sentence for the Bail Act charge and this was recorded as 'concurrent with the sentence for the main charge'.

POLICE DETENTION SHEET DATA

Information was collected on all accused who were arrested in each area during the 12 weeks that fieldwork was undertaken. This information was taken from the detention sheet which is completed for every individual who passes through the police station. The information recorded on the detention sheet is limited and details sex, age, address, the charge and, in Doon and Braid, whether the person was on bail. For the purposes of this research, cases were included for those accused who were detained in custody or released either on undertaking or for summons. Accused who were arrested on warrant were excluded. This group accounted for 12% (71) accused at Doon; 5% (46) accused at Tweed and 19% (270) accused at Braid. During the study period a total of 511 accused were charged and processed by police in Doon, 900 accused in Tweed and 1193 accused in Braid.

In Doon and Braid the detention sheet included a tick box for the bail status of the accused to be recorded. In Tweed, whether the accused was on bail was not recorded routinely on the detention sheet. Police there made efforts to record this information on the sheet in order to assist the research, however, the very low percentage recorded (3% of all accused) suggests that this information is unlikely to be reliable.

STUDY SAMPLE

The study sample was drawn so as to focus on those accused for whom a bail decision might be relevant. The sample comprised of all accused who were detained in custody or released on undertaking. Accused arrested on warrant were only included in the sample if the alleged offence had taken place during the time that fieldwork had been on-going in that area. Researchers asked decision making officers to identify and to explain the significance of factors which had affected their decisions to detain accused in custody or release on undertaking. In addition the case papers and attached Scottish Criminal Record Office (SCRO) print out of accuseds' previous convictions and pending cases were examined and information recorded on the characteristics of accused (age, sex, race and address) and their records (previous convictions in the last 3 years; whether similar convictions in the past year; number of previous custodial sentences; most serious previous sentence; whether the accused was on bail when arrested and details of any bail order; number of outstanding bail orders; number of pending cases and whether these were similar; details of any outstanding court orders including the length of any deferred sentence). Details of the offence were also collected, and on the victim of the offence (including age, sex, race and whether any relationship with the accused) and on a measure of the harm which the victim suffered. The value of loss was noted where appropriate and details of the physical harm suffered were also noted. The measure of physical harm was insensitive as little detail is included in the police report and this made it difficult to measure certain types of harm such as emotional distress. For this reason the discussion of the harm suffered by the victim does not include cases of sexual assault.

As with the census, the charge was selected at the beginning of the process as decision-makers respond to the offences which, at that time, they consider to be the most serious, though these may not, at the stage of final disposal, be the offences for which the most serious sentence is given. The over-representation of not guilty outcomes which we noted above for accused in census cases, needs also to be considered for sample cases. However, care has been taken to minimise the possibility of misinterpretation of the significance of not guilty outcomes. For example, at table 5.6 in chapter 5 we discuss those accused who were found not guilty after having spent time on remand. All this group with the exception of one in Braid, were not convicted of *any* offences. The accused in Braid had been found not guilty of housebreaking but was convicted of attempting to pervert the course of justice (having initially given a false name to the police) and fined £200.

PROCURATOR FISCAL OBSERVATION

Researchers were present to observe marking of individual cases in the sample. Either during marking or shortly after, the marking depute was asked about their attitude to bail and to explain their decision in a case. The discussion focused on the specific circumstances of the case, the record of the accused, their bail history if relevant, the assessment of risk to the community and harm to the victim and the depute was asked to outline relevant process factors. In this way, the researchers were able to form an account of the factors which influenced decision-making. In cases where the accused was on bail, the depute was asked if their decision would have been the same if the accused had not been on bail and similarly if the accused was of no fixed abode, the depute was asked what their attitude to bail would be if the accused was able to provide a suitable address. This information was supplemented by semi-structured interviews which were also undertaken with procurator fiscal staff in each area in order to establish more general views on bail and its operation.

COURT OBSERVATION

We observed the first court hearing for all summary cases in the sample. We were not able to observe first appearances in solemn cases as these are heard in private, but we observed as many as possible of the second appearances of accused who were remanded in custody at the pleading diet. In cases where the final appearance was not observed, the case papers were checked on regular visits to the courts for details of the progress of the case and its disposal. A researcher made the last visit to collect information on final disposal to Doon and Tweed in July 1992 and to Braid in September 1992. At this stage 25% of cases (82% of solemn cases) were outstanding in Braid as it was only 6 months since fieldwork had finished there. A further visit was made in March 1993 (11 months after fieldwork finished) to collect information on the final disposals of sample cases. In March 1993 only 6% were still outstanding (2% of summary cases and 21% of solemn) and a further 3% had warrants for their arrest after a failure to appear at court which had not been executed. The time gap between the date of the final disposal of these cases and the disposal being checked by the researcher (> 6 months) meant that it was not possible to check these cases for further alleged offences.

BAIL ABUSE

One of the aims of the study was to examine the significance of breaching of bail conditions (bail abuse). This was done in two ways: firstly, the process of each case was followed and it was recorded if the accused failed to appear at any diet. It was recorded if the fiscal libelled a Bail Act charge for this failure to appear although in some cases no action was taken as there was found to be a reason for the failure to appear or the accused was given another chance to attend court. Secondly an indicator of the level of offending on bail was formed by checking each accused's record on the Scottish Criminal Record Office computer to note the number of pending cases libelled between the date that the accused was liberated by the court and final disposal. It is possible that this is an over-estimate of the level of bail abuse as the individuals may be found 'not guilty' of the alleged offences. It is affected by the accuracy of information entered on to the computer. In Doon and Tweed it was possible to check the record for alleged offences within a few days of the case reaching final disposal but in Braid, the information was entered onto computer at regional police headquarters and there was a delay of 4 to 6 weeks before the information on the accused's alleged offences would be entered on to computer. During this period it is possible that some cases reached final disposal etc. This meant that it was not possible for the researchers to check the records and details were provided by SCRO. The details of individuals to be checked were sent in batches to SCRO and this meant that there was some considerable time (> 2 months) in between the case reaching final disposal and the record being checked. This time lag means that information for Braid is not as accurate as in the other areas. Cases reaching final disposal after the end of July 1992 in Doon and Tweed, and September 1992 in Braid could not be checked for bail abuse. This means that many of the solemn cases in Braid were not checked as few of these had reached final disposal by September 1992 and for this reason only information for summary cases is compared in the discussion in chapter 7. It should be noted that the sampling decision for this study could be expected to give a higher level of bail abuse than other studies as the perceived likelihood of the accused offending and/or failing to appear at court plays a part in the initial police decision to keep the accused in custody or release on undertaking rather than release the accused for summons.

SHERIFF INTERVIEWS

At the end of the fieldwork in each area semi-structured interviews were conducted with sheriffs from the study courts. Nine sheriffs were interviewed for about 30 minutes each. The topics covered included the patterns of bail use which had been identified in a particular court, views on the practical functions of ordaining, granting bail or remanding both pre-trial and post-conviction; Wheatley guidelines; bail abuse; views on the further release of accused alleged to be in breach of an existing bail order; the use of special conditions.

BAIL APPEALS

Cases where a bail appeal was lodged were noted and where possible we spoke to the defence agents about the grounds for the appeal. The research also had access to the statement which the fiscal compiled for the high court outlining their grounds for opposing bail. The result of the appeal was noted. In the study all appeals were by the accused. Though there were no examples of appeals by the prosecution, prosecution appeals were discussed in interviews with fiscals and advocate deputes.

THE HIGH COURT

Semi-structured interviews, lasting 30 minutes each, were held with two advocates depute who regularly appear in bail appeals. The topics covered included the bail appeal process; factors in considering attitude to bail at appeal; attitude to further release of accused alleged to be in breach of an existing bail order; views on Crown bail appeals; communication with local procurator fiscal offices; Wheatley guidelines.

Semi-structured interviews, lasting 30 minutes each, were held with two high court judges who regularly hear bail appeals.

The topics covered included the bail appeal process; factors in considering granting or refusing bail at appeal; the functions of bail; use of special conditions; attitude to further release of accused alleged to be in breach of an existing bail order; views on Crown bail appeals; communication with lower courts; Wheatley guidelines.

ANNEX 2

COURT CENSUS

Table 2A Court Census: Main Charges Libelled*

	Doon	*Tweed*	*Braid*
Serious/sexual assault	*5%*	*5%*	*8%*
Dishonesty	*33%*	*30%*	*32%*
Assault	*10%*	*15%*	*9%*
BOP	*16%*	*13%*	*12%*
Other *	*37%*	*38%*	*40%*
Total	*100%*	*100%*	*100%*
N=	1126	2511	1582

*Other = road traffic offences; offences against public justice; drugs offences; miscellaneous crimes and offences

Table 2B Court Census - Summary Cases: Plea Entered at First Calling*

	Doon	*Tweed*	*Braid*
Not guilty	*58%*	*41%*	*45%*
Guilty	*42%*	*59%*	*55%*
Total	*100%*	*100%*	*100%*
N=	944	2074	1284

* Accused for whom a warrant was issued after they failed to appear in Court have been excluded. (42 at Doon; 90 at Tweed; 30 at Braid). Cases continued without plea have been excluded (43 at Doon; 57 at Tweed; 27 at Braid)

Table 2C Court Census: Outcome of First Appearance by Charge Doon (solemn + summary cases)

	Bail	*Remand*	*Ordained*
Serious/sexual assault	*66%*	*21%*	*14%*
Dishonesty	*69%*	*14%*	*16%*
Assault	*70%*	*11%*	*19%*
BOP	*83%*	*4%*	*13%*
Other	*48%*	*11%*	*41%*
Total	*66%*	*12%*	*22%*
N=	534	94	181

TWEED (solemn + summary cases)

	Bail	*Remand*	*Ordained*
Serious/sexual assault	*58%*	*31%*	*12%*
Dishonesty	*47%*	*19%*	*34%*
Assault	*58%*	*12%*	*30%*
BOP	*52%*	*11%*	*37%*
Other	*34%*	*13%*	*53%*
Total	*47%*	*16%*	*27%*
N=	748	253	592

BRAID (solemn + summary cases)

	Bail	*Remand*	*Ordained*
Serious/sexual assault	*37%*	*56%*	*7%*
Dishonesty	*46%*	*40%*	*14%*
Assault	*51%*	*26%*	*23%*
BOP	*53%*	*28%*	*18%*
Other	*46%*	*21%*	*32%*
Total	*47%*	*34%*	*20%*
N=	502	360	209

Table 2D Court Census Initial 12 Weeks: Final Disposal for Individual Offence Types

Serious/sexual assault*

	Doon	*Tweed*	*Braid*
Imprisonment	*21%*	*27%*	*53%*
CSO	*0*	*9%*	*16%*
Probation	*14%*	*6%*	*0*
Monetary penalty(MP)	*21%*	*24%*	*3%*
MP + disqualification	*0*	*0*	*0*
Admonition	*14%*	*0*	*3%*
Not guilty	*29%*	*33%*	*16%*
Other *	*0*	*0*	*0*
Total	14	33	31

* Excludes 1 case remaining incomplete in Doon

Dishonesty*

	Doon	*Tweed*	*Braid*
Imprisonment	*18%*	*32%*	*42%*
CSO	*9%*	*7%*	*8%*
Probation	*10%*	*12%*	*3%*
Monetary penalty(MP)	*24%*	*24%*	*21%*
MP + disqualification	*2%*	*4%*	*6%*
Admonition	*4%*	*6%*	*8%*
Not guilty	*35%*	*14%*	*12%*
Other	*0*	*1%*	*0*
Total	*100%*	*100%*	*100%*
N=	135	215	106

*Excludes cases remaining incomplete = 3 in Doon, 19 in Tweed and 5 in Braid. Also excludes outstanding warrants - 2 in Doon, 4 in Tweed and 1 in Braid

Assault*

	Doon	*Tweed*	*Braid*
Imprisonment	*6%*	*7%*	*5%*
CSO	*6%*	*5%*	*10%*
Probation	*0*	*2%*	*0*
Monetary penalty(MP)	*58%*	*63%*	*55%*
MP + disqualification	*0*	*0*	*0*
Admonition	*6%*	*5%*	*5%*
Not guilty	*22%*	*18%*	*25%*
Other	*0*	*0*	*0*
Total	*100%*	*100%*	*100%*
N=	36	96	20

*Excludes cases remaining incomplete = 2 in Doon, 6 in Tweed and 1 in Braid. Also excludes 1 outstanding warrant in Doon and 2 in Tweed

Breach of the peace*

	Doon	*Tweed*	*Braid*
Imprisonment	*1%*	*10%*	*32%*
CSO	*3%*	*4%*	*4%*
Probation	*0*	*6%*	*4%*
Monetary penalty(MP)	*59%*	*55%*	*35%*
MP + disqualification	*0*	*0*	*0*
Admonition	*10%*	*11%*	*7%*
Not guilty	*24%*	*13%*	*19%*
Other *	*3%*	*1%*	*0*
Total	*100%*	*100%*	*100%*
N=	70	141	57

*Excludes cases remaining incomplete = 1 in Doon and 8 in Braid. Also excludes 1 outstanding warrant in Tweed

Other*

	Doon	*Tweed*	*Braid*
Imprisonment	*12%*	*5%*	*10%*
CSO	*<1%*	*3%*	*<1%*
Probation	*<1%*	*4%*	*1%*
Monetary penalty(MP)	*16%*	*17%*	*13%*
MP + disqualification	*50%*	*59%*	*67%*
Admonition	*6%*	*4%*	*4%*
Not guilty	*15%*	*7%*	*3%*
Total	*100%*	*100%*	*100%*
N=	142	313	206

* Excludes cases remaining incomplete - 4 in Doon, 8 in Tweed and 2 in Braid. Also excludes outstanding warrants - 2 in Doon and 3 in Tweed

ANNEX 3

CHARACTERISTICS OF ACCUSED AND CASES IN THE SAMPLE

Table 3A Accused Arrested by Police During the 12 Study Weeks: Age

	*Doon**		*Tweed*		*Braid*	
	All accused	Sample	All accused	Sample	All accused	Sample
Under 16	*9%*	*0*	*9%*	*1%*	*12%*	*1%*
16-20	*36%*	*44%*	*32%*	*27%*	*38%*	*42%*
21-30	*29%*	*33%*	*33%*	*45%*	*27%*	*37%*
31-40	*14%*	*11%*	*14%*	*17%*	*14%*	*12%*
41-60	*9%*	*6%*	*11%*	*11%*	*8%*	*8%*
61+	*3%*	*6%*	*1%*	*0*	*2%*	*0*
Total	*100%*	*100%*	*100%*	*100%*	*100%*	*100%*
N=	511	177	900	222	1193	178

* In 1 sample case in Doon the age of the accused was not recorded

Table 3B Social Characteristics of Accused in the Sample

	*Doon**		*Tweed*		*Braid*	
	Custody	U-taking	Custody	U-taking	Custody	U-taking
Age						
Under 16	*0*	*0*	*<1%*	*0*	*0*	*5%*
16-20	*46%*	*37%*	*25%*	*41%*	*40%*	*57%*
21-30	*30%*	*45%*	*47%*	*31%*	*39%*	*24%*
31-40	*12%*	*8%*	*17%*	*16%*	*13%*	*10%*
41-60	*5%*	*11%*	*11%*	*13%*	*9%*	*5%*
61+	*7%*	*0*	*0*	*0*	*0*	*0*
Total	*100%*	*101%*	*100%*	*101%*	*101%*	*101%*
N=	139	38	190	32	157	21

*In 1 sample case in Doon the age of the accused was not recorded

	*Doon**		*Tweed*		*Braid*	
	Custody	U-taking	Custody	U-taking	Custody	U-taking
Sex						
Male	*94%*	*97%*	*94%*	*84%*	*91%*	*81%*
Female	*7%*	*3%*	*6%*	*16%*	*9%*	*19%*
Total	*101%*	*100%*	*100%*	*100%*	*100%*	*100%*
N=	139	39	190	32	157	21

Address						
NFA	*18%*	*0*	*23%*	*0*	*17%*	*0*
Local (temp)	*10%*	*5%*	*8%*	*6%*	*3%*	*10%*
Local (perm)	*68%*	*51%*	*57%*	*94%*	*70%*	*81%*
Elsewhere	*4%*	*41%*	*12%*	*0*	*10%*	*10%*
Total	*100%*	*100%*	*100%*	*100%*	*100%*	*100%*
N=	139	38	190	32	157	21

*In 1 sample case in Doon the address of the accused was not recorded

Table 3C Sample Offence Type

	Doon		*Tweed*		*Braid*	
	Custody	U-taking	Custody	U-taking	Custody	U-taking
Serious/sexual assault	*12%*	*3%*	*15%*	*3%*	*19%*	*14%*
Dishonesty	*37%*	*28%*	*35%*	*6%*	*39%*	*48%*
Assault	*14%*	*31%*	*23%*	*19%*	*14%*	*5%*
BOP	*22%*	*36%*	*16%*	*72%*	*18%*	*14%*
Other	*15%*	*3%*	*11%*	*0*	*10%*	*19%*
Total	*100%*	*100%*	*100%*	*100%*	*100%*	*100%*
N=	139	39	190	32	157	21

Table 3D Sample Accused with Convictions in the Previous Three Years

	*Doon**		*Tweed*		*Braid***	
	Custody	U-taking	Custody	U-taking	Custody	U-taking
No previous convictions	*18%*	*49%*	*30%*	*56%*	*22%*	*29%*
Previous convictions	*82%*	*51%*	*70%*	*44%*	*78%*	*71%*
Total	*100%*	*100%*	*100%*	*100%*	*100%*	*100%*
N=	137	37	190	32	156	21

*In 2 custody and 2 undertaking cases the information was not available as there was no computer printout. 3 of these were not proceeded or went to the District Court

** In 1 case the accused was released for citation after a review of the decision

Table 3E Most Serious Sentences Served by Sample Accused with Previous Convictions

	Doon		*Tweed*		*Braid*	
	Custody	U-taking	Custody	U-taking	Custody	U-taking
Admonished	*4%*	*18%*	*4%*	*0*	*3%*	*0*
Monetary penalty	*44%*	*42%*	*36%*	*86%*	*42%*	*20%*
Probation	*7%*	*8%*	*8%*	*7%*	*2%*	*13%*
Com. Service Order	*15%*	*7%*	*8%*	*0*	*4%*	*20%*
Custody	*31%*	*11%*	*41%*	*7%*	*49%*	*40%*
Other*	*0*	*0*	*2%*	*0*	*0*	*7%*
Total	*101%*	*100%*	*100%*	*100%*	*100%*	*100%*
N=	110	18	132	14	116	15

*Other includes disqualification from driving, absolute discharge and offences dealt with by the childrens panel.

Excluding 3 accused in Doon and 5 in Braid who had previous convictions although sentence was currently deferred on these. Tweed - 1 case type of sentence was not recorded as no print out of the record was available with the case papers.

Table 3F Sample Accused with Cases Pending

	*Doon**		*Tweed*		*Braid*	
	Custody	U-taking	Custody	U-taking	Custody	U-taking
No pending case	*35%*	*63%*	*51%*	*88%*	*41%*	*43%*
Analogous pending case	*46%*	*21%*	*38%*	*3%*	*42%*	*38%*
Non-analogous pending case	*16%*	*16%*	*11%*	*6%*	*17%*	*19%*
Nature pending unknown	*3%*	*0*	*0*	*3%*	*1%*	*0*
Total	*100%*	*100%*	*100%*	*100%*	*101%*	*100%*
N=	138	38	190	32	157	21

*Doon 2 cases missing as there was no print out of the record available with the case papers.

Table 3G Sample Accused Subject to Current Court Orders (excluding bail)

	Doon		*Tweed*		*Braid*	
	Custody	U-taking	Custody	U-taking	Custody	U-taking
No court order	*73%*	*84%*	*68%*	*94%*	*73%*	*67%*
Deferred sentence	*17%*	*16%*	*22%*	*3%*	*8%*	*5%*
Probation order	*5%*	*0*	*1%*	*3%*	*4%*	*14%*
Com. Service Order	*1%*	*0*	*3%*	*0*	*<1%*	*5%*
Other*	*4%*	*0*	*6%*	*0*	*14%*	*10%*
Total	*100%*	*100%*	*100%*	*100%*	*100%*	*100%*
N=	138	38	190	32	157	21

*Other = warrant, licence, Matrimonial Homes Act interdict.
Doon 2 cases missing as print out not available with the case papers.

Table 3H Sample Accused on Bail when Arrested

	Doon		*Tweed*		*Braid*	
	Custody	U-taking	Custody	U-taking	Custody	U-taking
On bail	*33%*	*5%*	*28%*	*0*	*18%*	*24%*
Not on bail	*67%*	*95%*	*72%*	*100%*	*82%*	*76%*
Total	*100%*	*100%*	*100%*	*100%*	*100%*	*100%*
N=	139	39	190	32	157	21

ANNEX 4

SAMPLE PROCEEDED IN THE SHERIFF COURT

It was important to ensure a sufficient representation of dishonesties since previous research has shown that accused in this type of case may be more likely to be involved in offending on bail. The sample at Tweed was boosted to improve the representation by taking details of custodies with dishonesty charges from a neighbouring police division (together the two divisions cover the whole city of Tweed). This resulted in the addition of 13 accused. Sensitivity checks were carried out on the data to control for the possibility that the inclusion of the extra cases might bias the sample. These accused were not included in the discussion of police decisions as they were made in a different police office to that in which the research was located. They are included in the figures below. These figures exclude the no proceedings and district court cases.

Table 4A Sample: Case Type Proceeded in Sheriff Court

	Doon		*Tweed*		*Braid*	
	Custody	U-taking	Custody	U-taking	Custody	U-taking
Serious/sexual assault	*13%*	*3%*	*17%*	*5%*	*19%*	*16%*
Dishonesty	*40%*	*25%*	*38%*	*10%*	*40%*	*42%*
Assault	*17%*	*38%*	*24%*	*25%*	*14%*	*5%*
BOP	*24%*	*34%*	*14%*	*60%*	*18%*	*16%*
Other	**6%**	**0**	**8%**	**0**	**9%**	**21%**
Total	*100%*	*100%*	*100%*	*100%*	*100%*	*100%*
N=	115	32	168	20	152	19

ANNEX 5

COURT DECISIONS

Table 5A Sample Appearing from Undertaking: Outcomes of First Court Appearance for Accused in Summary and Solemn Cases

	Doon	*Tweed*	*Braid*	
	Summary	Summary	Summary	Solemn
Bail (standard)	*69%*	*5%*	*50%*	*0*
Bail (special)	*0*	*5%*	*6%*	*0*
Remand	*3%*	*0*	*13%*	*100%*
Ordained	*9%*	*45%*	*6%*	*0*
Final disposal	*19%*	*40%*	*6%*	*0*
Warrant	*0*	*5%*	*19%*	*0*
Total	*100%*	*100%*	*100%*	*100%*
N=	32	20	16	3

Table 5B Sample Appearing from Undertaking: Marking Deputes Attitude to Bail in Cases where Accused in Summary Cases Plead Guilty*

	Doon	*Tweed*	*Braid*
Agree	*88%*	*100%*	*33%*
Oppose	*12%*	*0*	*67%*
Total	*100%*	*100%*	*100%*
N=	8	9	3

*Excluding 1 case at Tweed and 3 cases at Braid where the accused failed to appear at court and a warrant was issued

Table 5C Sample Summary Cases Appearing from Undertaking: Application for Bail

	Doon	*Tweed*	*Braid*
Yes	*88%*	*72%*	*91%*
No	*12%*	*28%*	*9%*
Total	*100%*	*100%*	*100%*
N=	26	11	11

Table 5D Sample Summary Cases Appearing from Undertaking: Not Guilty Plea: Procurator Fiscal Atttitude to Bail by Outcome of Court

	Doon		*Tweed*	*Braid*	
	Agree	Oppose	Agree	Agree	Oppose
Bail (standard)	87%	100%	10%	88%	100%
Bail (special)	0	0	10%	13%	0
Remand	0	0	0	0	0
Ordained	13%	0	70%	0	0
Final disposal	0	0	10%	0	0
Warrant	0	0	0	0	0
Total	100%	100%	100%	100%	0
N=	23	1	10	8	1

Table 5E Sample summary cases appearing from undertaking: guilty plea: outcome of cour

	Doon	*Tweed*	*Braid*
Bail (standard)	13%	0	0
Bail (special)	0	0	0
Remand	13%	0	33%
Ordained	0	22%	33%
Final disposal	75%	78%	33%
Total	100%	100%	100%
N=	8	9	3

Table 5F Sample cases appearing from undertaking: final disposal

	Doon	*Tweed*	*Braid*	
	Summary	Summary	Summary	Solemn
Imprisonment	3%	0	25%	33%
CSO	0	0	0	0
Probation	6%	5%	13%	0
Monetary penalty	59%	65%	31%	0
Admonition	13%	5%	0	0
Not guilty	13%	15%	25%	0
No Proceedings	6%	0	0	0
Other	0	10%	6%	67%
Warrant	0	0	0	0
Total	100%	100%	100%	100%
N=	32	20	16	3

TABLE 5G Sample Accused: Final Disposal by the Outcome of the First Court (solemn and summary)

DOON

	Remand	Bail	Ordained	Final disposal
Imprisonment	20%(4)	7%(7)	13%(1)	12%(2)
CSO	10%(2)	3%(3)	0	0
Probation	15%(3)	6%(6)	0	0
Monetary penalty	10%(2)	44%(45)	25%(2)	88%(15)
Admonition	15%(3)	11%(11)	13%(1)	0
Not guilty	15%(3)	17%(17)	25%(2)	0
No proceedings	15%(3)	9%(9)	25%(2)	0
Other	0	2%(2)	0	0
Warrant	0	2%(2)	0	0
Total	100%	100%	100%	100%
N=	20	102	8	17

TWEED

	Remand	Bail	Ordained	Final disposal
Imprisonment	55%(17)	17%(16)	0	22%(9)
CSO	7%(2)	14%(13)	0	0
Probation	10%(3)	11%(11)	5%(1)	0
Monetary penalty	10%(3)	32%(31)	60%(12)	71%(29)
Admonition	0	3%(3)	5%(1)	5%(2)
Not guilty	6%(2)	14%(13)	10%(2)	2%(1)
No proceedings	3%(1)	1%(1)	0	0
Other	10%(3)	7%(7)	20%(4)	0
Warrant	0	1%(1)	0	0
Total	100%	100%	100%	100%
N=	31	96	20	41

BRAID

	Remand	Bail	Ordained	Final disposal
Imprisonment	42%(31)	24%(18)	0	56%(10)
CSO	3%(2)	9%(7)	0	0
Probation	5%(4)	4%(3)	0	0
Monetary penalty	15%(11)	30%(23)	67%(2)	33%(6)
Admonition	1%(1)	3%(2)	33%(1)	0
Not guilty	14%(10)	22%(17)	0	11%(2)
No proceedings	5%(4)	3%(2)	0	0
Other	12%(9)	3%(2)	0	0
Warrant	1%(1)	4%(3)	0	0
Total	100%	100%	100%	100%
N=	73	77	3	18

Table 5H Sample Accused: Final Disposal by Type of Charge (summary and solemn)

DOON

	Ser/Sex assault	Dishonesty	Assault	Breach of peace	Other
Imprisonment	13%(2)	17%(9)	0	8%(3)	0
CSO	0	6%(3)	6%(2)	0	0
Probation	6%(1)	13%(7)	0	3%(1)	0
Monetary penalty	38%(6)	26%(14)	66%(21)	50%(19)	57%(4)
Admonition	6%(1)	7%(4)	6%(2)	16%(6)	29%(2)
Not guilty	0	19%(10)	16%(5)	18%(7)	0
No proceedings	38%(6)	11%(6)	3%(1)	3%(1)	0
Other *	0	0	3%(1)	3%(1)	0
Warrant	0	2%(1)	0	0	14%(1)
Total	16	54	32	38	8

*Other = case incomplete (including deferred sentences), Hospital orders

TWEED

	Ser/Sex assault	Dishonesty	Assault	Breach of peace	Other
Imprisonment	24%(7)	29%(19)	17%(8)	14%(5)	23%(3)
CSO	7%(2)	12%(8)	4%(2)	6%(2)	8%(1)
Probation	10%(3)	12%(8)	4%(2)	0	15%(2)
Monetary penalty	45%(13)	26%(17)	54%(25)	49%(17)	23%(3)
Admonition	0	2%(1)	2%(1)	9%(3)	8%(1)
Not guilty	3%(1)	9%(6)	11%(5)	14%(5)	8%(1)
No proceedings	3%(1)	2%(1)	0	0	0
Other *	7%(2)	8%(5)	7%(3)	9%(3)	8%(1)
Warrant	0	0	0	0	8%(1)
Total	29	65	46	35	13

*Other = case incomplete (including deferred sentences), Hospital orders

BRAID

	Ser/Sex assault	Dishonesty	Assault	Breach of peace	Other
Imprisonment	34%(11)	43%(30)	14%(3)	27%(8)	39%(7)
CSO	3%(1)	4%(3)	9%(2)	10%(3)	0
Probation	3%(1)	6%(4)	0	3%(1)	6%(1)
Monetary penalty	9%(3)	23%(16)	27%(6)	37%(11)	33%(6)
Admonition	0	0	14%(3)	3%(1)	0
Not guilty	13%(4)	20%(14)	23%(5)	13%(4)	11%(2)
No proceedings	13%(4)	0	5%(1)	3%(1)	0
Other *	22%(7)	1%(1)	5%(1)	3%(1)	6%(1)
Warrant	3%(1)	1%(1)	5%(1)	0	6%(1)
Total	100%	100%	100%	100%	100%
N=	32	69	22	30	18

*Other = case incomplete (including deferred sentences), Hospital orders

ANNEX 6

ILLUSTRATIVE CASE HISTORIES OF ACCUSED ALLEGED TO HAVE OFFENDED ON BAIL

Accused identifiers prefixed by X are from Doon; by Y are from Tweed and by Z are from Braid.

Within 4 Weeks of Bail

X79 charged with **theft by opening a lockfast place, vandalism and offending on bail** (commercial property loss between £11 and £50 fully recovered) and was charged with **four further offences** within two weeks of his release on bail the first additional charge being **housebreaking**. X79, who was to appear in the sample on five occasions, had **no previous convictions** in the past three years but had been placed **on bail** for breach of the peace a fortnight earlier. He had three analogous pending cases. **Police** detained him as he and his co-accused were described as "**known active housebreakers**" who had admitted more offences when interviewed. The **fiscal agreed bail** as though X79 was on bail the present offence was described as "**trivial**". In **court bail was granted** with no discussion and a trial date was set. X79 appeared for each court date and was eventually **fined £40, ordered to pay compensation of £10 and admonished on the bail charge.**

Y97 was charged with having committed **seven further offences** the first of which was alleged to have occurred within two weeks of his release on bail. Originally charged with **conspiracy to steal a car** the first additional charge was that of **theft by shipbreaking**. In the initial incident he had been caught with a group of three other co-accused in possession of tools believed to be for stealing cars in an area where there had recently been a spate of car thefts. Y97 had similar convictions in the previous year, his most serious sentence had been probation, he was **not on bail at time of original arrest, had one bail conviction** in previous three years, three analogous pending cases and was currently on a three week deferred sentence. The **fiscal agreed bail** since they did not consider the offence to be very serious, although they wanted bail conditions to be attached to Y97's release as he had been kept in police custody. **In court bail was granted** and a trial set for three months later. On the trial date the accused pled guilty and had sentence deferred for a social enquiry report and a community service report. Bail was not continued and Y97 was simply ordained for the next court at which he was given **fourteen days detention.**

At the time of final disposal Z84 was charged with having committed **nine further offences** the first of which was alleged to have occurred within 2 weeks of his release by the court. Originally charged with **breach of the peace and shoplifting**, the first additional charge was that of **possessing an offensive weapon**. In the initial incident the accused was alleged to have been challenging members of the public to fight late at night. Z84 had similar convictions in the previous year, his most serious sentence had been a fine, he was not on bail at time of original arrest, had no history of bail convictions, five non-analogous pending cases. The **fiscal**, who described Z84 as a "continual thief" whose record was "getting close to a course of conduct" **had planned to oppose bail** at the initial court because he had **no fixed address**, although it was stated that if an address were to be offered bail would be agreed. However **no application for bail** was made at court because Z84 lacked an address and he was remanded. Five days later there was a **bail review** at which the accused offered an address and **bail was granted**. A month later he pled guilty and had sentence deferred and subsequently was sentenced to **200 hours community service.**

Within Eight Weeks of Bail

X90 was the same person as X79 but on this occasion he was charged with **housebreaking and breach of bail** (household, value **£101-£250 not recovered**). **He was charged with a** further seven offences the first of which was **theft by opening a lockfast place** and was within five weeks of this present bail order. He had **no previous convictions,** though he had been known to the children's panel, but had **two outstanding orders**, one of which had been granted the week previously (see X79) he had four pending cases and was now on a deferred sentence. **Police** had **initially** been **going to release X90 on undertaking** as the officer who had dealt with it would not be on duty to complete the enquiry. However, another officer thought that **since he was on bail, property was unrecovered and a third co-accused had still to be traced,** there should be no question of this being other than a **custody**. The **fiscal agreed bail** as though on bail, no previous convictions, the evidence was weak and X90 was only sixteen. He was not prepared to consider pending charges. At **court bail was granted** with no discussion. Subsequently X79 pled guilty, by which time he was on probation for other matters and sentence was deferred to obtain reports about his progress on probation. Finally he was given **100 hours community service.**

Y36 originally charged with **two breaches of the peace and one breach of bail (3(1)(b))**. At time of final disposal he was charged with **eight further offences** the first additional charge was that of **housebreaking** which was alleged to have occurred seven weeks after his release on bail. In the original incident he had been attempting to force entry to his parental home from which he was banned by interdict. **Detained by police** because he was **on bail,** had **similar convictions**, was NFA and police thought there would be difficulty in tracing him for court. There was a history of accused assaulting and associated offences against his parents. Y36 had **analogous convictions** in the **previous year,** two custodial sentences in the previous three years, was **on one bail order in relation to a charge of wilful fireraising, had three bail convictions** for offending on bail in previous three years and **one for failing to appear at court.** He had four analogous pending cases and was currently on deferred sentence by the court. The **fiscal opposed bail** because Y36 was on bail, was in **breach of interdict** and because of his **previous convictions.** In court he **pled guilty** and his agent offered an address. The fiscal narrated the incident, indicated that Y36 was on bail and sentence deferred and suggested that the pending charges were analogous and that the victims were always Y36's parents. The defence agent confirmed this and asked for a deferred sentence for psychiatric reports which had already been organised. Y36 was **ordained by the court** and subsequently **failed to appear** for his next court and a warrant was issued. He was arrested a month later and was sentenced to **two months imprisonment** on each charge concurrently.

Z156, originally charged with **housebreaking,** at time of final disposal was charged with one **further offence**, another **housebreaking,** which was alleged to have occurred

6 weeks after he had been released on bail. He was originally detained by the police because he had analogous pending cases and because the CID wanted to interview him on other matters. He had **similar convictions within the last year and five analogous pending cases.** He had **one conviction for breach of bail** within the previous three years and his most serious sentence had been a fine. The **fiscal agreed** bail because Z156 was not considered to have much of a record and **he was not on bail.** At **court** he pled not guilty and was **released on bail.** He **later pled guilty** and was **remanded** in custody for three weeks after which he received a 4 **month custodial sentence.**

Within Twelve Weeks of Bail

X174 originally charged with **assault and offending on bail** (victim had a broken nose), at time of disposal he was charged with a **further three offences** (two **assaults and a breach of the peace**) the earliest of which was eleven weeks after his release on bail. X174 appeared in the sample on two other occasions (X2 and X153 and accounts for 3 of the bail orders breached at Doon). Though he had convictions within the previous three years he had **no analogous convictions within the previous year,** his most serious sentence was a community service order and he currently had **two bail orders, one of which had been made about 2 months prior and the other a month prior to the present case.** They were for housebreaking, bail and a prevention of crime charge. X174 had four non-analogous pending cases and **one bail conviction** in the previous three years. **Police kept him because of the seriousness of the assault and the breach of bail.** The **fiscal agreed bail** (and sought bail conditions) because of the nature of the incident, which was described as 'bailable' and **his record was not considered to justify custody.** There was no discussion in court and **bail was granted.** Three months later at the trial date, the **not guilty plea was accepted.**

Y15 originally charged with **assault, breach of the peace, theft, breach of bail, possessing an offensive weapon** and subsequently charged with **theft,** had **five further offences** alleged at the time of final disposal of the original offence, the first of which was ten weeks after the initial release on bail. Y15 appeared in the sample on three occasions (Y2;Y34) and accounts for three of the thirteen accused identified as having potentially breached their bail. Originally detained by police because of an assault with a broken bottle (slight injury to victim) and theft valued between £50 and £100 (unrecovered), he was **detained by police because he was on bail.** Had he not been on bail police said they would have released him as he was only sixteen. He had **similar convictions in the previous year** but had no sentences as was on deferred sentence, though he had previously been under supervision of the children's panel. He had **one outstanding bail order granted three days prior to his arrest (linked to breach of the peace charges**), had two analogous pending cases and **no history of breaching bail.** Unusually for this area, the **fiscal** libelled a breach of bail charge for each bail order breached and **opposed bail** because the offence with the broken bottle was "semi-serious". The **fiscal** did not expect Y15 to be locked up because he had only one recorded previous conviction for which he was currently on bail, but argued that "it's my public duty to try and get him locked up if these (charges) are true". In **court** the fiscal opposed bail because of the recent bail order and the escalation in offending as charges related to two separate incidents. "There is no evidence that this young man's prepared to behave himself". The defence argued that though the record was not trivial it was not serious and there had been insufficient grounds put forward by the fiscal to deprive Y15 of his liberty, and drew attention to a medical condition which Y15 had. The **sheriff** was the same one who had previously granted bail to Y15 and stated that he was reluctant to lock up someone so young and with such a short record. **Bail was granted.** Y15 appeared for all subsequent courts, pleading guilty three months later and having sentence deferred for good behaviour. Two months after this he was given **80 hours community service.**

Z105 originally faced seven charges of **theft by opening a lockfast place and one housebreaking** (loss between £250 and £1000 - no recovery). He was on bail for a total of five months, had **four new charges** libelled in that period, the first additional charge was that of **housebreaking,** ten weeks after his release on bail by the court. He had **similar convictions within the previous year** and his most serious sentence had been a fine; he was **not on bail, had no history of breaching bail** and had one non-analogous charge pending. The **fiscal agreed bail** and though it was **granted by the court,** the sheriff made it clear that he did not think bail should have been granted stating that bail was given "solely on the grounds that there is no opposition". Z105 appeared for all six subsequent diets and was ultimately sentenced to pay **£50 compensation to each of his eight victims.**

After Twelve Weeks on Bail

X144 originally charged with a **police assault** (heavy bruising, suspected fracture)and with **trying to rescue a co-acccused who had been arrested,** was charged with **two further breaches of the peace** the first of which was twenty-one weeks after he had been released on bail. He had convictions within the previous three years though no **analogous convictions within the previous year,** his most serious sentence having been a fine. He was **not on bail,** and had **no bail convictions,** though he had five analogous pending cases. The **fiscal** agreed bail, although he described the incident as a"serious matter" as X144 was **not on bail.** The **court** granted bail after no discussion. X144 appeared for all subsequent courts and was eventually **fined £100.**

Y247 originally charged with **breach of the peace, police assault, attempting to defeat the ends of justice and offending on bail** twenty-five weeks later had **two further charges, shoplifting and theft motor vehicle.** Although he had convictions in the previous three years he had **no analogous convictions within the previous year,** his most serious sentence had been a fine. **On two bail orders** each about three months old (one for being found in circumstances likely to commit crime and one for theft by opening a lockfast place and breach of bail). He had nine non-analogous pending cases and had **one bail conviction in the previous three years. He had failed to appear to answer three deferred sentences.** The **fiscal** opposed bail as he was NFA and was on bail, though the depute would accept an address if one was offered. At court pled not guilty and the depute indicated that they would be opposing bail before the defence made an application. Defence made a bail application, pointing out that accused had to be taken to hospital as a result of his encounter with the police. The accused had been granted bail at the district court that morning and there had been no fiscal opposition to that, asks for probation on sentence deferred matters. The sheriff indicated that their initial response to the deferred sentences was to consider custody, however because there were few previous convictions Y247 was placed on probation for those matters and **granted bail** on the present charges "it would be pointless refusing you bail as you're going to be on probation". Y247 **failed to appear for one further court** but appeared for the other two and was ultimately given **1 month prison on these charges and two months prison for the bail charge** to run concurrently with sentences which he was receiving on other matters.

Z160 was originally charged with **breach of the peace, resisting arrest, police assault** and a district court warrant outstanding at the time of her arrest. Detained by the police because of a large number of previous convictions. She had previously been released by police for summons, had not appeared at court and a warrant had been taken for her arrest. Sixteen weeks after her release on bail she had **two further charges** alleged for **breach of the peace.** Although she had convictions in the previous three years she had **no analogous convictions in the previous year.** Her record showed that she'd had fifteen custodial sentences in the previous thee years, she was **not on bail at time of arrest although she'd had three bail convictions in the previous three years,** she had four analogous pending cases. The **fiscal** marked Z160's case as bail to be opposed on the grounds of her record and that she'd had **8 bail convictions in the previous four years** and described her as a "regular trouble maker". At **court** Z160 pled guilty, had her sentence deferred for three months for good behaviour and bail was continued. She **failed to appear** for her deferred sentence and appeared in court one month later facing a Bail Act charge 3(1)(a). She pled guilty and was sentenced to **three months** prison for the original charges and one month's consecutive imprisonment for the **bail offence.**

ANNEX 7

BAIL ABUSE

Table 7A Outcome for Sample Accused for Whom Warrant Issued After Failure to Appear*

	Doon	*Tweed*	*Braid*
Imprisoned	29%	30%	90%
CSO	14%	20%	0
Probation	0	10%	0
Monetary penalty	0	30%	10%
Admonished	14%	0	0
Not guilty	14%	5%	0
No proceedings	29%	5%	0
Total	100%	100%	100%
N=	7	20	10

*Excluding 2 accused in Doon; 1 in Tweed and 4 in Braid where the warrant was still outstanding; and 1 in Tweed and 2 in Braid whose cases were still outstanding

Court Census Data

Most of those recorded in the census did not have any bail or similar charge libelled. Of those who did, the most frequently libelled charge was that of offending while on bail. The differences between the areas were small although Braid, the area with the highest level of remand, had the lowest proportion of accused appearing with bail charges and Doon, the area which made the greatest use of bail, had the highest proportion accused of breaching bail. This pattern was reflected in the sample (see chapter 7).

Table 7B Census: All Accused with Bail Act or Similar Charges

	Doon	*Tweed*	*Braid*
Fail to appear - B(S)AS3(1)(a)	2%	1%	4%
Offend on bail - B(S)AS3(1)(b)	18%	14%	11%
Other B(S)Act	0	1%	1%
Fail to appear	1%	1%	1%
(Crim Procedure Act 1975 S338 & S295)			
Pervert course of justice	1%	2%	3%
No bail or similar charge	78%	82%	83%
Total	100%	100%	100%
N=	1126	2511	1582

Table 7C Census: Disposal of Bail Related Charge

	Doon	*Tweed*	*Braid*
Custody	6%	8%	25%
CSO	1%	1%	0
Probation	0	1%	0
Fine	11%	19%	17%
Admonish	10%	3%	7%
Concurrent *	47%	48%	37%
Not guilty	25%	19%	14%
Total	100%	100%	100%
N=	93	134	71

Braid 2 outcomes not recorded
*Disposal not separately stated from that for the main charge

A higher proportion of accused were found not guilty of bail act charges in Doon than in either of the other areas. In Tweed and Braid the proportion of accused found not to be guilty of bail act charges was higher than the proportion not guilty of all other charges. Although this was also true of Doon the difference in that area was negligible. (not guilty for all charges = 24% at Doon; 12% at Tweed and 9% at Braid).

BIBLIOGRAPHY

Brookes, S, 1991. **The Effect of 'Re-offending' on Bail on Crime in Avon and Somerset.** Avon and Somerset Constabulary.

Brennan, T, 1987. *Classification: An Overview of Selected Metholodigcal Issues* in Gottfredson, D M and Tonry, M (Eds), 1987. **Prediction and Classification: Criminal Justice Decision Making. Chicago:** The University of Chicago Press: 201-248.

Brink, B and Stone, C, 1988 (March). *Offenders who do not ask for Bail.* **The Criminal Law Review:** 137-196.

Docherty, M J and East, R, 1985. *Bail Decisions in Magistrates' Courts* in **British Journal of Criminology** Volume 25, No 3: 251-266.

Goldkamp, J S and Gottfredson, M R, 1985. **Policy Guidelines for Bail: an Experiment in Court Reform.** Philadelphia: Temple University Press.

Goldkamp, J S, 1987. *Prediction in Criminal Justice Policy Development* in Gottfredson, D M and Tonry, M (Eds) op.cit.: 103-150.

Goldkamp, J S, 1987. *Rational Choice and Determinism* in Gottfredson, M R and Hirschi, T (Eds), 1987. **Positive Criminology.** California: Sage Publications: 125-137.

Gottfredson, D M, 1987. *Prediction and Classification in Criminal Justice Decision Making* in Gottfredson, D M and Tonry, M (Eds) op.cit.: 1-20.

Gottfredson, M R and Hirschi, T, 1987. *The Positive Tradition* in Gottfredson, M R and Hirschi, T (Eds) op.cit.: 9-22.

Gottfredson, S D, 1987. *Prediction: An Overview of Selected Methodological Issues* in Gottfredson, D M and Tonry, M (Eds) op.cit.: 21-52.

Henderson, P F and Morgan, P M, 1991. **Remands in Custody for up to 28 days: the Experiment.** Research and Planning Unit Paper 52. London: Home Office.

Hucklesby, A, 1992. *The Problem with Bail Bandits.* **New Law Journal,** Volume 142, No 6549: 558-560.

Jones, C, 1988. *Jailing and Bailing: Understanding Bail and Custodial Remand in Scotland, England and Wales* in Backett, S, MacNeill, J and Yellowlees, A (Eds). **Imprisonment Today.** London: McMillan Press Ltd:16-35.

Jones, P R and Goldkamp, J S, 1991. *Judicial Guidelines for Pre-trial Release: Research and Policy Developments in the United States* in the **Howard Journal of Criminal Justice,** Volume 30, No 2: 140-160.

Macphail, I D, 1983. *Bail after Judicial Examination* in **Journal of the Law Society of Scotland,** Volume 28, No 2: 335-338.

Mair, G (Editor), 1989. **Risk Prediction and Probation: Papers from a Research and Planning Unit Workshop.** Research and Planning Unit Paper 56. London: Home Office.

Mair, G, 1988. **Bail and Probation Work: the ILPS Temporary Bail Action Project.** Research and Planning Unit, Paper 46. London: Home Office.

Melvin, M and Didcott, P G, 1976. **Pre-trial Bail and Custody in the Scottish Sheriff Courts.** Scottish Office Central Research Unit. Edinburgh: HMSO.

Moody, S R and Tombs, J, 1982. **Prosecution in the Public Interest.** Edinburgh Scottish Academic Press.

Morgan, P and Pearce, R, 1988. **Remand Decisions in Brighton and Bournemouth.** Research and Planning Unit Paper 53. London: Home Office.

Morgan, P M , 1992. **Offending While on Bail: a Survey of Recent Studies.** Research and Planning Unit Paper 65. London: Home Office.

Murray, D G, 1989. **Review of Research on Re-offending of Mentally Disordered Offenders.** Research and Planning Unit, Paper 55. London; Home Office.

Nicols, T and Ennis, J, 1991. **Offending on Bail.** Metropolitan Police Directorate of Management Services.

Northumbria Police, 1991. **Bail and Multiple Offending.** Northumbria Police.

Paterson, F, 1988. **Decision Making under the Bail etc (Scotland) Act 1980: Pilot Study Report** (Unpublished).

Paterson, F, 1993. *Bail Decisions: Risk, Uncertainty, Choice* in Adler, M, Millar, A and Morris, S (Eds). **Socio-Legal Research in the Scottish Courts** (Volume 3). Edinburgh: Scottish Office Central Research Unit Paper.

Paterson, F and Whittaker, C, 1993. *Criminal Justice Cultures: Negotiating Bail and Remand* (Unpublished Paper to the British Criminology Conference, University of Wales).

Roberts, C H, 1989. *The Potential of Predictive Instruments to Aid Clinical Judgement: The Case of Probation Officers and their Social Inquiry Reports* in Mair, G (Ed) op.cit.

Social Research Branch,1982. **An Analysis of Crown Office Bail Monitoring Exercise.** Scottish Office Central Research Unit.

Stewart, A L, 1990. **The Scottish Criminal Courts in Action.** Edinburgh: Butterworths.

Tarling, R, Jones, P and Sanders, A, 1986. *Police Bail.* **Home Office Research and Planning Unit Bulletin** No 21: 52-56.

Tonry, M, 1987. *Prediction and Classification: Legal and Ethical Issues* in Gottfredson, D M and Tonry, M (Eds) op. cit.: 367-413.

Tombs, J, 1988. *Prosecution Approaches and Imprisonment* in Backett, S, MacNeill, J and Yellowlees, A (Eds) op.cit.: 1-15.

Wozniak, E, Scrimgeour, P and Nicolson, L, 1988. **Custodial Remand in Scotland.** Edinburgh: Scottish Office Central Research Unit/SHHD Criminal Statistics Unit.

INDEX

Printed in the United Kingdom by HMSO Edinburgh
Dd 0287959 C10 4/94 (000055)